CURATING SUBJECTS

Paul O'Neill (Ed.)

De Appel

De Appel, Centre for Contemporary Art
Nieuwe Spiegelstraat 10
NL – 1017 DE Amsterdam

T +31 (0)206255651
F +31 (0)206225215
www.deappel.nl

Director: Ann Demeester
Publications: Edna van Duyn

De Appel is supported by the
Ministry of OC&W and the City
of Amsterdam.

First published in London 2007

ISBN 978-90-73501-71-3

Printed and bound in Europe

CURATING SUBJECTS

De Appel

Søren Andreasen & Lars Bang Larsen
Julie Ault
Carlos Basualdo
Dave Beech & Mark Hutchinson
Irene Calderoni
Anshuman Das Gupta & Grant Watson
Clémentine Deliss
Eva Diaz
Claire Doherty
Okwui Enwezor
Annie Fletcher
Liam Gillick
Jens Hoffmann
Robert Nickas
Hans Ulrich Obrist
Sarah Pierce
Simon Sheikh
Mary Anne Staniszewski
Andrew Wilson
Mick Wilson

Paul O'Neill (Ed.)

Table of Contents

INTRODUCTION

Paul O'Neill Interviewed by Annie Fletcher

ANNIE FLETCHER   Everywhere we turn these days, there seems to
be a new book by curators on curators and curating, analysing the
contemporary circumstances of our production, weighing up the
methodologies and approaches used to frame contemporary artistic
practice or questioning the exhibition models currently in use. How
do you explain this hyper-critical introspection seemingly inherent
to our profession at the moment? Do we really need another book
about curating?

PAUL O'NEILL   Absolutely. I actually think we need many more, but
with more heterogeneous approaches both to the issues around
curating and the format these discussions take. As curatorial practice
continues to evolve, we need publications that respond critically to
such an evolution. Many of the books you refer to appeared very
recently; they are retroactive and respond to considerable gaps in
historical knowledge. The last twenty years have seen radical shifts
in the perception of what the curator does, but curatorial criticism
and the specific critical discourse surrounding curating has been
slow to respond, inform or critique these modifications in a productive
way. Curatorial histories are currently in the process of becoming
part of this discourse and this is still at a very early stage in its
development — there is a lot of catching up to do.

AF   Are you saying that, despite all the output on the latest
developments in curatorial knowledge, we in fact have a limited
vocabulary to represent these changes and a restricted understanding of these transformations? How does that manifest itself?

PO'N   Both of your assertions are true, but it manifests itself
specifically in relation to the vocabulary. There was a shift away from
the predominant notion of the professional museum curator in the
1960s, when the terms *Ausstellungsmacher* (in German) and *faiseur
d'expositions* (in French) were being used to represent an
intellectual figure operating counter to the museum, who organised
large-scale, independent exhibitions of contemporary art and was
understood as someone who had spent a long time operating within
the art world, usually without a fixed institutional post, who
influenced public opinion through their exhibitions. We have seen
a gradual change from the perception of the curator as carer and
behind-the-scenes aesthetic arbiter to a more centralised position
on a much broader stage, with a creative, political and active part
to play in the production, mediation and dissemination of art itself.
In the English speaking world, the closest under-standing of
Ausstellungsmacher was of a kind of author as independent
"exhibition-maker", primarily referencing the activities of a few
curators who began operating between the 1960s and 1970s, in
particular Harald Szeemann, Seth Siegelaub, Pontus Hultén and
Kasper König.

It wasn't until the 1990s, when curating became less of an accidental career choice, that the noun "curator" was supplemented by a new application of the verb "to curate", neither of which you will find in the Oxford English Dictionary or your Microsoft spell-check. So, even the most fundamental terms are floating signifiers, fluctuating between different meanings. Key mobilisations have seen the amplification of the notion of the curator as an agent responsible for overall exhibition structure and narrative, and the now-ubiquitous usage of "curated by" (in the context of exhibition invitations, press releases and catalogues) being established. But, we still have more of an understanding of who certain curators *are* than what they actually *do*, which may also be the result of a celebrity culture and the popularisation of art as part of the global entertainment industry. In addition, although curating now takes on many diverse forms of practice, beyond the traditional exhibition space, the critical focus is too often on outcomes (exhibitions, catalogues, projects) rather than the reproductive process of institutional power structures. Many exhibitions have moved beyond the predominantly illustrative, singly-authored narrative; indeed, exhibitions are not the only outcome of curatorial ideas. Curating is an adaptive discipline, using and adopting inherited codes and rules of behaviour.

There is already a long list of metaphors trying to grapple with these transformations, ranging from medium, midwife, DJ, agent, manager, platform provider, self-promoter and scout to the more ridiculous such as diviner, fairy godmother or even god. As part of a more recent trend, curating is represented as having contingent forms of social exchange, with the allocation of associative words such as caregiver, collaborator, cultural mediator, facilitator, negotiator, and cultural agitator. Some of these terms have been useful, as a way of widening our understanding during such a dynamic phase. In their essay for *Curating Subjects*, Søren Andreasen and Lars Bang Larsen have added to this list the concept of the curator as "middleman", in an attempt to analyse how acts, ideas and products are authorised and made credible through processes of mediation and communicative exchange.

AF   In a way it sounds like a very performative practice, which gets played out through the verbal. Can one trace the development of this vocabulary? Is there a clear genealogy of curatorship through anthologies?

PO'N   Well, beginning in the 1990s, most anthologies tended to come out of international meetings between curators, as part of curatorial summits, symposia, seminars and conferences, although some may have taken local curatorial practice as their starting point. [1] Without exception, and some more than others, they placed an emphasis on individual practice, the first-person narrative and curator self-positioning — articulated through primary interviews, statements and exhibition re-presentations — as they attempted to define and map out a relatively barren field of discourse. The ascendancy of the curatorial gesture in the 1990s also began to establish curatorial practice as a potential space for discussion, critique and debate, where the evacuated role of the critic in parallel cultural discourse was usurped by a neo-critical space for the practice of curating. More recently, art magazines have taken curating as one of their key subjects for debates which have, in turn, been led by invited curators. One explanation for this focus may simply be that many critics are now primarily curators, but I would argue that the basis for this concentration is manifold. A parallel publishing industry responded to the growth of the curator's visibility within the field of contemporary art, where the ubiquity of the curator, a precise lack of criticality around the efficacy of the expanding field of curating and, most significantly, the growth of a new audience meant an ever-increasing number of curators, curatorial students and graduates were in search of relevant material. This was also a period of professionalisation for both curators and artists; there was a new market and a new-found subject.

AF   What motivated you to make this book? How is *Curating Subjects* different from what we have already?

PO'N   Although many of those anthologies were essential, I grew tired of reading curators discussing their own projects. I felt urged to compile a book that went beyond the first person narrative. Instead, I wanted to get curators and artists from diverse curatorial positions to comment, critique or speculate upon the practice of other curators, their predecessors and their peers.

AF   Given that we can, apparently, note the moment when the activity and analysis of curating seemed to emerge and then increase exponentially, do any of the texts in *Curating Subjects* actually discuss the development of "the curator's moment" or "the turn towards curating" in the 1990s?

PO'N   Yes. Jens Hoffmann's essay looks directly at certain tendencies in the 1990s by connecting François Truffaut's theory of the *auteur* to the practice and conditions of recent exhibition-making as a means of analysing the emergence of the concept of the "curator-as-creator". Eva Diaz takes a specific 1990s exhibition, *Laboratorium* (1999), as her departure point, to examine how traditional and innovative notions of the experiment could benefit current and potential future curatorial methodologies. And Mick Wilson's essay explores the inter-relationship between curating, participatory cultural processes and the turn towards the discursive in more recent practice. It was also important that the book was an extension to some of my conversations with curators, who put together their first exhibitions in the 1990s, with whom I had some of my most evocative discussions about the expanding curatorial field.

AF   The anthologies you referred to primarily focused on curating during the 1990s. What about practices that go back further? Will they be represented in the book? Do any of the texts critique the historicity of the discipline, as it is understood now?

PO'N   The history of curating has yet to be fully established as an academic field of enquiry. Much of the corresponding literature, for even our most contemporary curatorial projects, is missing. Hans Ulrich Obrist's ongoing project, interviewing curators from the last century, is producing important historical material. One of these interviews, with the late Jean Leering, Director of the Van Abbemuseum in Eindhoven in the early 1960s, is published here for the first time as part of what Obrist calls "a protest against forgetting". More generally, the contextualisation of space and its rhetoric have been overshadowed by the context of art in terms of epochs and an artist's *œuvre* since early modernism in spite of the fact that 20th century exhibition installations have had such a crucial effect on how meaning was produced in art. Aside from Brian O'Doherty's essays that made up *Inside the White Cube* (1976), there wasn't much subsequent literature until the 1990s. One of the most significant, for me, was Mary Anne Staniszewski's *The Power of Display* (1998), which looked at exhibition designs, displays and installations as part of the history of the Museum of Modern Art in New York. Staniszewski was key in highlighting how "amnesia" towards such innovations can raise serious questions about responsibility, in both creating institutional conventions and in constructing the ideological and historical processes of curatorial praxis.[2] It was for this reason that I invited her to bring her project up to date, with a critical review of the new MoMA space and the re-hang of their collection.

AF   What of that other development — which seems to have slipped so easily into the curatorial repertoire — the advent of biennials and the figure of the nomadic, global curator in the 1990s? Surely, this development alone has had profound implications for how one thinks about the socio-political framing of artistic practice, and for how the curator is positioned as a cultural commentator in the broader contemporary sphere?

PO'N   Since the late 1980s, the group exhibition has become the primary site for curatorial experimentation and, as such, generated a new discursive space around artistic practice. As Okwui Enwezor reflects in my interview with him, the group exhibition — in particular the biennial — has become a dominant model, showing the vital and productive messiness of the contemporary. The group exhibition

works contra to the canonical model of the monographic presentation and, by bringing a greater mix of people into an exhibition,
the biennial model creates a space for defining multifarious ways
of engaging with disparate interests, within a more trans-cultural
context. The last decade also brought cheaper air travel, a greater
mobility of populations and the advent of the Internet, enabling
art professionals greater access to places, peoples and cultures.
There was a radical increase in the number of recurring, large-scale,
international exhibitions — resulting from the structural
consequences of an expanding art market — with certain curators
becoming internationally-networked service-providers, offering
their skills to a diverse exhibition market. One accomplishment of
biennials is how they have helped to shape new social, cultural and
political relations in a more globalised world, while maintaining the
traditional model through discourses on cultural policy, national
representation, internationalism, cultural travel, urban regeneration
and local tourism. However, biennials have also become polarising
spaces for the legitimisation of certain forms of artistic and curatorial
activities, with the most effective successfully engaging with politics
as a cultural, rather than an institutional, practice. Most recently,
as Claire Doherty has argued in her chapter, the international
scattered-site exhibition has begun to employ the rhetoric of "local
place" as a retort to the accusation that biennials operate merely as
stopovers on the international circuit, for the frequent-flyer tribe of
nomadic artists and curators, and have little or no lasting impact on
the inhabitants or cultural life of their host cities.

AF   You haven't mentioned the changes in artistic practice in
the 1990s. Do you think that it was artwork itself which catalysed
many of the changes in curatorial practice or the other way around?
Do you deal with how artists have specifically contributed to
curatorial knowledge?

PO'N   I would say that it was primarily curatorial practice that
changed in the 1990s, as well as becoming more responsive to
artistic practice that incorporated curatorial, organisational,
relational or distributional strategies into its remit. The impact of
artist-curating had already gathered momentum in the 1980s —
with artists such as Group Material, General Idea, Louise Lawler,
Fred Wilson, Judith Barry and also the many other artists linked to
institutional critique — although you could trace these origins back
a lot further. In recognition of this phenomenon, Julie Ault was invited
to look back on three influential exhibitions curated by the artists
Group Material during this period. It was also vital to represent the
descendants of such initiatives and Clémentine Deliss's essay looks
at the curatorial intentions behind recent exhibitions by artists
John Bock and Thomas Hirschhorn. I also invited the artist Sarah
Pierce, whose work is often described as curatorial, to provide a text

that examines more recent artist-curatorial models such as Fucking Good Art magazine in Rotterdam, D.A.E. in Donostia-San Sebastián and Orchard, a gallery founded by artists on the Lower East Side of Manhattan.

AF   Given that you were determined that the book shouldn't reside in the realm of the anecdotal, or as an account of the authors' own practice, was there a specific brief for contributors? How did you manage to avoid the tendency for this emerging discourse to refer to itself only in terms of its immediate present or its urgent future?

PO'N   I wanted to document the inter-dependent relationships between the curatorial past, present and speculative futures. Each contributor was invited to provide a text for one of three categories: 1)   Curating and under-represented historical projects/existing paradigms; 2)   Under-considered current curatorial issues, and; 3)   Potential or desirable futures for contemporary art curating. The book has three equal and loosely aligned time zones, intermingled in the final design and layout. The brief was initially open-ended enough to enable a diversity of stylistic approaches — ranging from Anshuman Das Gupta and Grant Watson's semi-fictional narrative about a Bauhaus exhibition that may have taken place in Calcutta in 1933 to Dave Beech and Mark Hutchinson's performed dialogue about "anti-curation" — whereas Simon Sheikh's essay actually fits into the past, present and future as he discusses how exhibitions use specific, inherited modes of address to construct meaning for audiences that are both real and imaginary publics. The only restriction placed upon the authors was that they try to resist writing about projects that they themselves have taken part in, although both Liam Gillick and Andrew Wilson found productive ways to critique my own criteria in their texts on two exhibitions they have been involved with: *Utopia Station* (ongoing since 2003) and *Made New* (1996), respectively. In divergent ways, both of these essays look very closely at the more hidden historical and procedural infrastructures of specific curatorial projects. The overall result is a wide range of responses demonstrating a pluralist, dynamic and emergent curatorial discourse, where critical essays, theoretical explorations, academic papers, propositions, historical overviews, polemics, exhibition critiques, interviews and fictional accounts sit side by side. *Curating Subjects* is about bringing three time frames together and representing them in one volume.

AF   How did you research and choose the contributors and the topics they discussed, especially if they were not accounting for their own practice? Is there a relationship between your own curatorial practice and the editorial process here?

PO'N   Like any curatorial project, I wanted the idea to gather form over time. I commissioned contributions one by one, instead of coming up with a set list from the outset. When one proposal was accepted, I then invited a new contribution that took a different approach or introduced a subject contrary to what was already in the book. Of course, not everyone could take part and there are inevitable omissions and contradictions. I wanted to preserve a sense of ongoing conversation throughout the editorial process, where each new text would influence, and be in dialogue with, what would be commissioned next. For example, after I invited Carlos Basualdo to publish his essay about the biennial as an unstable political and cultural institution, he suggested I should contact Irene Calderoni, who was doing detailed historical research into curating in the 1960s. Basualdo is an advocate of the biennial model, as is Okwui Enwezor, so I wanted a soft critique of the generic biennial experience, which Robert Nickas provided in the form of a users' guide that could be read every two years. Topics were gradually added, juxtaposed and intercepted.

In the end, anthologies are similar to exhibitions. They are testing sites that evolve through variable degrees of dialogue, semi-autonomous participation and self-determined modes of resistance. A curatorial strategy should provide a useful opening-out of potentialities and enable multiple responses to the same question, while incorporating failure as a disruptive ingredient within the overall structure and conceptual framework of the project. In the beginning, there is only a vague idea for the future. Over time, it fragments, mutates and eventually amalgamates, until the overall subject matter becomes clearer. Once a semi-public space becomes available for an eventual outcome, there is a prospective future time line in place, and it was the dynamics of this temporal transition that I wanted to maintain as much as possible throughout the content, structure and form of the book.

1.   Ute Meta Bauer, ed., *Meta 2: The New Spirit in Curating* (Stuttgart: Künstlerhaus Stuttgart, 1992); Peter White, ed., *Naming a Practice: Curatorial Strategies for the Future* (Banff, Canada: Banff Centre for the Arts, 1996); Anna Harding, ed., *Art and Design Magazine: On Curating — the Contemporary Art Museum and Beyond, No.52* (London: Academy Editions, 1997); Mika Hannula, ed., *Stopping the Process: Contemporary Views on Art and Exhibitions* (Helsinki: NIFCA, 1998); Barnaby Drabble and Dorothee Richter, eds., *Curating Degree Zero, An International Curating Symposium* (Nuremberg: Verlag für Moderne Kunst, 1999); Catherine Thomas, ed., *The Edge of Everything: Reflections on Curatorial Practice* (Banff, Canada: Banff Centre Press, 2000); Dave Beech and Gavin Wade, ed., *Curating in the 21st Century* (Walsall & Wolverhampton: The New Art Gallery Walsall / University of Wolverhampton, 2000); Susan Hiller and Sarah Martin, eds., *The Producers: Contemporary Curators in Conversation* (Series 1–5), (Newcastle: Baltic and University of Newcastle, 2000–2002); Carolee Thea, ed., *Foci: Interviews with 10 International Curators* (New York: Apexart, 2001); Paula Marincola ed., *Curating Now: Imaginative Practice? Public Responsibility* (Philadelphia: Philadelphia Exhibitions Initiative, 2001); Carin Kuoni, ed., *Words of Wisdom: A Curator's Vade Mecum* (New York: Independent Curators International (ICI), 2001); Melanie

Townsend, ed., *Beyond the Box: Diverging Curatorial Practices* (Banff, Canada: Banff Centre Press, 2003); Christoph Tannert, Ute Tischler and Künstlerhaus Bethanien, eds., *MIB — Men in Black: Handbook of Curatorial Practice* (Frankfurt am Main: Revolver, 2004); Liam Gillick and Maria Lind, eds., *Curating With Light Luggage* (Frankfurt am Main: Revolver, 2005).

2.   These included Douglas Crimp, *On The Museum's Ruins* (Cambridge, Massachusetts: MIT Press, 1993); Bruce Altshuler, *The Avant-Garde in Exhibition: New Art in the 20th Century* (Berkeley and Los Angeles: University of California Press, 1994); Bruce Ferguson, Reesa Greenberg and Sandy Nairne, eds., *Thinking About Exhibitions* (London and New York: Routledge, 1996); Mary Ann Staniszewski, *The Power of Display: A History of Exhibition Installation at MoMA* (Cambridge, Massachusetts: MIT Press, 1998) and the republication in 1999, thirteen years after its last pressing in 1986, of Brian O'Doherty, *Inside the White Cube: The Ideology of the Gallery Space* (Berkeley, Los Angeles and London: University of California Press, 1999). At the very end of the 1990s, publications also began to appear that focused on individual curatorial innovations from the 20th century such as the exploration into Marcel Duchamp and Salvador Dalí's curatorial roles in the Surrealist exhibitions of the 1930–40s in Lewis Kachur, *Displaying the Marvellous: Marcel Duchamp, Salvador Dalí and Surrealist Exhibition Installations* (Cambridge, Massachusetts: MIT Press 2001); Sybil Gordon Kantor, *Alfred H. Barr, Jr. and the Intellectual Origins of the Museum of Modern Art* (Cambridge, Massachusetts: MIT Press 2002); Alexander Alberro, *Conceptual Art and the Politics of Publicity* (Cambridge, Massachusetts: MIT Press 2003), which focused on Seth Siegelaub's curatorial practice of the 1960s, and two recent monographs on Harald Szeemann, both published after his death: Hans-Joachim Müller, *Harald Szeemann: Exhibition Maker* (Ostfildern-Ruit: Hatje Cantz, 2005) and Tobia Bezzola and Roman Kurzmeyer, *Harald Szeemann: with by through because towards despite — Catalogue of All Exhibitions, 1957–2001* (Vienna and New York: Springer-Verlag, 2007).

THE MIDDLEMAN: BEGINNING TO TALK ABOUT MEDIATION

Søren Andreasen & Lars Bang Larsen

The mediation that communicates the work is, in principle, total.
Hans-Georg Gadamer, *Truth and Method,* 1960

With an idealistic critical approach, we set out to describe 'the means of production', with view to analysing divergent models of artistic activity from the last 30 years. Unsurprisingly, in the end we didn't get very far. We were struck by our inability to describe the basic structures of contemporary art production, and the concepts of materials, tools, work and value.

By revising existing notions of production through a focus on mediation, we began to examine how objects are altered and transformed during the processes of exchange. Eventually, we went in search of the flow of production with the purpose of reading the subject who mediates — the mediator, the intermediary, or what we propose to call here the middleman. This is an investigation motivated by self-interest as a way of conceptualising what we do as producers, consumers and communicators of art. We wish to question the mechanisms through which acts, ideas and products are authorised — how is art made, and for whom is it produced? How is it recognised and made credible through mediation?

The figure of the middleman is typically seen as a conformist, parasitical agent responsible for short-circuiting authenticity. The middleman has an aura of mediocrity. The middleman is average, and a suspect character. There is always the risk that he knows more than he should and that he feathers his own nest. In other words, the middleman has an opaque presence in social space.

In his text from 1963, "A Revolutionary Proposal: Invisible Insurrection of a Million Minds", the Scottish novelist and situationist Alexander Trocchi called for an empowerment of the intelligentsia through the takeover of universities and other knowledge-producing institutions. He writes: "Our first move must be to eliminate the brokers". [1] For Trocchi, "Cutting out the middleman" became a means of accelerating cultural transformation. Similarly, in the late 1960s, Joseph Kosuth argued that conceptual art should eliminate the role of the art critic. By using text as the primary medium for art, unmediated relations were now possible between work and viewer, without the interference of commentary.

1.   www.notbored.org/invisible.html

In other words, mediation represents all that modernism hated about modern life. There was not much to choose between mediation and alienation. In his seminal book *Inside the White Cube* (1976), Brian O'Doherty writes:

[It is inescapably modern that] alienation may now be a necessary preface to experience… much of our experience can only be brought home through mediation. …In most areas of experience there is a busy traffic in proxies and surrogates …as with other mediated experience, "feeling" is turned into a consumer product. [2]

Is the mediator, or the figure of the middleman, as bad as modernism wanted us to believe, and as insidious as neo-liberalism makes them appear? Gilles Deleuze thought differently. In an interview from 1985 called "Mediators", he challenges contemporary thought to intervene in or connect to what is already there. What is important, he says, is not to be the origin of an effort or to ponder eternal values, but instead to participate in movements: to put ideas into orbit and to get caught up in perpetual motion. He also urges modern thinkers to stop being custodians and to "get into something". For Deleuze, movement / flow is creation itself, and the mediator embraces movement in order to keep the world open and alive.

Mediators are fundamental. Creation's all about mediators. Without them nothing happens. They can be people – for a philosopher, artists or scientists; for a scientist, philosophers or artists – but things too, even plants or animals (…). Whether they are real or imaginary, animate or inanimate, you have to form your mediators. It's a series. If you're not in some series, even a completely imaginary one, you're lost. I need my mediators to express myself and they'd never express themselves without me: you're always working in a group, even when you seem to be on your own. [3]

But 'mediation' is a concept that is already contested by its different significations. It is typically taken to mean conflict management, as when an impartial expert such as Kofi Annan steps in to mediate a high-

2.   Brian O'Doherty: *Inside the White Cube. The Ideology of the Gallery Space*, University of California Press, London 1986, pp. 52–53.
3.   Gilles Deleuze: "Mediators". In *Negotiations 1972-1990*, Columbia University Press, New York 1990, p. 125.

level military or political confrontation. It also signifies organisational development or restorative justice. It remains uncertain what charge the term has when it is used in an art context: how much significance is retained from that of conflict management related to the hermeneutical term *Vermittlung*, which signifies mediation in the sense of interpreting a given object with a view to communicating it? What kind of 'mediation' is at stake in the work of artists and curators — conflict management or *Kunstvermittlung*?

By reconsidering the grey areas of mediation, we propose to explore the term 'middleman' rather than 'mediator'. As already suggested, 'mediator' is an imprecise term that risks giving 'the intermediary' the benefit of the doubt through its heroic connotations. In spite of its inescapable sexism, 'middleman' is useful to explore because it denotes a subject unaccounted for in discussions of the significance and the potential concepts of mediation. We put forward the 'middleman' because it denotes a supplementary subjectivity or a subject who is out of place, and because of its usage by French historian Fernand Braudel, which we shall discuss in more detail.

The question is why do we tend to instinctively mistrust the middleman? Are we right or wrong to be suspicious? What is the potential of the middleman? The figure of the midwife has been a staple of Western philosophy since Socrates, as someone who helps give birth to knowledge, so is it because of the metaphorical charge of the pedagogical midwife that we find him or her more worthy of trust than the middleman?

The Historical Rise of the Middleman

For Fernand Braudel the 'middleman' is a key agent in the development of capitalism. Braudel sets out to make a historical investigation of the influence of economical activity on everyday life and vice versa — a work that lasted 25 years and materialised in three huge volumes called *Civilisation and Capitalism,* which was published in the mid-1970s.

Braudel's focus of attention is the market economy: i.e. the origin and possible end of market economy and the rise of capitalism. The basis is the elementary markets, which are simply linking production and consumption:

[The elementary markets] form a frontier, a lower limit of economy. Everything outside the market has only "use value"; anything that passes through the narrow gate into the marketplace acquires "exchange value." [4]

Nothing passes through the narrow gate into the marketplace by itself. The transformation from use value to exchange value involves a deliberate action and 'a someone'. Braudel pays a lot of attention to this agent of the market economy, which corresponds to our interest in 'the subject who mediates': the agent of exchange, linkage and transformation.

Only if he crosses the frontier into the elementary market is the individual, or "agent," included in the exchange, in what I have called economic life, in order to contrast it with material life and also in order to distinguish it from capitalism [...]. [5]

The ability to cross the frontier of the marketplace is a precondition to participate in economic life. At the elementary marketplace, producers and consumers link up directly to exchange goods and services but gradually the marketplace is divided into two levels: a lower one, which comprises markets, shops, and peddlers, and an upper one, which includes fairs and bourses. This development of specialisation and hierarchy within the marketplace is a precondition of capitalism, which according to Braudel is a different activity from market economy. The rise of capitalism takes place outside the marketplace — at the outskirts of every market town:

From time to time three people [...] are involved [in the exchange]; that is, an intermediary, a third man, appears between the client and the producer. This dealer can, when the occasion arises, upset or dominate the market and influence prices by stockpiling goods; even a small retailer can flout the law and deal with peasants as they enter the town, purchasing their goods at a lower price, then selling them in the market. [6]

4.   Fernand Braudel: *Afterthoughts on Material Civilization and Capitalism.*
John Hopkins University Press, Baltimore 1977, p. 17.
5.   Ibid. pp. 17–19.
6.   Ibid. p. 50.

This third man, this intermediary, agent, or dealer, operating at the outskirts of every market town breaks off relations between producer and consumer, eventually becoming the only one who knows the market conditions at both ends of the chain. He literally establishes a 'super-market' transforming both use value and exchange value into capital value — doing so by representing and speculating in the interests and needs of producers and consumers and thus regulating the link between the market and the everyday life. Braudel calls this type of economical activity 'opaque' as the transparent exchange of the elementary marketplace is transformed into a 'sphere of circulation' that escapes the regulation, control and competition of the market economy.

Capitalist economy is about regulating and controlling access to the market — eventually becoming itself the only available passage between the market and everyday life. A passage that is materialised as a 'sphere of circulation' — a super-market — which brings to mind Henri Lefebvre's statement that capitalism, like an artificial intelligence, has learned to survive its crisis through the consumption and production of social space.

This very rough résumé of Braudel's history of economics is obviously a tendentious means of reflecting upon our own pursuit of the 'middleman'. Two aspects of Braudel's theory fuelled our discussions: first of all, he detects and describes the rise to power of the intermediary agent who not only breaks up the relations between consumers and producers but takes over the relations itself. And secondly, how this takeover is actually situated in the various spheres of circulation that represent and speculate in the needs and interests of consumers and producers.

When we read the subject who mediates — the middleman — we take it as a precondition that contemporary art is produced, consumed, and communicated in a capitalist society, what Guy Debord calls "bureaucratic capitalism" in his *Comments On The Society Of The Spectacle* (1988). This historical situation was also foreseen by Braudel who claimed that "Capitalism only triumphs when it becomes identified with the state, when it is the state" and more recently, it is directly proclaimed as the current political agenda named 'The Third Way', which has the integration of state and economy as its big vision. [7]

---

7.   Ibid. p. 64.

Curating's Crisis of Representation

Braudel's mediating subject is the archetypal intermediary who is not equivalent with the market but controls access to it. In this way middlemen have worked for centuries at the ringside of the marketplace, floating prices and fixing exchange rates. It could be argued that the development of capitalism and its technologies are reflected at any given time in intermediary subjectivity. A contemporary incarnation is the spin-doctor, for example, whose intervention in the market of mass-communicated images makes political events difficult to verify empirically.

It should be added that the intermediary is not necessarily a capitalist agent. The traditional revolutionary subject becomes a middleman in spite of herself by being an intermediary identified with a utopian view or a desire for a different socio-political order: not because of the real political hustle it takes to usher in utopia or social change, but simply because the intention of taking over the means of production in order to build a better future for the people in itself is an act of representation.

It is therefore futile to speculate about the possible elimination of mediation and intermediaries ala Joseph Kosuth. Instead, we must zoom in on intermediary subjectivity and try to analyse it. The art field offers an extensive palette of 'mediating functions', which take part in the production of art. This involves all the usual suspects of course, with the dealer as the art world equivalent of Braudel's middleman, but in different ways the artist herself and arguably the beholder as well. In the following, we will focus on another significant mediating subject — the curator — who operates with global cultural capitalism as the backdrop for her activities.

It is sometimes said — and more often implied — in discussions about curating that it is a 'reactive profession'. Bearing in mind that any mode of authorship is a complex and variable function of discourse, and as such cannot be isolated from the apparatuses of representation surrounding it, it doesn't seem tenable to depict curating in this way. First of all, to describe it as reactive removes the role of the curator from that of the public intellectual to being a purely professional agent. Secondly, to qualify the curator as 'reactive' implies orthodoxies that determine the artistic function as being primary, positing artistic work as the primal scene.

Curating sometimes appears to be a self-conscious profession. The contemporary artist is often put on the spot, but for all the right reasons so to speak. If the artist's work is 'incomprehensible' it is because she is a struggling intellect. If art is a fraud it is because it reveals that all of our capitalist culture is a fraud. Above all, it is pretty clear what the artist does, because the artwork is signed. The classical Philistine questions as to 'what is art supposed to look like?' or 'What does it mean?' are, in the case of the curator, displaced towards her own agency and subjectivity: 'What is a curator?' It is a question that doesn't make sense, because the curator is not something; the curator does something. There is no ontology of the middleman: she is a performative and exemplary agent, acquiring subjectivity in and by the act of mediation.

Perhaps it is unsurprising that the discourse(s) on curating are very complex, when dealing with highly specific pragmatic issues (budgets, deadlines, names, and places) at the same time as being rather elusive. Perhaps this is due to the culture of mobility as one of the parameters of curatorial work when mobility denotes a culture of experience, not of knowledge – it is the accumulation of events. However, this is not so different from the work of the itinerant artist, but the work of the artist belongs to a different economy of representation. For example, why is the monographic catalogue on the work of the curator the exception when it for artists is the rule? The idea of a curator's catalogue may seem redundant to many. Is a banal observation, but perhaps symptomatic of the difficulties we have with representing the curatorial signature. The 'curator's monograph' that exist typically filter curatorial work through text about art, architecture, design etc. rather than discussions about the production of space or about the curator as an authorial subject. For example, a curator does not publish a book about their work in which they invite critics to comment, as is the case with the artist's monographic catalogue. [8]

Let us stay with the question of writing. In the words of English curator Andrew Renton, there are only few examples of rigorous discourse on curating. Renton proposes that the best way to represent curating might be to explore *around* curating. He cites as an example that Hans Ulrich Obrist's theoretical solution to writing is the interview, "a theoretical route that is a discourse with many people." [9] That is, a kind of writing-in-progress, an infinite conversation.

8.   For "curator's monographs" see *Hans cUlrich Obrist: Prefaces 1991–2005.* Lukas & Sternberg, New York 2006; Hou Hanru: *On The Mid-Ground.* Selected texts Ed. Yu Hsiao-Hwei. Timezone 8, Hong Kong 2002; and the posthumous Hans-Joachim Müller, ed., *Harald Szeemann: Exhibition Maker.* Hatje Cantz, Ostfildern-Ruit 2006.
9.   "A Conversation Between Andrew Renton, Sabine Brümmer and Sophie von Olfers". Arco News 2005, Madrid, p. 33.

Renton further states that curating is about "seeing where the creative act can possibly go... and we don't know where it can go". To Renton, the curatorial obligation to be closely involved in processes further complicates or even eliminates the act of writing, because you are trying "to keep track of what's unknown... the minute you write it down on paper, it would be redundant almost that second". [10] You could argue that exhibition making is a form of writing too: but a form of writing with visual, spatial properties, and one whose further existence always hinges on its reception and "translation" into academic or critical text. So while there is an abundant production of text in the art world, it would seem that writing rarely appears as curatorial practice.

In the lecture "Everything is In-between", Hans Ulrich Obrist talks about how curators in the past have reached out from the art system and have pioneered the inclusion of other cultural fields in their work. In what he calls "curatorial positions of in-betweenness" it is striking how he qualifies his argument with figures of speed and instability. He talks about elasticity, transformation, dynamics, oscillation, mobility and mutation. [11] There seems to be no standing still.

Of course, it is quite justifiable to say that we don't know how curatorial practice will develop, especially as especially as Renton argues that it is a discipline still in its infancy. Moreover, the courage to fight for a radical openness in terms of outcome is a badly needed perspective in any kind humanistic research. However, this does not tell us why the symptom of the curatorial text is a focus on the unpredictable and the unstable: the curator may be an unformed subject, but she is also a highly operational one. One conclusion would be that curating refutes its own description through the 'speed of art'.

It is significant in this respect that Obrist call his historical precursors mediators rather than curators. As mentioned above, the term 'mediator' has rather heroic connotations, implying a neutral and resourceful individual who intervenes in an existing conflict situation with high-level troubleshooting, in order to restore order. There is a major difference between 'intermediary' and 'mediator'. The intermediary lies low and is not supposed to appear, whereas the mediator's success is determined in great measure by her public authority in matters where consensus is sought. So why is the curator described as a mediator and

10.   Ibid. p. 34.
11.   www.thing.net/eyebeam msg00373.html

not as an intermediary, or better still, why is the curator not seen as an interlocutor, or as one who participates in movements (with all the political implications of that term)?

Fernand Braudel claims that capitalism only succeeds when every thing is ready for it to take over, just like the middleman who starts operating at the outskirts of the elementary market and inserts hierarchies within it. But maybe several middlemen can function as intermediaries for each other and create delays and diversions inside the spheres of circulation? To put it polemically: to start making conflicts instead of solving them, to see how ideas collide rather than creating consensus? Here it is interesting to link to Jacques Rancière's notion of 'in-betweenness' as political subjectification. Subjectification, he writes,

> Is the formation of a one that is not a self but is the relation of a self to an other... [a] subject is an outsider, or more, an in-between... Political subjectification is the enactment of equality – or the handling of a wrong – by people who are together to the extent that they are between. It is a crossing of identities, relying on a crossing of names: names that link... a being to a nonbeing or a not-yet-being. [12]

On the face if it this sounds like another way of saying "we don't know where it can go". Arguably Ranciére and Renton are alluding to a related set of problems: the 'being-in-process' of curating could be seen as a crossing of identities where 'difference' shares a desire for resistance to that which could bring processes of betweenness to completion. However the bottom line is that globalised culture's reproduction of itself issues a formidable challenge for us to develop discursive tools with which we can pick up, qualify and interpret forms of being still to come.

One might argue that to place artist and curator side by side as intermediaries ultimately levels out the difference between the two, thereby opening up claims that the curator also is an artist. She probably isn't, but that is not the point; this is basically the equivalent of asking 'what is art?' That is, whether we talk about the art object or communicative roles in art, ontological criteria that claim to be capable of installing privileged access to historical truths is unproductive. Similarly, positions which are optimised through capital's spheres of circulation (for example

12.   Jacques Rancière: "Politics, Identification, and Subjectivization." *October* 01 (Summer 1992), New York, p. 60–61.

by employing managerial paradigms on the making and communication of art) always run the risk of becoming purely formal relations that bring processes of 'in-betweenness' towards some form of closure. A critical and hermeneutical work that deliberates art's transformative power needs to address the experiences of art making, communication and spectatorship in a way which allows for different levels of experience to be synchronised not only between artists, curators and critics, but in the wider representational spaces we inhabit as citizens. This could be a point of entry into a more productive discussion about the making and communication of art today.

THREE SNAPSHOTS FROM THE EIGHTIES: ON GROUP MATERIAL

Julie Ault

Exhibitions are crucial junctions within which art and artifacts are made accessible to audiences, and particular narratives, histories, and ideas are activated. Furthermore, every mode of display establishes relationships between artist, art, institution, and audience and generates routines and rituals for looking. It is precisely because of the power that exhibitions have in assigning or opening up meanings, in creating contexts and situating viewers, that standardized exhibition methods and formats as well as display conventions need to be critically rethought and potentially subverted. Contextual strategies of exhibition making can defy and challenge the categorizations and hierarchies through which relations in the art industry, and in culture at large, are reproduced.

For the artists' collaborative Group Material, which I was a part of between 1979 and 1996, the temporary exhibition was a medium through which models of social and representational structures were posited, and through which rules, situations, and venues were often subverted. Specific exhibition projects evolved from and expanded upon the collaborative process of discursive engagement, its principles of practice. What follows are sketches of three such projects with different impetuses that range from an exhibition in Group Material's storefront gallery planned to articulate a specific geographic community, to an institutionally specific exhibition that critically challenged the museum context it acted within, to an exhibition conceived of and constructed around urgent sociopolitical issues.

The People's Choice (Arroz con Mango) 1981

In 1980 Group Material rented a storefront space on East Thirteenth Street in New York City: The intention, to make a room of our own as a laboratory within which exhibitions and events driven by our engagement with social themes and topical issues would be staged. For the first year or so the group consisted of thirteen members. [1] Balancing multiple audiences and constituencies, we sought to develop relationships with people living in the neighborhood, with colleagues, like-minded cultural producers, and with the more abstract 'art world'.

1.   Hannah Alderfer, George Ault, Julie Ault, Patrick Brennan, Liliana Dones, Yolanda Hawkins, Beth Jaker, Mundy McLaughlin, Marybeth Nelson, Marek Pakulski, Tim Rollins, Peter Szypula, and Michael Udvardy.

From that year on Thirteenth Street, *The People's Choice* is the project that functioned most effectively for engaging questions about cultural values, and redressing notions of public. The curatorial process began on January 1, 1981 when the group distributed a letter door-to-door to residents living on the block. In part it read:

Dear friends and neighbors of 13th Street. Group Material is having an exhibition and you're invited. Group Material is the gallery that opened this October at 244 East 13th. We are a group of young people who have been organizing different kinds of events in our storefront. We've had parties, art shows, movies and art classes for the kids who are always rushing in and out. *The People's Choice* is the title of our next exhibition. We would like to show things that might not usually find their way into an art gallery. The things that you personally find beautiful, the objects that you keep for your own pleasure, the objects that have meaning for you your family and your friends. What could these be? They can be photographs, or your favorite posters. If you collect things, these objects would be good for this exhibition. [2]

Unfortunately this letter didn't elicit participation as intended. We anticipated a rush of deliveries from smiling neighbors enthused by the idea of "making your own show". But people were slow to respond, and understandably questioned how their belongings would be cared for and used. We sought to articulate our desires and intentions for the show, and, got more aggressively personable in our solicitations. The process gained steam: as people saw their neighbors bringing in their family pictures and favorite things, their exhibitor fantasies were fueled and competition became a motor. Soon, everyone wanted a piece of the action, a place on the wall. Everything brought in was installed. Over the following weeks more and more items were brought in until the walls were covered in a salon-style display. The exhibition manifest as an eclectic collection of everyday objects usually kept in homes, brought into an exhibition space accessible to all passerby and visitors.

The People's Choice was intended to interrogate the traditional museum collection model of what is culturally and symbolically valuable by posing a collection determined by people not usually identified or professionalized as cultural experts. It was not Group Material's inten-

---

2.   Letter to residents of E. 13th Street, January 1, 1981.

tion to instrumentalize or attempt to sociologically trace or distinguish a group. The aim was to construct a particular notion of what constitutes a public display. [3] As a process *The People's Choice* provided a concrete framework for working in the immediate neighborhood — a geographically and economically determined community — drawing on its resources, reflecting, and providing something in return. As a representational space the exhibition was meant to render a portrayal of the block told through common objects, a community-based narrative of everyday life rather than one imposed by distanced experts.

Americana 1985

Group Material's first exhibition sited in a museum addressed hierarchical positionings of cultural production, including through display itself. An invitation was extended by curator Lisa Phillips from the Whitney Museum of American Art for the group to participate in the 1985 Biennial by making a new installation. [4] It was at that time rare for artists without gallery representation and without commercial circulation to be included in the Biennial, except within the film/video category.

Since the Whitney Museum defines its biennial exhibition as a survey of the most significant recent art, its very structure raises questions about criteria for selection, the politics of inclusion and exclusion, and the consequences of museum validation. In Group Material's view generally the Biennial expressed an overdetermined narrow vision of art practices and production, manifest as a greatest hits of what had been previously validated through sales in the commercial galleries, with a trade-fair environment, and didn't attend to broader definitions of cultural production or social contexts.

Given that 1985 was the pinnacle of activity and interest in the East Village art scene as well as the key moment when many were proposing pluralism as a paradigm, that year's Biennial attempted to be more inclusive than earlier versions. Hence, the invitation to Group Material.

With this context in mind we developed an exhibition titled *Americana*, and engaged critically with notions of what American culture

3.   See also Thomas Lawson, "The People's Choice," in *Artforum*, April, 1981.
4.   In 1985 Group Material consisted of Doug Ashford, Julie Ault, Mundy McLaughlin, and Tim Rollins.

is and how curatorial practices have supported a monolithic notion of American art. Group Material decided to make a model of our own biennial, a salon des refuses, of what was significantly absent, excluded through curatorial business-as-usual from the Whitney Museum. *Americana* took issue with the exclusivity and whitewashed picture of American art proposed and supported by dominant cultural institutions such as the Whitney, and in a non-didactic manner opened curatorial practice to scrutiny.

    Americana included work by overtly socially engaged artists many of whom were women and artists of color, and popular "commercial artists" as well as store-bought objects from so-called low culture. In terms of the look of the show, it was designed to be dense and layered, viewed first as a whole (as democratic) rather than as discrete (autonomous) objects. We purchased many rolls of Contact Paper, the inexpensive decorative self-adhesive wallpaper, in diverse patterns, mostly coded as "American." Strips of the patterned paper were laid like stripes from floor to ceiling, forming a ground of diverse designs upon which objects were hung. Over fifty artists' works were selected for inclusion, as well as products from supermarkets and department stores. Store-bought items, such as a selection of laundry detergents, were installed in groupings that — with a degree of irony — demonstrated "freedom of choice." A television was hooked up which broadcast whatever was on major network programming continuously. A washing machine and dryer dominated center stage as the only other sculptural elements. A soundtrack made up of songs "representative of America" sampled from various genres was on continuous play. The total effect of *Americana* was over-stimulating with no space in the room left "neutral." In *Americana* space was densely instrumentalized distinct from the rest of the Biennial, which, except for a couple installations, was installed on the standard 60" hanging line.

    One organizing goal was to schematize and make material some problematic divisions and hierarchies within the art and culture industry. The boundaries between "high" and "low" culture were symbolically dislodged in *Americana*. Another aim of bringing in mass-produced products was to link choices — including aesthetic ones — people make when shopping with the decisions curators make when shopping on a grander scale for a museum collection. The exhibition aimed to be a catalyst for thinking about the function of cultural representation and hierarchies of cultural production.

How did these two exhibitory entities cohabitate? How did *Americana* and the Biennial itself identify with each other and inflect respective readings? A cynical viewer might say that the context and authority of the Biennial eclipsed Group Material's installation. Group Material viewed public institutions as platforms and places that we wanted to affect through participation. The coexistence of our "model biennial" and the official exhibition made visible the paradoxical character of such institutions, and such institution-specific practices. In a review in the Village Voice weekly newspaper Kim Levin cited *Americana* as representative proof of the low level that art had sunk to:

If Group Material's titillating, weakly rebellious installation lacks the grubby strength of the Times Square Show nearly five years ago, it does provide a hook to hang this year's Biennial on: commodity time is here... It's nice that Group Material tried to outwit the Whitney curators with its laundry room, even if it ended up doing the dirty work for them. [5]

In the letter of response to the critic, published in the May 21, 1985 issue of The Village Voice, Group Material stated:

Contrary to Kim Levin's assumptions, Group Material wasn't used by the Whitney to any greater extent than its resources and visibility were used by us to present a critical model of what we believe an American museum's biennial should be... If you really want a "radical shakeup," why stop at the Biennial? The entire culture industry needs to be overhauled. *Americana* is but one small demonstration toward a program of cultural change. It was not designed for the Whitney, or for art critics, but for the large public which Levin contemptuously reduces to "students, tourists, novices, and art investors." [6]

5.   Kim Levin, "The Whitney Laundry," in *Village Voice*, April 9, 1985. Other reviews of Americana were more positive than Levin's, including Dan Cameron writing in the Summer '85 issue of *Arts*: "Like all good installations, Americana needed a lot of looking and contemplating, and actually required a form of attention that entirely transcends the normal experience of art. That this project could have occurred at all, much less with its integrity fully maintained, is as commendable a sign as we have ever seen of the Whitney's ultimate good intentions."
6.   Group Material, Letter to the editor, *Village Voice*, May 21, 1985

AIDS Timeline 1989

In 1988, after seeing Group Material's *AIDS & Democracy: A Case Study* at the Dia Art Foundation, curator Larry Rinder of the University of Berkeley in California invited Group Material to make another AIDS-related project. Given the urgencies relevant to AIDS and that by 1989 there had been ten years of the epidemic with severely inadequate public response, we determined a map of the interlocking conditions that transformed the epidemic into a crisis was in need of articulation for the discourse about AIDS. [7] A social landscape of history was needed and seemed apt for an exhibition about, from, and nearby a context of AIDS. Keeping in mind the university population would be the primary audience an information-heavy installation was produced.

AIDS Timeline was envisioned as a textual and pictorial chronologically structured exhibit about the development of the AIDS crisis. A timeline in which the chronological format is in itself a guiding operation and orientation for viewers seemed an expedient organizing device for bringing into proximity seemingly incompatible information and material.

Research in several areas: medical and scientific industries; governmental statistics and policies; media representations of the AIDS crisis, particularly stigmatization of people with AIDS which linked representation to public opinion, allocations of resources, etc.; grassroots community and activist responses by affected communities was conducted by the group with help from research assistant Richard Meyer. Artifacts intended to mark cultural events (i.e. The Empire Strikes Back top-grossing movie of 1980) and catalyze memory in viewers were included in the display as well as artworks made by individuals and collectives.

The materials and information were presented not as disparate facts but as a web of intertwined events and association of ideas, in order to describe social processes and demonstrate that actions and events have consequences and interconnections with other actions and events. Within such an exhibition artworks being produced in relation to AIDS were contextualized.

Although the timeline format at first glance promoted a linear reading, once one got into the material and the histories and stories being

7.   In 1991 Group Material was composed of Doug Ashford, Julie Ault, Felix Gonzalez-Torres, and Karen Ramspacher.

traced cross-referencing was inevitable. The arrangement of the art and artifacts chosen posited a history of the political and social conditions in which AIDS was allowed and encouraged to become a national crisis, and represented some exemplary responses to those circumstances. It also indicted the government and populace at large for its "inaction." Group Material's prefatory statement about the project read:

> Like any representation of history, this project is subjective in that it includes certain information and excludes other information... The timeline documents the impact that homophobia, heterosexism, sexism, and racism have had on the formation of effective public policy. Virtually all the major social inequities that compromise democracy in the US are reflected in the decade-long history of AIDS. [8]

* * *

These examples suggest models of exhibition practice that rely on collaborative process, and exhibition structures which rely on conceptual interweaving. They share decentralized spatial arrangements that encourage cross-referencing and catalyze meanings within themetized fields. They also combine various kinds of cultural production — artifacts, art, documentation, and mass-produced objects — in a single space. These examples should be understood as counter-positions to academic curatorial or exhibition-making practices which are centered around strictly defined art historical methods, linearity, master narratives, and upholding divisions between art and artifact, "high" and "low," practitioner and spectator.

There are two significant social sites inherent in the exhibition form: the political process of exhibition-making which reflects, represents, and produces particular social formations, and, the shared environment exhibitions are received in. In the eighties Group Material proposed that these social sites be discursive formations, and to some degree, function as models or forums for participation.

8.   Group Material, artists' pages in *1991 Biennial Exhibition* (New York: Whitney Museum of American Art and W.W. Norton Company, 1991).

THE UNSTABLE INSTITUTION

Carlos Basualdo

In 1531 Titian bought a house with a garden near the lagoon on Venice's north side from which he could, on a clear day, make out the mountains surrounding his hometown of Pieve di Cadore. Biri Grande, in the parish of San Canciano, no longer exists. The Fondamente Nuove, a half a mile of docks along the island's northern edge, was built in its place just a few years after the artist's death. Unprepared pedestrians walking along the docks might take the possibility of seeing the Alps as an amusing happenstance. And to be sure, the smog and air pollution seem to conspire in order to limit the landscape to the classical silhouettes of Italian cypresses in the San Michele Cemetery and some campanile or other on Murano Island. But nevertheless, they were there. I can guarantee that the day we left Venice, from the vantage point of the boat that took us to the airport with all our baggage, we were deliciously surprised to see the silhouette of the Alps.

* * *

Even things that are most categorically evident can occasionally seem invisible. Not because they do not exist, but rather because, at particular moments, some act of intellectual conjuring, some configuration of actions and thought is able to hide them from the horizon of perception. Paradoxically, I have the impression that something similar happens with large-scale international art exhibitions. It is not that they literally become invisible, since they are precisely a staging of enormous mechanisms of visibility, but rather that the singularity of their meaning seems to conceal itself from the myriad of journalists, critics, historians, and pundits who, as one might imagine, come to be their privileged spectators. [1] Of course, I am not saying that these events do not stir up opinions; on the contrary. Opinions abound, but not because common criteria exist that can be used to evaluate this genre of events. For example, reviewing the critical articles that refer to the most recent edition of the Venice Biennale as well as to the latest Documenta in Kassel, we may observe an enormous discrepancy, not so much with regard to the shows themselves, but rather regarding the expectations that the critical and journalistic realms

1.   It is important to note that one of the motives for this text stems from my participation, in various capacities, in three of the exhibitions mentioned: as a panelist in the "100 Days / 100 Guests" at Documenta10, and as a member of the curatorial teams of Documenta11 and the 50th Venice Biennale. In particular, my work in the latter two events allowed me to interact intimately with both their organizational and their conceptual aspects.

seem to have formed for the events. The insistence on leaving aside the explicit intentions that — following the organizers' criteria — try to justify the realization and the subject matter of the shows would not be so serious, especially if it were a matter of a voluntary stance; but perhaps the fact that they are analyzed from perspectives that end up making those intentions invisible should indeed be taken seriously. One gets the impression, for example, that many critics respond indignantly to any insinuation of subordination of the individual works to an overly complex thematic frame, as if the primary function of these shows were that of freeing the art from its intellectual overdeterminations. In other cases, the absence of theme is perceived as an inexcusable lack. Only rarely is the exhibitive structure of the event itself or its frequent extra-artistic ramifications given serious consideration — and this in spite of the fact that quite often these latter are structurally constitutive elements in terms of the explicit goals of their organizers. Reviewing the bibliography might seem funny if it weren't a truly uncomfortable, and even, at times, pathetic exercise [2]. Reproached for the frequent occurrence of errors and omissions, the careful reading of many journalistic reviews allows us to deduce that the author was not even able to visit the entire show. On the other hand, would have to be acknowledged that in many cases these are events that were simply not designed to be seen in their totality, both on account of their sheer size and on account of the fact that they are made up of a large number of components whose duration by far exceeds that of an average visit. Critics attempt to ignore this explicit intentionality and tend to react with disdain, without stopping to analyze their possible consequences. The lack of a frame of reference that could allow us to interpret these events becomes ever more evident as its development becomes ever more urgent. And this, by virtue of verifying that the type of specific operation that these shows carry out in the field of art and culture turns out to be hardly perceptible (if at all) through the opinions of a large part of their commentators. Titian's mountains blend into the mist that conceals and disguises them. From the printed page, only the repeated, interchangeable silhouettes of the cypresses can be discerned.

2.   For a paradigmatic historical example of this kind of coverage see: Brice Kurtz. "Documenta 5: A Critical Preview." *Arts magazine*, Summer 1972, Vol. 46, N° 8. Pag. 30, which contains, in a nutshell, most of the usual misunderstanding about these kind of events.

With regard to the rivers of ink that these shows release, both in the specialized press and in the mass media, the academic critical literature that specifically tackles these events is relatively scarce: barely a dozen books, divided into two or three languages, largely published in the last decade [3]. Perhaps both phenomena are related. Shows like Documenta or the Venice Biennale have acquired an unprecedented visibility in the area of contemporary art — a field of culture that, until recently, almost exclusively interested a more or less limited group of specialists. That same visibility suddenly turns them into desirable and even, occasionally, income-generating instruments for the political and corporate sectors. At the same time, it makes them anathema for the very intellectual spheres whose analytical capacity should (supposedly) help to elucidate their current meaning and possible potential. The majority of the few voices stemming from the circles of academic critics that mention these events tend to be unanimously discrediting. In most of their view, it is a case of an epiphenomena of mass culture, of the indisputable symptoms of the assimilation of the project of the avant-garde by the culture industry. Pure and simple spectacles whose logic is nothing more than that of capitalism in its late stage; that is, the progressive suppression of the multiple system of values and its trans-lation into a universal equivalent, namely, exchange value. In a certain way, this direction of analysis seems to imply that the oppositional nature, which characterizes the critical project in modernity, would be largely foreign to these kinds of shows that are unequivocally associated with the realms of marketing and consumption. Following this line of reasoning to the end, we may conclude that the apparent lack of criteria that journal-istic criticism underscores when referring to these kinds of events, as

3.   Altough there is certainly a profuse bibliography on museums, there seems to be no single publication on the subject of large-scale international exhibitions alone. Some of the most recent publications on the subject of exhibitions/curatorial practice are: Bruce Altshuler. *The Avant-Garde in Exhibition: New Art in the 20th Century*, Harry N. Abrams, 1994; Emma Barker ed. *Contemporary Cultures of Display*, Yale University Press, 1999; Reesa Greenberg, Bruce W. Ferguson, Sandy Nairne, ed. *Thinking About Exhibitions*, Routledge, 1996; Bernard Guelton. *L'Exposition: Interprétation et Reinterprétation*, Harmattan, 1998; Anna Harding, ed. *Curating the Contemporary Art Museum and Beyond*, London, Academy Editions, 1997; Susan Hiller and Sarah Martin, ed. *The Producers: Contemporary Curators in Conversation I, II, III, IV*, Gateshead Baltic, 2000–2003; Bern Klüser and Katharina Hegewisch, ed. *L'Art de l'Exposition*, Editions du Regard, 1988; Carin, Kuoni, ed. *Words of Wisdom: A Curator's Vade Mecum on Contemporary Art*, Independent Curators International, 2001; Paula Marincola, ed. *Curating Now: Imaginative Practice/Public Responsability*, Philadelphia Exhibitions Initiative, 2001; Dorothee Richter and Eva Schmidt ed. *Curating Degree Zero: An International Curating Symposium*, VG Bild-Kunst, 1999.

mentioned above, is nothing more than a symptom of the expiration of its traditional function in this specific stage of the development of the culture industry.

Art criticism emerged in a fashion parallel to the formation of an international circuit in which artists, galleries, and museums each found their own place. It is obvious that academic criticism, linked to universities (and overwhelmingly to the discipline of art history), finds its place in this same system as another of its institutional moorings. Artistic modernity is thus presented as a constellation of specific practices and institutional settings charged with discerning — and assigning — the relative values that incorporate them. The ensemble is determined by a certain way of representing the singularity of its own history and of articulating the value system that it produces. These institutional instances regulate the relationships between the individual parts that constitute them, at the same time as they restrict their degrees of freedom. Naturally, the assembly is not synchronic; it was not produced all at once. Instead, it is a more or less unstable product of a series of historical processes that, like sedimentary strata, wound up pairing off slowly in order finally to produce an impression of totality. For their survival, institutions require the illusion of everlastingness, since this is what, in the final analysis, safeguards them against their contingent character. In Western countries, modern art was thought to be structured around the relative balance between a number of institutions founded on a common history or histories; that is to say, on shared values. In this order of things, the tension between production and the market would have something like referees of criticism and museums [4]. We could say, very schematically, that the duty of criticism had been that of inscribing production into a symbolic field in a way that simultaneously made it accessible to the effects of the mechanisms of production of exchange value; and the duty of art history was that of recovering the specific differential in the work that hinders its complete subordination to exchange value. Between the two, the Museum — an institution that from its origins has had a fundamentally ideological character — sanctioned the value of the work as an exchange value, but not without first disguising this, hiding it in the folds of a particular

4.   A complementary account of the tension — concerning issues of taste and value — between the audience and an institution devoted to the public education and promotion of art can be found in: Seth Koven. "The Whitechapel Picture Exhibitions and the Politics of Seeing," in Daniel Sherman and Irit Rogoff, ed. *Museum Culture: Histories, Discourses, Spectacles*, Minnesota University Press, 1994.

historical narrative that it would supposedly be in charge of preserving and intensifying [5]. Obviously, it is not difficult to imagine that a case of exhibiting and producing works that is not immediately associated with either galleries or museums — and although it maintains a dialogue with both the market and history, nevertheless does not exactly respond to the expectations of either — may suddenly become at least partially illegible for the system in which it should supposedly operate.

But at this point I should clarify the types of events to which I am referring. Are we dealing with large-scale shows in general? With the international biennial circuit? Perhaps more importantly, are we dealing with a characterization that exclusively concerns the size of the exhibition — that is, the size of its budget and the number of works included — or could this also have to do with other factors, such as the nature of the institutional framework from which events like these are generated? Although an archeology of the large-scale international exhibition model would have to include many shows organized by more conventional art institutions, it seems fair to argue that Biennials represented them at their most exemplary. At first glance, biennials seem to have only their name in common. The Venice Biennale was carried out for the first time at the end of the nineteenth century, modeled on the world expositions that had been so popular throughout that century. It would take five more decades and two world wars to found the São Paulo Bienal, which, like Venice, has been taking, place ever since. In the brief interlude of fifteen years, from 1984 — the year in which the first edition of the Havana Bienal took place — to the present, over fifteen international biennials have been established, including those of Istanbul (1987), Lyon (1992), Santa Fe (1995), Kwan Ju (1995), Johannesburg (1995), Shanghai (1996), Berlin (1996), Montreal (1998), and others. [6] Moreover, the specific conditions in which these shows were established are as diverse as their resources and the attraction they exert, both on the specialized press and on the general media. The Venice Biennale served as a model for the São Paulo Bienal, and the initial function of the latter show had been to set itself up in conjunction with the former and with the Carnegie International (founded in 1896) in international events able to back the position of their respective cities — and countries — on the map of modern culture. In 1984, the first Havana Bienal obeyed a very clear

5.   See Theodor Adorno. "Valéry Proust Museum, in Prisms", MIT Press, 1982.
6.   See Paula Latos-Valier, "Biennales Big and Small," *Info* (bulletin of the 25th Biennial of Graphic Art in Ljubljana [Slovenia]), 2003.

ideological goal: to stimulate communication between artists and intel-
lectuals of the southern hemisphere, with the purpose of preventing the
distribution of contemporary art from being monopolized by the centers
of economic power. Havana's success was capitalized by a number of
biennials that emerged afterward, with the obvious function of granting
visibility to local productions and of promoting the cities and countries in
which they were carried out.

Nearly all the shows of this type rely on the official economic
support of their respective countries or cities. The presence of a
marketing component is therefore common to all. It is a question of
publicizing the artistic and cultural potential of a city, a country, and a
particular region. The origin of few has perhaps been as ideologically
marked as in the cases of the Havana Bienal and, of course, Documenta,
which since 1955 has been carried out — first every four years, and now
every five — in the German city of Kassel. On one hand, Documenta is a
fortunate subproduct of the Cold War, and on the other, it stemmed from
the need for postwar Germany to bring itself up to date with the evolution
of modern and contemporary art, leaving behind the painful excesses and
omissions of Nazism — which, among other things, affected the practice
and appreciation of modern art in that country [7]. In all cases, diplomacy,
politics, and commerce converge in a powerful movement whose purpose
seems to be the appropriation and instrumentalization of the symbolic
value of art. The specific motives change — Venice originally dealt with
the updating of a universalistic ideology clearly related to European
colonialism; Havana, on the other hand, staged an ideological project of a
diametrically opposing nature — but the type of operation is curiously the
same. Another point of agreement consists in the fact that the majority of
these shows emphasize the internationalist nature of cultural and artistic
production. It is not a question of a unified vision, but rather of considering internationalism a term literally in dispute, specifically interpreted in
highly diverse ways. The nature of the interests that generate the events
and their common commitment to a possible horizon of internationalism
seems to associate these shows in an intimate way to the ups and downs

7.   For a discussion on the connection between the first Documenta and the
"Degenerate Art" show see: Walter Grasskamp. " 'Degenerate Art' and Documenta I:
Modernism Ostracized and Disarmed," in Daniel J. Sherman and Irit Rogoff ed.
Museum Cultures: Histories, Discourses, Spectacles, University of Minnesota
Press, 1994. For Grasskamp, the tension between Documenta as an exemplary art
institution of post-war Germany and the questions posed to Modern art by the Nazis
would ultimately only be acknowledge in their full implications by the curatorial team
of Documenta 5 in 1972.

of modernity — and to the range of its possible interpretations. Their unstable nature — in a certain way, tentative, incomplete, and always subject to negotiations and readaptations — does nothing more than reinforce this tie.

In 1983, barely a year before the first edition of the Havana Bienal was carried out — the success of which in part led to the proliferation of these types of shows executed since then — Professor Theodore Levitt of Harvard University wrote in the *Harvard Business Review:* "the globalization of markets is at hand." This was one of the first texts that used a term that would become progressively more common in following years. The globalization to which Levitt referred consisted in the extension of the logic of economies of scale to a planetary level, and it was grounded in the supposed world convergence of consumer tastes. In an article written for the 20th anniversary of the publication of Levitt's text, Richard Tomkins states: "Prof. Levitt's message was simple. As new technology extended the reach of global media and brought down the cost of communications, the world was shrinking. As a result, consumer tastes everywhere were converging, creating global markets for standardised products on a previously unimagined scale." [8] The publication of that essay coincided with a period of market openness that, although in a less pronounced way, still continues today. In predicting a supposed convergence of consumer tastes, Levitt does not seem to take into account that, as a consequence of the spread of new technologies and the ever more decentralized use of information made possible as a result, the nature of the demand itself becomes more specialized. From the current perspective we could affirm that the value of Levitt's thesis consists mostly of its symptomatic character. Coinciding with the information revolution associated with the use of Internet and the progressive development of communications possibilities in general, Levitt's text foresees a period of progressive integration on a world level, although not of decentralization. In the realm of contemporary art, that phenomenon is reflected precisely through the growing proliferation of these unstable institutions of the megashows. We could venture the hypothesis that the biennials that have emerged in the last two decades have done so completely in tune with these transformations, as a result of the contrast between the tendency toward centralization typical of the integration of the markets on a global

8.   Richard Tomkins, "Happy Birthday, Globalisation," "Features," *Financial Times,* May 6, 2003.

scale and the increasing dissemination of information, which provides a growing visibility for local situations and problems. This tension is obviously essential in the case of institutions of this type whose aim, to a large extent, consists precisely of its representation and analysis.

It is evident that these institutions have been created with a clearly instrumental purpose: to respond to the interests that brought them about; that is, to promote the contexts in which they are carried out, giving them greater visibility on an international scale, supplying them with a patina of prestige, and ratifying the supposed commitment of these different contexts to modernity in general, and specifically to the processes of economic integration associated with late capitalism. The aura of prestige that surrounds art in general, and modern and contemporary art in particular, adapts perfectly to this task. What is instrumentalized through these types of events is precisely the symbolic capital of modern art, tied to its own presumed autonomy and independence from market logic. Following this line of reasoning, we could arrive at the paradoxical conclusion that the relationship between the supposed aim of art biennials and the traditional function of museums would simply come to be one of continuity. The symbolic value created initially by museums — as a concealed affirmation of the exchange value of the objects and artistic practices — is ultimately transformed by the biennials into pure utility. Perhaps this has been (and in many cases, continues to be) the ultimately credulous reasoning of the instigating institutions of many of the biennials. And in some cases it may even be partially proved. Nevertheless, this equation assumes a complete identity between what is exhibited in the museums and what is exhibited in the biennials. Furthermore, it assumes an agreement between the conceptual and ideological frameworks of both types of institutions. Both of these assumptions are erroneous.

The configuration of interests found at the core of institutions like biennials clearly differs from the configuration that gave rise to the institutional circuit traditionally linked to modernity in art: museums, criticism, and galleries. The commercial fate of the works, for example, is neither evident nor even strictly necessary in the case of such shows, for the simple reason that the bulk of the financing that concerns the realization of the event and the production of many of the projects is largely independent from collecting (either private or state-funded). This factor facilitates the inclusion of practices of a non-objectual nature, as well as works of an interdisplinary nature and even practices pertaining to other fields of cultural production — such as cinema, design, architecture, etc. — and it indirectly winds up stimulating the problematization of the notion of art as an autonomous activity. The inclusion of works of an interdisciplinary nature, as well as the insistent integration of discursive elements in these kinds of events, has progressively become a constant. [9] Moreover, the sheer size of these shows — necessary to achieve the impact on a marketing level that is expected of them — makes their insertion into highly particularized interpretative systems indispensable. Without these systems, the shows would lose their ability to communicate as discrete singularities; that is, they would lack all identity. In many cases, it is even manifestly expected that the conceptual framework charged with giving these events legibility is related to local questions — at least as far as the inclusion of elements tied to the local culture is concerned. This gives rise to the appearance of the figure of the curator as the event's conceptual organizer. In comparison with the traditional role of the curator at a museum, this more recent incarnation seems to have been endowed with a higher degree of autonomy. It is no longer a question of the discerning critic or the interpretive historian regarding a specific tradition, but rather of a relatively unfamiliar figure in charge of negotiating the distance between the value system that those other figures had traditionally established and the ideological pressures and practices corresponding to the institutional setting in which these kinds of events emerge. But the appearance of this specific incarnation of the curator is no mere accident; since this is a professional in the field of art situated in the position of responding to a number of extra-artistic conditionings and questions, her work is necessarily different from that of the figures that preceded her. [10] The type of knowledge that s/he puts into practice becomes less and less retrievable from the perspective of the critic or art historian, even if we are still dealing with a highly particular and specific knowledge. The chain of meanings that will make sense of the group

9.   Suffice it to mention the examples of "100 Days/100 Guests" at Documenta10, the four "Platforms" at Documenta11, and the events surrounding the "Archive of Contemporaneity" at the 50th Venice Biennale.
10.   See: Karsten Schubert. *The Curator's Egg: The Evolution of the Museum Concept from the French Revolution to the Present Day*, London, One-Off Press, 2000. In several chapters of the last section of his informative introductory account of the history of museums in the West, Karsten Schubert tackles on the changes experienced by the role of curators in the last three decades. Although his observations are primarely concerned with curators working at museums, they nonetheless seems inspired, or at least parallel and certainly more pertinent, to the transformation of the curatorial role as it takes place in regards to large-scale international exhibitions.

of practices gathered for a show of this type will, then, necessarily be constructed around an interrogation of the local histories and contexts, always in terms of their possible relationship to a presumed internationalist horizon. The curator's work is riddled with and overdetermined by these kinds of problems. Perhaps we could say that the curator's ability to produce a highly differentiated form of knowledge is related to the degree of fidelity that ties her to the ensemble of unique situations around which s/he develops her practice. This type of work thus implies the articulation of a reflection capable of linking forms of local culture and history with that horizon of internationalism that appears as one of the founding elements in these events. Finally, partially freed — or better yet, made independent by force — from the constrictions associated with the supposed autonomous nature of artistic production, the curator finds herself in the position, and with the need, to expand not only the canonical apparatus that articulates the historical narratives linked to the production of modern and contemporary art, but also the very definition of that which constitutes an artistic practice in a specific context. [11]

The supposed instrumental nature of biennials may thus serve, paradoxically, to try out a series of operations whose scope is largely radical when considered within the institutional context traditionally linked to (Western) modern and contemporary art. We could synthetically classify these operations into two types: on one hand, those of a revisionist sort, which lead to a reconsideration of the canonical mechanisms established in the historical narratives produced almost exclusively in Europe and the United States; on the other hand, the exploration of the position of the artwork in a wide cultural context in connection with a variety of symbolic practices to which it would supposedly not be related. An exhaustive revision of the canon and a reexamination of the autonomous nature of the work of art are actually two sides of the same coin, since an inquiry into the mechanisms that structure art history's narrative will inexorably lead us to consider historical discourse as highly ideologized and, therefore, the inevitable result of the intersection of heterogeneous and diverse practices and interests. The relationship with

11.   The consideration of art as an autonomous activity certainly leads to the inclusion of highly specialized practices in historical narratives. When this framework disappears as a prime intellectual motive, it becomes possible — and to a large extent, compulsory — to explore an expanded field of cultural production, since it would be a matter of understanding artistic practices in their relationships to the economic, political, and social context. To a certain extent, we could say that Documenta10 thematized precisely this process of canon revision.

the local context, which is usually mandatory in these events, becomes an opportunity to exercise the historical revisionism that, in the final analysis, inescapably ends with a questioning of the ideological base that articulates the institutions of artistic modernity. With respect to the traditional institutional structure, the events to which I am referring carry out a sort of surreptitious short circuit. Their supposed instrumentality, signaled by a sector of academic criticism as a function of their dependent relationship with the culture industry, would conversely be revealed as the juncture that facilitates the expansion of the canon and the exploration of an expanded notion of that which would set itself up as an artistic practice in a specific context. Needless to say, although this range of possibilities appears inscribed in the very institutional structure of these types of events, it is no guarantee of their realization. The figure responsible for actualizing this range of possibilities is, inevitably, that of the event's curator. And this is because the determinations that could guarantee the effectiveness of her practice — in the case of this type of show — are in no way predetermined by the institutional framework in which that practice is carried out, unlike what happens when the curator joins the traditional structure of the museum. The curator's inevitable lead role in such shows has recently given her an exaggerated, and clearly equivocal, level of visibility in the cultural field. It is a question of a misunderstood celebrity status. Between a mere instrument of the culture industry and one of the most recent incarnations of the model of the independent intellectual, the possible range into which the curator's decisions are introduced is at once remarkably vast and dangerously undefined.

The invisibility to which I referred at the beginning of this text is clearly related to the position that these shows occupy with respect to the traditional circuit of criticism, the museum, and galleries. They never completely belong to the system of art institutions in which they are supposedly inscribed, and the range of practical and theoretical possibilities to which they give rise often turns out to be subversive — let's not forget that museums are first and foremost Western institutions, and that the global expansion of large-scale international exhibitions performs an insistent de-centering of the canon and of artistic modernity. In a growing fashion, one has the impression that the vitality of these kinds of shows seems to be a direct function of the number of visitors that they attract and the dissemination that they achieve in the media, and in inverse relation to the appreciation of specialized criticism — in terms of the politics of exclusion historically enacted by the institutions of modernity, large-scale international exhibitions, as was the case with theater in the High Renaissance, could perhaps be considered as "a force for the breakdown of class distinctions, even for democratization" [12]. However, that vitality is undoubtedly the best guarantee of their survival. To a large extent, the conceptual horizon that shows such as the two latest editions of Documenta or the first Havana Bienal have opened still remains largely unexplored. There is no doubt, however, that many aspects tied to these kinds of events have been partially absorbed and recycled by museums and galleries — a process that is not at all recent, although it has visibly sped up over the last decade. One instance is exemplified by the fact that in that short span of time a significant number of artists have effectively been incorporated into the canonical narrative of the postwar period. Many conventional museums have resourced to the implementation of Biennial or Triennial showcases as a way to increase the number of their visitors and attract the attention of the press. In some cases, a clear and direct influence of these types of shows on the traditional institutional circuit is confirmed; in others, it is more a question of partial coincidences in the development of independent — though without a doubt, simultaneous — processes, as that form of internationalism that has been labeled "globalization" increasingly determines the financing and programming of a large part of the museums in Europe and the United States. Beyond these transformations and a sense of growing interdependence among traditional modern institutions and these types of shows, the implications of the latter do not yet seem to have found a framework of appropriate analysis. These events are insistently evaluated in terms of the logic of the institutions of modernity and not in relation to the challenges that they embody. A proper historic account of the emergence of these institutions is still required. A clearer understanding of their implications in terms of an interrogation of the canon and the modern notion of the autonomy of art is equally needed. Although the project of the formulation of alternative versions of (Western) modernity seems to have been a driving force for many of these institutions from

12.   William J. Bouwsma. *The Waning of the Renaissance: 1550–1640*, New Haven and London, Yale University Press, 2000. Pag. 131. An interesting paralellism could be established between the emergence of teather as a cultural practice in the High Renaissance and the position that large-scale international exhibitions occupy in today's cultural lansdcape. Both originally distrusted for their connection to spectacle and commerce, their artistic evolution being partially function of their growing popularity, are examples of a complex relation between culture and spectacle that the institutions of modernity traditionally rejected.

their very beginning, the implications of such a radical move remained yet to be theorized. The development of large scale exhibitions can be associated with the economic and informational transformation of late capitalis — like the expansion of tourism at a global scale and the concurrent rise in the number of museum visitors worldwide; in sum, a growing process of democratization of culture that is caracterized by an increasing intermingling between education and entertainment. Large-scale exhibitions could be referred to as one of the possible responses to these phenomena from the cultural field. Nonetheless, there is little understanding of their position in terms of the cultural industry and the institutions of artistic modernity. Their contribution to the cultural field has barely been accounted for. Perhaps it is precisely in an inquiry of this nature where we could find the possibility of giving the kind of visibility to these events that would allow us, among other things, to articulate an effective reform of the institutions of modernity. [13]

13.   A number of institutions founded in the postwar period and dedicated to exhibiting modern and contemporary art shared — at least if we take their original intention into account — several aspects in common with the events to which I am referring. One particularly remarkable example is that of the Georges Pompidou Center, established as an interdisciplinary laboratory for research on modern and contemporary cultural production. Although the Pompidou's activity under the administration of Pontus Hultén seemed headed in the direction of satisfying these aims, it later began to transform progressively into a more or less conventional modern art museum. On rare occasions, some exhibitions still conserve an interdisciplinary and revisionist nature that nevertheless does not dominate the entire program.

INCONSEQUENTIAL BAYONETS? [1]

A CORRESPONDENCE ON CURATION, INDEPENDENCE AND COLLABORATION

Dave Beech & Mark Hutchinson

MARK HUTCHINSON   Independence is always independence from something. In art, there is a first-order sense of independence, in which the artist is an independent practitioner. In this aesthetic version of self-employment, the artist can make what he or she likes in self-determined activity. It is precisely through this aspect of self-determination that Steve Edwards can interpret art as resisting the division of mental and manual labour, which he uses in putting forward art as a model of utopian work. However, this first order independence is predicated upon the freedom of the market. The market allows anyone to bring their goods to it (in principle) and enter into relations of exchange with other commodities. This is one of the conditions for Modern art's independence. As Terry Eagleton reiterates in *After Theory*, it is capitalism, which is disinterested not dons. But here, being independent is also being isolated: it is commodities not persons that the market brings into relationship with each other.

The relation of the curator to the first order independence of the market is, perhaps, harder to gauge. The curator works directly at the point of arts reception: the job of curation is to mediate the reception of art. It is worth remembering how new this contemporary idea of the curator is: if it first emerged in the 1970s, it is only in the last ten years that it has become such a prominent and pervasive presence in the art world.

I am tempted to speculate that there is a connection between the recent rise of specialist, technical jobs at the point of arts distribution and the recent changes in contemporary capitalism. It is well documented how contemporary capitalism has evolved logic, which is 'cultural' rather than productivist. There is an inversion of the relationship between the commodity and its image: whereas the image used to support the sale of the commodity now the commodity supports the sale of the image. Companies such as Nike no longer own the means of production of Nike goods; the ideal state for such global corporations is to own nothing — to outsource all production. What Nike sells is not so much trainers and the like, but ideas. And isn't art in a similar position? With hindsight, the conceptualist scrutiny of the ontological status of the artwork coincided with capitalism's shift from things to ideas. No wonder that ideas of dematerialization became prevalent in art at a time when this was exactly what was going on with capitalism? So, perhaps it is possible to link the rise of the structural position of the curator within art's social relations with an ontological shift in capitalism itself. This is not to suggest that all (or any) curation can be reduced to the economic. It is to suggest one way, at least, in which curation is dependent on ideological, hegemonic structures. Furthermore, any curation which wishes to assert its independence must do so from a position which acknowledges its dependence: that it does not operate under conditions of its own choosing.

It is tempting to think of independence as only being possible as a kind of second order independence. That is, it is not possible to be independent of the existing dominant institutions of art unless you are also within them. If the fault line of divisions, absences, aporias, lacks, ills and so forth does not run between art and everything else but rather through art and everything else, then tackling art politically is going to be a matter of attending to division within art. The adoption of the philistine is predicated on seeing the negations within art as co-terminus with the negations inherent to capitalism. It is not possible to be independent as an individual. If dependence is about the relationship one has with others, then so is independence. Independence must be a collaborative project.

For curation, an essential question is something like: how is the position of the curator placed within the existing divisions of art? For example, it is hard to think of any advertising agency as ever being in a position to be politically radical. Advertising is trying to sell you things you don't want, and as such is a vital component in the running of contemporary capitalism. Now it is possible to study (and presumably practice) such a thing as "ethical advertising." But it is hard to think of a better example of what Zizek calls "interpassivity." Making advertising ethical is a way to change things to stop them really changing: indeed, of avoiding thinking the kind of change that would be necessary to bring advertising to an end. Is curation in a similar irredeemable position? Perhaps we could ask the question this way: is it possible to have philistine curators? Or, perhaps, is it possible for the philistine within each curator to have expression in what the curator does, qua curator?

How might we think about what it is that the curator does? One way of thinking of the curator is as a kind of expert of display. I think that this is a fairly dominant self-image of much contemporary curation. Bolstered by a myriad of theoretical terminology, the curator deploys techniques, strategies and methodologies. As an expert, such practice can be thought about in terms of efficiency, accessibility, transparency and the like: technical criteria for a technical practice. In one sense, this is all well and good: being incompetent is not easily reconciled with radical practice.

What is interesting, is what the idea of expertise leaves out, or cannot address. At one level, it is hard to imagine that this view of curation could be become critical of its own constitution and conditions of possibility: of its own political and social determinations. But to view the curator as an expert on display is also to think of the curator as an expert on art. And here there are certain difficulties. If we take art to be a critical project of self-making and self-transformation, then it is difficult to see what an expert on art is an expert in? The old fashioned (pre-1970) curator was a keeper of a particular collection: someone who had expert knowledge precisely because the object of their knowledge was fixed and finite. The curator of a diverse, troublesome and changing art, surely needs to begin from a position of doubt and uncertainty, or, indeed, from a position of listening. The curator *qua* expert is someone who knows in advance what is art and what is good for art. The curator qua listener is trying to find out what a particular piece of art might need. That is, what this latter curator might do is going to be determined by entering into a reciprocal and collaborative relationship with artists. A condition for this possibility is the independence of the curator from institutional and established ties, both contractual and ideological.

In a way, this is to suggest the possibility of the curator becoming a co-producer with the artist. This is dangerous territory, re relational aesthetics and all that. We need some analysis of different kinds of collaboration and agency.

For the Lacanian psycho-analyst, what defines the analyst is not that he or she is the subject supposed to know but that he or she knows that the subject supposed to know doesn't in fact know. The purpose of analysis is not to impart the analyst's expert knowledge but to provide the conditions in which the patient can disabuse him or herself of the belief in the subject supposed to know. In as much as the investment in a guarantor of meaning is the negation of agency of the subject, psycho-analysis is the negation of a negation. It is a process not only without compensation but also against compensation: the outcome of psycho-analysis is that the patient accepts that there are no guarantees, which includes abandoning a model of compensation.

The curator could be imagined as a subject supposed to know. What would be interesting would be to imagine the curator, as someone who knows this and knows that the subject supposed to know doesn't exist. Of course the artist is not exactly in an equivalent position to the analysand — or is she? One way to describe the analysand might be as someone who is not independent enough — someone who is not able to act outside of an economy of guarantees and compensations: someone who is watchful of being watched. And is not the danger for the artist to be making work in relation to the (false) universal Art — to be looking to Art as a guarantor of his or her actions as an artist?

The problem with curation is not that it mediates the reception of art (how could the reception of art not be mediated?) but that it so often adopts a position of expertise in a way that implicitly asserts an authority over art. This is the assigned position of curation within the dominant modes of distribution for art: a practice that deals in cultural capital. But it is not the only possibility for curation. A curation that is sure of itself, in the sense of not having a critical self-awareness of its own agency, goes to reproduce the accepted norms and authority of art and to elide the contradictions and divisions of art. A critically self-aware curation would have to enter into a mutual and dialogical relationship with artists. It might not even be clear that such a practice was curation at all. Such a practice would have to live with doubt and conflict.

DAVE BEECH   The question that haunts the critique of curation is this: how can individual curators exceed the political economy of the curator as subject to a discipline, as an historical figure and as an institutional functionary? Or, less optimistically: what prevents curators from *doing something else*? Anti-art is, here, preferred as a model to profession-alism, competence, skill and so on. *Doing something else* thus stands in for a range of activities and positions that resist complicity. If, as you say, independence is always independence from something, then complicity is always complicity with something — a market, an institution, a history, a conception of art's social value, an anthropology of the art-goer — and, therefore, *doing something else* means resisting the specific constraints of the market, art's institutions, art's histories, etc. As we learn from anti-art, resistance to complicity (to complicities) does not derive from isolating one's practice from the social world, but from interrupting and infecting art with social contexts that are suppressed or excluded by art's official discourses.

Have there been any anti-curators? The über-curators can be radical, innovative, challenging, interesting... but none of the key players in curating have been anti-curators, have they? Quite the opposite (and your point about authority comes in here): the curator has taken up the mantle of the author after artists have adapted to the death of the author. In order to get a glimpse of what an anti-curator might be like, then, we need to look at artists curating. Bank exhibitions such as *Zombie Golf, Cocaine Orgasm, Bank TV, Dog-u-Mental* and *Charge of the Light Brigade* were gloriously incompetent curatorial projects, crackling with division, conflict and contingency rather than orchestrated according to professional standards of museum display. What is significant, here, is not that Bank and other anti-professional artist-led projects might offer some bad tempered model for ill-at-ease curators. Quite the inverse. What artist-led projects suggest is that the question of the critique of curating is actually a broader question of how art is organised socially. Curators, then, are not the experts of display, reception and interpretation; they are collaborators in art's social relations. In this respect, perhaps, the analogy with the analyst (as the one who is supposed to know) is not required except insofar as the curator has taken on the institutional role of the one who knows. Curators have become an additional slice of management only by concealing their dependence on the knowledge of others. In fact, this concealed dependence on others is true of all post-Taylorist managers: the division between mental and manual labour, that is the separation of organisation from activity, is always dependent on workers sorting out problems 'on the ground'.

In a recent email exchange with a young curator, some of these issues have come up. His curatorial strategy — which is not uncommon — seems to involve coming up with a vague framework and hoping that the artists will save his blushes. When confronted with this he said, "I trust the capability of critical/engaged/political cultural producers to express any thoughts, concerns and solutions regarding the 'theme' with their work". If there is anything wrong with his curatorial framework, then, he is confident that the artists will rectify the exhibition for him. His dependence on the artists is concealed by the explicit commitment to the critical engagement of artists, which the curator forgoes. Art & Language, in a public talk at Tate Britain a couple of years ago, took issue with curators of this sort by making something of the possibility that an artwork might stand out from the institutional framework that is supposed to bring meaning to it. "The group show can be bad while the individual works were good", they speculate, concluding, therefore, "paintings [by which they mean 'internally complex artworks'] are subversive of the institution." If my young curator is anything to go by, on the contrary, such internally complex — "good" — artworks are manna from heaven for the institution.

Art & Language's either/or argument (either object or institution) is ontologically blunt because they want to preserve a space for artworks to outrank the institution; they want the artist to resist the bullying of the curator. This is ontologically unsustainable, though, because it involves splitting off the artist and the art object from the totality of art's social being. You wouldn't even have an artist to split off from the institution if art's institutions had not fostered the modern conception of the artist in the first place! Similarly, our critique of the curator can neither begin with nor hope for the splitting off of the curator from art's social being. What's more, if the curator is to be able to *do something else*, then curating must be rethought as embedded in social being. In other words, if the objectionable tradition of curating is based on the curator being split off from art, culture and society, the radical critique of curating needs to reinsert the curator back into the cultural totality. Doing something else means being something else.

MARK HUTCHINSON   If, for the curator, doing something else means being someone else, then it seems important to stress that this "being" encompasses the occupation of existing structures in a different way. It is not being something other than a curator. The institutional role of curation is predicated on a de-totalizing split in art's social relations. Such a split is both a necessary condition for the constitution of the curator and what is maintained by the very idea of the curator. The curator is always already embedded in social relations. The problem of rethinking the curator as embedded in social relations is the question of what that embedding might be. The conventional and objectionable tradition of the curator does not so much split off the curator from art, culture and society than preserve a separate sphere of action and influence *within* art, culture and society: a sphere that conceals and denies the existing social relations of art (and therefore of the curator him — or herself). Curation has been, perhaps, not so much split off from art, as the demarcation of a split within the totality of art's social being. The political task for curation, in overcoming the de-totalizing split inherent within curation, is not to formulate some alternative, positive model of curation. On the contrary, if the de-totalizing split inherent in curation is the negation of certain experiences and so on (the negation of modes of being), then the uncovering of the concealments, refusals and denials hitherto present in curation is the negation of these negations.

Anti-curation, along the lines of the anti-art, might offer a way of thinking through the predicaments of curation. However, if this is an act of "interrupting and infecting art with social contexts," then this could also be the invoking or remembering of that which has been repressed, excluded and denied. Social contexts, I want to say, have always been present in art and "art's official discourses." they are present as the cause of symptoms rather than the condition of agency (in Bhaskar's sense). That is to say, they are present as absences.

If anti-art infects art with social contexts then anti-curation infects curation with social context, likewise. Anti-art is not "not-art" and anti-curation is not "not-curation." The subversive potential of anti-art is not about championing something outside of art (the excluded, the everyday, etc.) at the expense of art: rather it is about confronting art with what is internal to art but which art itself refuses to countenance. In this precise sense, anti-art is the dialectical transformation of art: the absenting of absences. Anti-art implies that there is something about art worth transforming. My hesitation over the word "infects" is because it implies that there is something pure, complete or uncontaminated, which falls prey to an outside force. Whilst this captures both the violence of the situation and the self-image of art in art's dominant discourses as something positive and pure, it misses out on the way that art is always already marked by splits and absence. Remembering the past might offer another metaphor, if we think of remembering as a repetitive nightmare rather than misty nostalgia: the repression of a traumatic event making itself felt. Could we say, perhaps, that anti-art haunts art like a nightmare?

And what of curation? Anti-curation implies that there is something about curation (in the social relations of curation) worth transforming: that it is worthwhile for the curator to be something else. The point about artists doing curation is that these artists were anti-curators to the degree that they transformed the social relations involved in producing the shows that they did. Needless to say, there are plenty of artist-curators, whose curation does not question how art is organized socially: who are following a conventional career path. As Art & Language might put it, they are quite happy to bully themselves. We need to take care to see the divisions between curators, artists and other art profes-sionals as secondary divisions: as themselves upshots of the divisions internal to each and internal to art and culture as such. That is to say, the social relations between artist, curators and so on, follow the internal repression in art of certain knowledges, experiences and so on: art's current social relations are built on the concealment and denial of these primary divisions.

DAVE BEECH　　You hesitate over the use of the word "infects" because it implies that there is something "pure, complete or uncontaminated" which anti-curation spoils. I don't think this conception of infection implies a pure, complete or uncontaminated curator; I think it implies a conventionalised identity that acts as a horizon for practice. Infection does not presuppose a closed totality of this sort. On the contrary, it is the resistance to the idea of an outside to curation that implies the closed totality. I'll explain this in a second. First I want to dwell a moment on how much we agree.

　　Curation has to be seen as riddled with absences, splits, ills and contradictions — despite its apparent, ideological and institutionalised professional identity. In fact, that apparently cohesive identity is itself an absenting force. And in this sense you are absolutely right that anti-curation confronts curation with what is internal but repressed in curation: anti-curation thus absents the absences of curation. Repressed absences, such as the social relations of curation, are already absented, so anti-art has to absent those repressions as well as absent (ie transform) those social relations. Of course, if curation were not characterised by these sorts of absences and ills then anti-curation would be indefensible. It is because curation is riddled with all manner of absences that anti-curation is called for.

　　However, I am concerned here about turning curation into a closed totality for which absences and constraints will only ever be internal ones. Bhaskar makes this point in relation to Hegel's dialectic. Hegel follows a set pattern in his dialectic characterised by preservative sublation. This is because Hegel's conception of totality is closed. All sublation therefore preserves and overcomes internal limitations on truth. Bhaskar argues that this is false by showing that there are also external constraints and also that no preservative sublation can avoid loss of some sort — something has to be lost, even if it is only time. So, the idea of infection, of an external force, can't be ruled out. In fact, the force which curation needs in order to absent its own absences is likely to be an external one if curation is the result of the sort of detotalizing split that you refer to. What curation needs now, I would argue, is an infection of that from which it has split in order to shape itself as a separate practice.

Hence, when and if the curator does something else — and *becomes* something else — I agree that this 'being' occupies existing structures differently but I want to go further and suggest that this "being" also occupies *different structures* differently. So, I want to add something to your insistence that doing something else "is not being something other than a curator". I want to add this: doing something else means being something other than a curator *as a curator*. It is this collision of otherness and identity that I am thinking of according to the model of infection — it is not a question of discovering what is already internal to the curator or of abandoning the curator altogether; it is a question of transforming the curator by infecting the curator with that which is other to the curator. Like anti-artists who resisted the institutional tramlines of artistic and aesthetic practices, the anti-curator needs to resist the horizon of curation. It is to the outside, the other, the external and the alien that the curator needs to turn, and to turn into.

1.   The title derives from Tristan Tzara's first Dada Manifesto from 1918. The opening sentence of the manifesto is as follows: "DADA is our intensity: it erects inconsequential bayonets and the Sumatral head of German babies; Dada is life with neither bedroom slippers nor parallels; it is against and for unity and definitely against the future; we are wise enough to know that our brains are going to become flabby cushions, that our antidogmatism is as exclusive as a civil servant, and that we cry liberty but are not free; a severe necessity with neither discipline nor morals and that we spit on humanity".

63 – 79

CREATING SHOWS: SOME NOTES ON EXHIBITION AESTHETICS AT THE END OF THE SIXTIES

Irene Calderoni

The history of art exhibitions of the 20th century is riddled with attempts to amend the relationship between the development of artistic tendencies and the experimentation of new display concepts. Avant-garde art exhibitions often tried to model themselves after the characteristics of the art they displayed for the public, thus manifesting themselves as works of the same genre they were showing. [1] From this perspective, an analysis of a group of exhibitions held at the end of the sixties, at the time of the emergence of practices related to post-minimal art, conceptual art and Arte Povera, seems particularly relevant. The curatorial practice of this period was also profoundly involved in the evolution of artistic languages, to the extent that the exhibition medium, as well as the role of the curator itself, was drastically redefined. Therefore, an examination of a sample of these shows becomes significant, not only for documentary purposes, but also for an analysis of the questions that were raised then and continue to be a concern within the contemporary context.

"Museographical Emergency" is the term Tommaso Trini coined in 1969 when he addressed the problems generated by the introduction into the museum context of a kind of art that tried to strain all the assumptions of traditional aesthetics. [2] For Trini, the dilemmas raised appeared to be unresolved and irresolvable, since the fixity of the museum space could not handle the process-oriented dimension of these art interventions. Others, however, believe that the shows Trini referred to are the sole examples of a successful symbiosis between artistic research and exhibition aesthetics. *Teatro delle Mostre* (Galleria La Tartaruga, Rome, 1968), *Nine at Leo Castelli* (Castelli Warehouse, New York, 1968), *January 5–31, 1969* (Seth Siegelaub, New York, 1969), *Op Losse Schroeven/Situaties en Cryptostructuren* (Stedelijk Museum, Amsterdam, 1969), *Live in your head: when attitudes become form* (Kunsthalle, Bern, 1969), *Anti-Illusion: Procedures/Materials* (Whitney Museum, New York, 1969), *Spaces* (MoMA, New York, 1969), *557,087* (Art Museum, Seattle, 1969) and *Information* (MoMA, New York, 1970),

1.   See Bruce Altshuler, *The Avant-garde in Exhibition*, New York: Harry N. Abrams, 1994. Compare the concept of "ideological exhibition" proposed by Lewis Kachur with regard to historical avant-garde shows in Lewis Kachur, *Displaying the Marvellous: Marcel Duchamp, Salvador Dalí and Surrealist Exhibition*, Cambridge, Mass.: MIT Press, 2001. A very interesting assertion in the question of exhibition aesthetics seems to have been put forward by Bruce W. Ferguson, who, promoting the adoption of analytic tools from semiotics, worked on the concept of exhibition as medium and speech. See Bruce W. Ferguson, "Exhibition Rhetorics: material speech and utter sense" in Reesa Greenberg, Bruce W. Ferguson and Sandy Nairne, eds., *Thinking about Exhibitions*, London: Routledge, 1996.
2.   Tommaso Trini, "The Prodigal Master's Trilogy", *Domus* 478, September, 1969.

are all examples of exhibitions which have gone down in history as not just functioning as the vehicles of the movements they rendered visible, but also as works in themselves which managed to express a level of meaning and experimentation of their own. [3]

Multiple aspects, ranging from display techniques to catalogue design and from advertising strategies to the artist-institution relationship, rendered these shows innovative with respect to traditional shows. The innovation, or, rather, the common matrix connecting them all, lies in the fact that, from hereon, the spatial and temporal context of artistic production would coincide with the context of the exhibition. In most cases, the works did not pre-exist the shows, but were created for and within them, with relevant consequences for the status of both the work and the exhibition medium. This resulted in the emergence of an awareness of the centrality of the presentation of the artwork, as well as the idea that the artwork operates as a function of, and is limited to, that place and that moment.

In the previous decade there had already been some shows which, in ways similar to those analysed here, had tried to test the limits of the exhibition medium, and had turned themselves into event-shows where the works "happened", and where the space and time of the exhibition merged into those of the artistic interventions. Some of the most notable examples are the experiences of the Gutai Group, whose exhibitions, between 1955 and 1958, were crucial precursors both to Happenings and Performance art, and to the development of process-oriented art practices in general. By staging the process of creation of the work of art, particularly pictorial, these artists brought the core of Action Painting to its extreme consequence — turning painting into pure action. The action then becomes the very work of art beyond the finished object. By 1969 Robert Barry, one of the key figures in the conceptual revolution, would have declared, "The *word* art is becoming less of a noun and more of a verb". [4] Another important example can be identified in the history of

3.   One of the most recent and comprehensive chronologies has been compiled by Susan Jenkins, "Information, Communication, Documentation: An Introduction to the Chronology of Group Exhibitions and Bibliographies" in Ann Goldstein and Anne Rorimer, *Reconsidering the Object of Art: 1965-1975*, exhibition catalogue, Los Angeles: MoCA, 1996. Already in 1973, Lucy Lippard with *Six Years* had offered a complete recording of the events in *quasi* real time. Lucy R. Lippard, *Six Years: The dematerialization of the art object from 1966 to 1972*, New York: Praeger, 1973. Rpt., Berkeley: University of California Press, 1997.

4.   Robert Barry quoted in Alexander Alberro, *Conceptual Art and the Politics of Publicity*, Cambridge, Mass.: MIT Press, 2003, p.55.

installation as an artistic medium. In this case the place of the exhibition and the work of art become a single entity. The relationship with the surrounding architectural space assumes a new and dominant role, one in which the work invades the environment, absorbing it and modifying it according to its objectives. From Lucio Fontana's *Ambiente Nero* (1949) to Yves Klein's *Le Vide* (1958), from Arman's *Le Plein* (1960) to Oldenburg's *The Store* (1961), the exhibition space emptied or saturated, highlighted in its essentiality or altered by the invasion of alien objects, is brought to the forefront, and becomes the very material of the artwork.

Space and time, architecture and theatre: it is between these poles, and within the precarious balance of these dimensions as well as in the hybridisation of these 'other' genres that the museographical challenge, posed by art at the end of the sixties against traditional exhibition structures, unfolds. It was a matter of fitting square pegs into round holes, of giving fluidity to something that was typically fixed, of making temporary what has always been characterised by its ambition for permanence.

On a base level, it can be argued that works of art which have been specifically created for an exhibition are at the same time both site-specific and time-specific, their *raison d'être* being that they were designed for the exhibition's particular space and time. It is within the here and now of the show that this signifying relationship, which generates the expressive similarity between exhibition medium and exhibited works, can be drawn. This essay will consider the three relevant components: space, time and institution. However, these aspects will not be examined as different inflections within the definition of context. Instead, each of them will be viewed in light of different articulations of the connections between art and exhibition. Usual approaches consider these components as a unity, underlining their interdependence, but here I would argue that the distinctions must be maintained, even though the period in question witnessed the relevance of their emergence as a whole. In other words, although it can be said that in works created for specific exhibitions an inclination towards site, temporality and to the institutional framework are essential elements, the nature and treatment of these same elements are characterised by different levels of complexity, with regard both to artistic practices and curatorial strategies.

Consequently, it becomes necessary to examine these exhibitions and the art they presented in order to establish how, in each case, curatorial and artistic decisions contributed to the creation of the supposed identity and affinity of their vocabulary. Of particular importance is the understanding of how the process or contextual elements emerged. How did these aspects influence the exhibitions as works in themselves? How did they define their aesthetics? From which perspective can we consider these shows as experimental contexts for the exhibition language and the institutions? How did they amend the relationship between artists and institutions, specifically between artists and curators? Have the innovations of the past become institutionalised?

This last point is of particular relevance when current exhibition practices are taken into account. In the nineties, Andrea Fraser carried out a vast survey of post-studio practices and interventions in the public sphere. The survey dealt with questions raised by practices usually referred to as project-work, which she renamed *service-oriented*, and which have been included with great difficulty in the context of the exhibiting institutions. In fact these institutions, which are geared toward the exhibition of objects, are unable, according to Fraser, to accommodate the specific needs and features of these procedure-based activities. [5] Fraser placed some of these characteristics in connection with artistic tendencies, which emerged at the end of the sixties. This period, and particularly the shows which this essay will discuss, witnessed the shift in orientation toward service and thus the simultaneity of the production and consumption of the product. If these shows managed to align curatorial practices with artistic ones, it was not only due to the contemporaneous nature of the works' creation and fruition, but rather caused by a deeper revision of the exhibition medium with respect to the expressive requirements of the work.

I will not go into detail about whether exhibiting issues raised by current art practices were caused by an involution which followed the innovations introduced within artistic institutions at that time, or whether contemporary art practices pose a completely different set of questions which require specific tools and solutions. Nevertheless, it seems relevant to examine a period which was important specifically for the intensity of both its artistic and curatorial research and experimentation. As Catherine David noted, regarding current tendencies which are characterised by very complex processes and often lack proper conclusions, a new planning of exhibition times and models becomes necessary,

5.   Andrea Fraser, "What's Intangible, Transitory, Mediating, Participatory, and Rendered in the Public Sphere?" in *Museum Highlights. The Writings of Andrea Fraser*, edited by Alexander Alberro, Cambridge, Mass.: MIT Press, 2005.

one which takes into consideration the different levels of complexity and meaning. [6] In this way, a multiplication of spatial and temporal contexts, which give visibility to a single art project, could succeed the simultaneity of creation and fruition in the context of the show.

From Studio to Museum: The Space Invasion

The work of art's belonging to a specific place, its being deeply rooted in it, its immobility, the attention to the concrete aspects of a space, be it architecture or nature: these are the defining features of site-specific practices at the end of the sixties. From Robert Smithson's "Site Selection Study", [7] which states that the artist's role is to explore a site in order to disclose and exhibit it, to Robert Barry's installations, which, according to the artist, could not be moved without being destroyed, from the interdependence between work and site declared by Richard Serra, for whom the work performs a critical analysis geared toward the alteration of a site, to Daniel Buren, who wrote that any work which does not take into account the architectural framework in which it is inserted runs the risk of being reduced to nothing, site-specificity is not only a way of working but also a central theme of the interventions.

The desertion of the atelier as the place traditionally devoted to the conception and creation of art was the necessary consequence of site-specific practices and, at the same time, the expression of the rejection of modernist concepts of the artist and of the institutional structures. The studio crumbles like the House of Usher, declared Smithson. The studio must be eliminated since it is a sclerotic habit of art, according to Buren. It is a pillar of a system to be deconstructed, that triad studio-gallery-museum that Harald Szeemann also considers as a target to hit and sink. [8]

6.   Catherine David, writing in "Inquiry. Learning from Documenta", *Parkett* 64, 2002.

7.   Robert Smithson, "Towards the Development of an Air Terminal Site", *Artforum*, 5:10, June 1967.

8.   Robert Smithson, "A Sedimentation of the Mind: Earth Projects", *Artforum*, 7:1, September 1968; Daniel Buren, *Les Écrits (1965–1990),* Bordeaux: capcMusée d'art contemporain de Bordeaux, 1991, Vol. I: 1965–1976; Harald Szeemann, introductory text to *When Attitudes Become Form*, exhibition catalogue, Bern: Kunsthalle Bern, 1969. Post-studio artists was a term used by Carl Andre to refer to the fact that artworks were not physically produced by the artist anymore, this aspect being delegated to other people. However, as Scott Burton noted in his essay in the catalogue of *When Attitudes Become Form,* the term can be more widely adopted to include a variety of artists whose practice makes the relationship between art and site more complex and meaningful.

Evidently, the reference is to the economical and social aspects of the art system, which impose ways of production and distribution of works as commodities, as autonomous objects, which consequently, are more vulnerable to the market's logic. [9] Thus *in situ* work has the goal of giving the artist more control over his/her work and over its circulation and presentation in the exhibition context, therefore attempting to reduce the mediating role carried out by artistic institutions. [10] Site-specific practices then become a way of reconstituting the work's use-value, which has supposedly been superseded or replaced by its exchange-value. However, as it has been argued, the shift from studio to museum as the place of creation is also a consequence, and subsequently the origin, of the exasperation of another kind of value — the exhibition value. [11]

The exhibition space becomes the first and only context for the realisation of the artwork and, at the same time, the site in which the work adapts itself and also modifies. This last point is particularly relevant, since it constitutes one of the main aspects of the novelty introduced by the shows to be examined. In fact, if site-specific practices emerged at the moment when artists worked directly within the exhibition context, developing their projects in the space and in response to this space, the level of freedom they were permitted in the alteration of display habits and architectural environment was a new and peculiar phenomenon. That the exhibition spaces leave themselves at the mercy of artists is most evident and most extraordinary in the case of museums, which by definition are institutional and inflexible.

Minimal sculpture had opened up the investigation of the relationship between the art object and the space of its insertion, but its framework of physical and ideological reference continued to be the white cube, with which its confrontation had started and ended. The ascetic

9.   Andrea Fraser, "What's Intangible, Transitory, Mediating, Participatory, and Rendered in the Public Sphere? Part II", in *Museum Highlights*. Since the sixties, questions linked to a social history of art, and then to a sociology of art, have become a central concern for artists and for the works of art themselves. What is relevant in this kind of approach is how the variables are always considered in their interaction. From this perspective, the withdrawal from the studio cannot be considered solely as the product of an art poetics or of individual intentionality and thus it becomes necessary to examine the circumstances, which made this gesture possible. This approach is also what obviously legitimates the study of artistic and exhibition practices through their joint evolution.

10.   See Veronique Rodriguez, "L'atelier et l'exposition: deux espaces en tension entre l'origine et la diffusion de l'œuvre", *Sociologie et sociétés* 34, Autumn 2002. Daniel Buren is one of the artists who most fiercely sustained this position in practice and also through fundamental theoretical work.

11.   Rodriguez, "L'atelier et l'exposition"

and idealising space, neutral only in appearance, is what site-specific practices attempt to overthrow; an alteration which curatorial choices accept and accentuate, consciously working on the model, which then becomes a kind of myth, of the museum as studio or creative laboratory. From this perspective, the deconstruction of the space, the aggressive and sometimes destructive interventions, together with the desertion of traditional display canons, the division and hierarchical ordering of works according to genres and styles are all consequences of the artist's invasion of the exhibition space. The final display is produced by their interventions, but also by a specific curatorial strategy, that is, a complete submission of the exhibition context to the logic of the works.

Concentration, to the extent of overcrowding, becomes a characteristic of some of these shows, a feature that seems to be designed to convey the idea of mixture, without any style-dependent order. This sometimes produces confusion in the spectator, as well as an appearance of chaos, as noted by a review of the *Anti-Illusion: Procedures/Materials* show at the Whitney:

Such a welter of concepts and formal manifestations are bound to look confusing, and only certain features are shared, sometimes very marginally. There was an attempt to include so many people in so broad a view that space did not allow for a really clear-sighted organised installation. [12]

Yet curators, in their catalogue texts or in subsequent recollections, recognise and affirm the originality of this method, which left habitual curatorial practices in the dust and entailed the assumption of significant risks on the part of curators and institutions. As Marcia Tucker, co-curator of *Anti-Illusion,* explained:

I knew that there were two ways of doing exhibitions, one didactic, the other investigative. The first was the gold standard: art historians organised exhibitions in order to share their expertise with the public, to show them what was worth looking at and how to look at it. The

12.   Robert Pincus-Witten, "New York", *Artforum,* 8:1, September 1969, p.57.
The most violent critiques, in this sense, are addressed to the Bern show, especially from the local press, as seems evident from the titles of the press review compiled by Szeemann in his diary of the show. See Harald Szeemann, "How Does an Exhibition Come into Being?" in *Painting Object Film Concept: Works from the Herbig Collection,* New York: Christie's, 1998.

investigative model was rarely used because it meant organising a show in order to learn something, moving full-tilt ahead without really knowing what the end result might be. It's what artists do all the time, of course. With the exception of the hacks, they always work without knowledge of the outcome. Scary, but then, artists always were the intrepid ones. Why not take a clue from them?[13]

If in the case of *Anti-Illusion* the curators had nonetheless avoided distorting features of the white cube, allowing the revolutionary strength of the work to emerge within a formal setting, in other instances the alteration of the museum space became the very theme of the shows and of the curatorial policies, as in the case of *Spaces* at the MoMA. Here each artist was invited to create an environment, an on-site installation, which would integrate into a gallery's space and give this space back as a work of art. Similarly, *Using Walls* at the Jewish Museum employed site-specific interventions, on the walls within the museum as well as on the exteriors of other buildings, as the subject and generating principle of the works and of the show as a whole.

Dissemination or movement pushes the limits of the museum even more extremely, when the works leave the exhibition space and go out in the urban or natural environment, in a specific place or in relation to a functional site.[14] This latter is more typical of conceptual practices, which find a recurring object of analysis in the idea of space, even if devoid of the physicality usually associated with site-specificity. So Seth Siegelaub, one of the most radical experimenters of the exhibition medium, fragments the show in different and distant places, which are physically unified not only in the catalogue space, but first and foremost, by the curatorial concept which is at the base of

13.   Marcia Tucker, "Anti Illusion, 1968", 3 March 2005, www.marciatucker.com/excerpts.html#november. I owe Marcia Tucker a special acknowledgement for helping me recall this experience, as well as for her valuable suggestions on the topic of this essay.
14.   See James Meyer, "The Functional Site", *Documents Journal 7*, Fall 1996.

the exhibition project and to which the artists are called to answer. [15] Likewise, some exhibitions find their way onto magazines pages, as with the prime example of *July – August 1970*. [16]

From Object to Process: The Delayed Time

As with site-specific practices, the investigation of the temporality of the work of art is a major and recurring issue in artistic research of the period in question. It takes many forms including methodological approaches and objects of analysis, critiques of traditional artistic practice and attacks on the status of the work of art as a finished and durable object. In the shows here analysed, the relevance of this dimension emerges in two different aspects: the procedural and the ephemeral.

As suggested by critic Maurizio Calvesi in the catalogue text from *Teatro delle Mostre*, artists' interventions focus on the unfolding of a process, rather than on the occurrence of an event, as in Happenings or Performance Art. [17] The process that is to be staged is the creation of the work, from the elaboration of the idea to its (possible) concrete realisation. Thus the stage is the exhibition, the context which defines the times and modes of representation. At the end of the spectacle the work disappears, it is often destroyed, since it cannot live on without arresting its flow.

This dimension of transience is evidently and strictly connected to site-specificity, as pointed out by a critic in his review of the exhibition organised by Robert Morris at the Castelli Warehouse:

15.   This is an exhibition system different from the one that is characteristic of the beginnings of Land Art. In both cases documentation is the work's communication and distribution medium, but in Siegelaub's shows the exhibition's parameters are established in advance, i.e. the exhibition framework pre-exists the single interventions. That was the case of *March 1969,* the calendar-show scattered between America and Europe, and of *July August September 1969.* Another relevant example is offered by *Sonsbeek 71,* the periodic public sculpture exhibition in Arnhem, which in the 1971 edition Wim Beeren exploded into a multiplicity of sites, as well as artistic media. See Wim Beeren, "From exhibition to activity" in *Sonsbeek buiten de perken/Sonsbeek 71,* exhibition catalogue, Arnhem: Centrum Park Sonsbeek, 1971.
16.   In this circumstance Siegelaub invited six critics to curate their own section/ show in the context of that issue of Studio International. That the situation was fit for a "curatorial game" is perfectly and ironically exemplified by Lucy Lippard's contribution, where she asked each of the artists involved to act as curator for another artist, establishing a context within which to intervene.
17.   Maurizio Calvesi, "Arte e tempo" in *Teatro delle Mostre,* exhibition catalogue, Roma: Lerici Editore, 1968.

It is not that we are irritated by a disdain for permanence, but we are touched by the knowledge that these works cannot even be moved without suffering a basic and perhaps irremediable shift in the way they look. The life and salience they have as objects, rather than the intactness of their medium, is, therefore, of a pathetic transience. [18]

Since the work of art's meaning is centred on the operation rather than on its result, on *praxis* rather than on *poiesis*, [19] the permanence of the object produced by the action loses relevance, while its disappearance helps emphasise the new aesthetics and the fight against the commodity status of the work of art. Yet the joint analysis of these shows reveals that the continuous repetition of the same actions upon different exhibiting occasions runs the risk of restoring permanence. In other words, the recreation of ephemeral works reconstitutes the object as a durable entity. [20]

The fact that the works' existence has the same duration as the shows which contain them is nevertheless of extreme importance for the change it introduces within the meaning of exhibitions as medium. From hereon, and for this reason, the exhibition context acquires the status of the circumstance of the work's coming into being. Thus the moment of the work's creation is identified with the moment of its fruition. Moreover, since the works draw attention to their duration and development in time, the temporal and procedural dimensions of the shows are also highlighted. Consequently, exhibitions attain a more manifest character of specificity in opposition to the stability of museum display. In some instances this aspect is emphasised by a dynamic exhibition formula, which develops in time through the fragmentation of the exhibition's entirety, resulting in a situation where each time the show is made up of the single exhibited work, as in *Teatro delle Mostre* and *March 1969,* where each day was devoted to the intervention of a different artist.

18.   Max Kozloff, "9 in a Warehouse", *Artforum,* 7:6, February 1969, p.38.
19.   For this terminology and for a critical discussion on the emergence of the value of process in contemporary art practices and the aesthetic discourse, see Giorgio Agamben, *L'uomo senza contenuto,* Macerata: Quodlibet, 1994.
20.   See Bruce Altshuler, who, in the analysis of *When Attitudes Become Form* argues that Szeemann's main operation was to reproduce a bunch of shows typical of the time. Bruce Altshuler, *The Avant-Garde in Exhibition*. With regard to paradoxes of the repetition of site-specific works, and more in general, on the relationship between ephemerality and site-specificity, see Miwon Kwon, *One Place After Another,* Cambridge, Mass.: MIT Press, 2002. Kwon supports the usefulness of differentiating between works, which are physically and conceptually site-specific, and a dependence on site, which is exclusively conceptual.

Here both the ephemeral and performative dimensions, which are recurrent in all these shows, are pushed to their limits. The spectacle of art in its making goes beyond the primary notion of process art, that is of a work whose formal features are dependent on the realisation procedures, the material characteristics and their interaction with physical and natural laws. The artists' presence in the exhibitions, creating on-site or installing their pieces, the workshop atmosphere, the museum turned into a meeting point or a discussion forum, are thus enhancements of the sense of mobility and incompletion that this type of art disseminates. In fact, this situation is most typical of the installation phase of the exhibitions, the energy loaded and art world-ridden pre-opening days, a situation, which depreciates as soon as the doors are opened to the general public. However, it can be argued that it is precisely this environment which has been taken as the model for the currently prolific artist in residency programs in museums, where the notion of museum as studio has been literalised, in a sometimes naive notion of process, in order to render the mystery of creation, not to mention the exposure of curatorial and administrative aspects, visible.

If, however, the attitude and the gesture of making art prevail over the finished product, which in the case of conceptual practices can even be absent as a tangible object, the exhibition itself is questioned at the very moment in which it acquires this status. In fact, paradoxically, process-oriented practices render the exhibition medium both essential and superfluous at the same time. As stated before, the exhibition medium is more significant because it constitutes a specific stage of the project, which is not autonomous from its conditions of circulation. Yet it is less significant since visualisation, image making and the work's showing itself off, becomes circumstantial and not substantial. Likewise, the relationship between event and process is problematic within the exhibition context. The event finds its defining feature in being bound to a particular time and place — its uniqueness and unrepeatable qualities are stressed in the realm of the spectacle. Meanwhile, process relies on fragmentation, recurrence and development. It leans toward a temporality that is delayed rather then condensed. The exhibition is closely related to the logic of the event, and even more so when dealing with time and site specific art, a fact that raises a basic contradiction with a poetics based on process and its particular communication needs. The spectacle of process can be a simple but unfair way to overstep the impasse, a fake solution, which occasionally appeared in the aforementioned exhibitions, but currently seems to be the rule of the day.

In fact, these exhibitions often result in catalogues which function as the place where the process dimension emerges. This can be read both as a retreat and as the will to involve all the supports in the communication of the same message. Exhibition catalogues do not present finished works, even in the case when these ones are present; rather they include artists' sketches, projects and works in progress. What more, they act as the logbooks, recording the construction phases of the exhibition itself. The introductory texts become tales, which relate the paths travelled, rather than critical essays with scientific approaches. Notably, the curators' use of the first person immediately indicates the rejection of a supposedly neutral enunciation position, which at times is substituted by a quasi-mythical narration. In a similar vain, many catalogues allow the artists to edit their own pages, a strategy which not only turns this instrument into another creative medium, but also amplifies the suggestion of a continuous and spreading artistic production. Ultimately, the most serious and evident threat to the exhibition medium derives from the tendency to dematerialise the art object, pushed to its limit by conceptual artists, so much so that, in some cases, the catalogue is considered as the primary, even the only, medium through which to "exhibit" these art forms.

From Artist to Curator: The Creating Institution

The institutional dimension will not be dealt with here as the context in which artists address their interventions, that is, from the institutional critique perspective. In that it performs a role of resistance to the art system, aiming at decoding the institutional conventions which surreptitiously influence works of art and their supposed autonomy, the approach of institutional critique does not represent a field of investigation other than the ones considered above, but it is rather transversal or, in some cases, superimposed upon them with regard to the adopted practices. What seems instead worth noticing here is the way the exhibitions under examination are characterised by a sequence of changes in the relationships between artists and institutions and, in particular, in the collaboration between artists and curators in the realisation of works and shows.

The first aspect of newness is evident, as it derives from what has been already observed. Since artists work site and time specifically, a show's organisation is not based on the selection of works, which would subsequently be installed by curators, but rather it is the artists themselves who are selected. This shift has relevant consequences on the whole process which leads to the installation of an exhibition, as it generates a necessary and composite co-operation between artists and curators. From the project submitted by the artist for his/her contribution to the finding of the materials necessary for its completion and maintenance, throughout the show's duration as well as in the objects and situations in evolution, the curator is a present and involved party, and here begins to play a fundamental role in the actualisation of the artistic works.

The awareness of this new function and of the importance it holds in artistic production is evident when considering again how catalogues often contain not only the art projects but also the correspondence between curators and artists, from the first contact with the invitation to take part in the show throughout the progression of the work. Often in the catalogue pages, and always with great enthusiasm, curators recognise the sometimes-invasive position they occupy in the process of the creation of the works on display.

The curator's involvement, however, is not limited to an operational function, but entails a general attitude of support for the new art, a side-taking which departs from the traditional objectivity of the museum keeper and comes closer to the complicity of the militant critic. This attitude turns out to be more legitimate, and sustainable in the long run, for those curators who work on their own, independent from any specific institution. It is not by chance that some museum curators, such as Wim Beeren and Harald Szeemann, left their positions in their respective institutions as a consequence of the shows they had organised and the controversies which were raised by them. Thus emerged the figure of the independent curator; one who is not necessarily linked to the idea of militancy or support for a definite artistic tendency, as exemplified by Szeemann's eclecticism, but rather is related to the notion of poetics, in that autonomy is mainly functional to a project of meaning.

When working inside the museum, on the other hand, the curator holds a mediating role between artist and institution; a particularly complex role not only for the production process he/she must manage, but also due to the critical stance against art institutions that many artists assert and put into practice through their works. Indeed, museums are charged with more responsibility and greater influence on the works, through their commissioning function, at the very moment when, and in response to the fact that, artists counter their formative principles. Art challenges museums. Artists come head to head with their new patrons in a manner never before so extreme, and yet never so accepted by museums. Curators find themselves in the middle of the skirmish, repre- senting the institutions while at the same time supporting the artists, in a period when artistic revolutions are accompanied by wider claims, on the part of artists, for social and economic recognition. Jennifer Licht, curator of *Spaces* at the MoMA, the first show in which artists received a fee for their contribution to the museum institution, presented her project to the museum staff in this way:

Some of the aims of the recent artists' protests have been directed toward dissociating art from the marketing system, and demands were made of museums to accept some direct responsibility. The works for this exhibition will be created especially, and dismantled afterwards. Here we can assume a role that belongs uniquely to the public institution and lies outside the domain of the art dealer. [21]

Following the experience of *Spaces* in 1971, MoMA launched the *Projects* series, to which the museum's contribution to contemporary art would be limited. In a renowned interview published on *Artforum* in 1974, William Rubin defended the MoMA from allegations of not being on the front line in presenting new artistic productions, arguing that contem- porary art itself was opposed to the museum, and purposefully rejected it. The concept of museum is not infinitely expandable, and cannot evolve in accordance to the needs of artistic practices, which programmatically challenge it, since this would entail a basic contradiction. [22] Rubin is still speaking as a museum official, requesting a position of critical distance between the museum and art in its making, while the curatorial figure which emerged at the end of the sixties, explicitly aimed at being contaminated by artistic practices, and at playing a major role in their procedural dynamics.

21.   Jennifer Licht quoted in Julie H. Reiss, *From Margin to Center. The Spaces of Installation Art,* Cambridge, Mass.: MIT Press, 1999, p.94.
22.   Lawrence Alloway and John Coplans, "Talking with William Rubin: 'The museum concept is not infinitely expandable'", *Artforum,* 13:2, October 1974.

This development, notably, raised some questions in relation to the respective domains of the activity of artists and curators. In this light, it is worth quoting a passage from Lucy Lippard's *Six Years,* itself a catalogue/show/project sui generis:

> Conceptual art, with its transformation of the studio into a study, brought art itself closer to my own activities. [...] If art could be anything at all that the artist chose to do, I reasoned, then so could criticism be whatever the writer chose to do. When I was accused of becoming an artist, I replied that I was just doing criticism, even if it took unexpected forms. [...] I also applied the conceptual freedom principle to the organisation of a series of four exhibitions, which began in 1969 at the Seattle Art Museum's World's Fair annex. [23]

As Andrea Fraser suggested with reference to the work of curators like Lippard and Siegelaub, their exhibition concepts represented a new way of working in that they established not only the themes of the shows, but also the procedures and situations within which artists were asked to work. [24] This aspect, from its inception, elicited more perplexity and critique from observers, the most frequent accusation being that these shows turned the curator into the main artist. Such critiques included Jack Burnham on Lippard and Siegelaub, Les Levine on Kynaston McShine (curator of *Information),* and Daniel Buren in his infamous accusation, effectively titled "Exhibition of an Exhibition", against Harald Szeemann's Documenta in 1972. [25]

On the one hand, the curators' adoption of an exhibition poetics in accordance with the exhibited art, one that rejects the falsity of neutrality, is aimed at a presentation which draws its strength from its coherence and faithfulness. On the other hand, this approach is accused of being too invasive in both the artists' role and their works' freedom of assertion. The debate, so recurrent in discussions about curatorial and exhibition practices, emerged for the first time at the moment when exhibitions became the context where speculative discourses about art merged with

23.   Lucy R. Lippard, *Six Years*, p.x.
24.   See Andrea Fraser, "What's Intangible, Transitory, Mediating, Participatory, and Rendered in the Public Sphere? Part II".
25.   Jack Burnham, "Alice's Head. Reflections on Conceptual Art", *Artforum*, 8:6, February 1970; Les Levine, "The information fall-out", *Studio International* 934, June 1971; Daniel Buren, "Ausstellung einer Ausstellung", *Documenta 5*, exhibition catalogue, Kassel: Bertelsmann, 1972.

artistic praxis. As argued above, this is due both to the characteristics of the art of this period, which gave a completely new importance to the exhibition dimension, as well as to the evolution of the role of the curator, which in this view invaded, not so strongly the field of the artist, but rather that of the critic. The exhibition turns into the vehicle through which critical thinking about art is developed. This is succinctly expressed in the previously quoted words of Lippard, and is perfectly summarised by Kynaston McShine in his text for the *Information* catalogue:

I have purposely made this text short and very general. *Information* will allow for a more careful and thorough analysis of all the aesthetic and social implications of the work. My essay is really in the galleries and in the whole of this volume. [26]

26.   Kynaston L. McShine, ed., *Information*, exhibition catalogue, New York: The Museum of Modern Art, 1970, p.141.

BAUHAUS CALCUTTA [1]

Anshuman Das Gupta & Grant Watson

In December 1933, 'The Fourteenth Annual Exhibition of the Indian Society of Oriental Art' was held at Samavaya Bhavan, number seventeen Park Street. With its impressive façade, this street cuts away at an angle from Chowringhee whose grand buildings confront the park with different styles (the grandest of all being the Indian Museum), presenting a slice of colonial architecture pasted onto an irregular metropolis that sprawls out from it in all directions.

By all accounts the opening of the Fourteenth Exhibition drew a large crowd, from Calcutta's artistic circles and from the city's high society. The inauguration began with the governor's speech and the protocol of lighting the lamp (in accordance with Hindu custom), a ceremony that was performed on this occasion by the dignitaries Mr Havell and Mr Abanindranath Tagore. Visitors to the opening including many of the city's foremost artists, as well as literary people, students, bureaucrats, government officials, businessmen, critics and of course the poet Rabindranath Tagore, whose backstage influence must have been in part responsible for the configuration of works on display. The exhibition was divided into two discrete groupings. On the left wall were paintings by artists from the 'Bengal School' such as Ksitindranath Mazumdar, Asit Halder, R.N. Chakravarty and others, all members of the Indian Society of Oriental Arts. Most of these artists painted in a manner, which would have been recognisable as that school's invention, a particularly Indian signature style, with mythology a preferred subject. There were pictures delineating gods and goddesses, idealised scenes from village life and there were works using caricature and satire to poke fun at Calcutta's rich. One prominent painting was of Siva meditating at the mouth of the Ganges, sitting motionless in an alcove of rocks as the river pours through his lap and down to the Gangetic plains below. Another was of a woman crossed legged in the doorway of a simple rustic dwelling, a parrot perched lightly on her palm. The artist Gaganendranath Tagore negotiated a broad spectrum of genres from Art Nouveaux, Cubism, South East Asian and specifically Indian traditions to polemical cartoons. His painting was called 'Puppets at Play'. It evoked an historically ambiguous but perhaps 'medieval' world, inhabited by elaborately styled mannequins positioned before some ornamental city ramparts. And everywhere there was the play of numerous cultural traditions, evident in the manipulation of style and content (a synthesis between the self-consciously 'oriental' and the 'occidental') with the paintings arranged as a decorative yet decidedly political statement.

Hung on the other side of the hall was a large selection of works from the Bauhaus. These works were not entirely a novelty in Calcutta, as several visitors to the exhibition would have seen similar things in reproduction — brought back to India by Tagore and kept in his library at Santiniketan. However such a comprehensive range of material, experienced first hand, must have made a strong impression on those present and provoked some interesting reactions. On loan from the Weimar was an extensive display of watercolours, drawings, woodcuts and other graphic works from several leading Bauhaus members, including Klee, Itten, Feininger, Macke and Kandinsky (as well as a selection of projects produced by their students) — representing the largest and most comprehensive exhibition of that school seen anywhere outside of Europe.

Also present that night was the pioneering critic and great connoisseur of the Indian art world O.C. Ganguly, the main force behind the publication Rupam and also the Journal of the Indian Society of Oriental Arts. He was by popular consent the best writer in Calcutta, and had been personally entrusted with the job of deciphering this work from an Indian perspective by Rabindranath Tagore himself. Apparently in an aside, Tagore had said to him: 'Ordhendu, now you have the originals before you, you shouldn't have any more qualms about the difference between the originals and the copies. I hope we can all expect a flurry of very illuminating writing from your pen.' Brought face to face with these paintings for the first time, the critic rose to the occasion and set about putting the case before his Bengali readership, touching in particular on the abstract, expressive and generally unaturalistic character of the Bauhaus school. He wrote:

These artists are no longer concerned with forms derived or deduced from nature but are free to play with forms devised in their own imagination and arranged in a new order, with new emotional stresses and juxtapositions.

From this Ganguly drew a more general conclusion believing that something of greater importance was afoot then merely the invention of a new style, something which could have implications beyond the European context from which it emerged. He recognised abstraction as a watershed, and saw in the use of purely formal criteria, the potential for an increasingly democratic art historical understanding to unfold — one which would trouble the classical cannon as it was perceived and reverse the hierarchy of values imposed on the East by the West.

In the past we used to differentiate artworks and award them merit in relation to their origin. Value was to do with precedent and lineage. So for example, a work from Ming China or Sunga or Gupta era of India were nothing in front of a Greek sculpture. But now a Sunga or Sung sculpture will be judged by the formal qualities, the form becomes the ultimate judge and that represents a sort of new and democratic objectivity. Now you see an open door through which light is seeping, what do you see abstract value, volume, intensity, form.

However, Calcutta audiences did not universally approve of the exhibition and different constituencies took offence for divergent reasons. Some believed it to be counterproductive to show European art at a time when the emphasis (as demonstrated by the Bengal School) was on working towards a regeneration of Indian painting. Other more conservative commentators felt that the works were variously incomprehensible, barbaric, ugly and even political subversive — and accused the artists of setting out to shock, by deliberately behaving in a gross and uncivilised manner. Ganguly staunchly rebuffed these complaints, and defended the Bauhaus on the grounds that even if viewers were unable to take an aesthetic pleasure, then they must at least respect the work for its conceptual beauty.

He wrote:

This so called Bolshevism or anarchist art as you call it, will not languish under your dismissal or accusations of its being hideous, barbaric, clumsy, perverse, idiotic, insane or pathological. The exponents of this new movement have come forward with an elaborate philosophy and comprehensive theory of art that defend their point of view which is itself a valuable contribution to aesthetic theory.

Perhaps sensing that there might be some scepticism, the most spirited defence came proactively in the Indian Society's own catalogue essay, which naturally enough sought to persuade its readers. Here the claims made on behalf of the Bauhaus artists (in the florid style of the times) reach their most lyrical and wide ranging.

It is for the first time that Western art is represented in India by a number of the most advanced and most sincere works of continental artists. They do not belong to any school but come from different parts of Europe: each having his own manner and technique. The artists met in Weimar and in spite of their variety of form found themselves united in their aim to realise the eternal truth of all art and to visualise it, by the means supplied by the present age, in their creed. They joined hands and became the masters of a state – school of art, and the method of their teaching is to hold up an example of their own inspired truthfulness and severe discipline. Neither masters nor students are followers of any' isms' although they are bound to make use of them to a greater or smaller extent. For 'Cubism' or Post Impressionism' are conventions of form, developed out of the need of the moment, and no one in whom the present is alive can escape their formulae. Kandinsky the Russian painter has been for more than ten years the herald of the 'Spiritual in Art'. His power of abstraction is unswerving, put into action as it is by the fervour of mysticism which has no other name than that of Russia. He was the first to paint pictures without any subject matter. He avoided all allusions to literature and nature and so made himself free to infuse his inner experience into mere lines and mere colours which are organised into compositions of intoxicating harmony. Kandinsky is the 'expressionist amongst the painters. If the end of civilisation foretold for Europe of the present day is to come true, it must be said that the artists are fighting heroically their last forlorn fight. But all death means resurrection and art itself is immortal. The Indian public should study this exhibition, for they then may learn that European Art does not mean 'naturalism' and that the transformation of the forms of nature in the work of an artist is common to ancient and modern India and Europe as an unconscious and therefore inevitable expression of the life of soul and the artistic genius.

Despite the immediate discursive flurry inspired by the show, today, 'The Fourteenth Annual Exhibition of the Indian Society of Oriental Art' exists as a fragment of art historical folklore and few records of it remain. It circulates like a rumour amongst interested parties, or as a footnote in the biography of one or other of the Tagore family (as the Bauhaus exhibition that occurred in Calcutta of all unlikely places) hinting at something about the city perhaps previously unimagined. Revealing, its cosmopolitanism, its cultural milieu linked up to the international avant-garde and the intense discussions that circulated around the question of modernity in India at that time, which, the critical reception of this exhibition attest to. While the paintings hung on two separate walls representing two apparently incompatible genres, their proximity in that context constituted an important curatorial juxtaposition — a moment in the history of exhibitions, which if it were to be repeated today would still seem audacious. Because while we sometimes imagine that miscegenation, cross-referencing and disjunction are peculiar to our own times, by all accounts things have always been that way. The desire to look and compare, to influence, to copy — the wish to learn — fuelled by competition, trade, scholarship, the side effects of colonial rule or just curiosity precedes us, stretching backwards into the past as a constant given.

1.   This essay is a semi fictional account of the *Fourteenth Annual Exhibition of the Indian Society of Oriental Art* that took place in Calcutta in December 1933. It has been put together using a mixture contemporaneous reviews and the exhibition catalogue text.

EXPLORE OR EDUCATE?

Clémentine Deliss

Exhibitions are ambivalent spaces whose ability to evoke passionate subjective responses is intimately connected to the way in which they transmit the potency of the experiential to the viewer or participant in excess of the artwork. It is easier to bridle in the unforeseeable and encourage restraint and contemplation than to meet with unknown responses. Sadly this act of domestication that cleans up and orders museographic displays affects us early on in life. How many adults do you know who, having been taken to museums as small children, dragged through portrait galleries, forced to breathe in the stagnant air of congealed paint or stand motionless before canvas, marble and bronze, still retain an ambivalent and sometimes nearly terrorised response to the enforced didacticism of exhibition displays? Perhaps the question of aesthetic edification never fell thick and heavy onto your junior legs as it did mine, forcing me to drag them across the wax patina of parquet floors, through endlessly interconnecting and well-lit chambers until suddenly everything went blank and, forgetting where I was, I screamed to go home? At moments like these, the museum and its worthy exhibition designers transform the unknown of the world ahead and the elaborate wonders that artists have produced into a badly oxygenated education game. For if a game is at stake than ideally it should be one that reinforces the playful, episodic encounter with phenomena that elude the pragmatic logic taught in the classroom, the mind's eye of school-teachers, or even the reassuring mood of collective consensus that can be found at the local cinema.

Two exhibitions that I visited in the autumn of 2004 made me wonder about certain changes in the relationship between art practice, experimentation as an integral part of the make-up of exhibitions, and concepts of instruction or didacticism. At John Bock's 'Klutterkammer' (ICA, London) and Thomas Hirschhorn's '24h Foucault' (Palais de Tokyo), I felt caught between a sense of knowing and a feeling of blanking out, confronted with retro time-lapses and recastings of works or figures from the past. This sensation leads me to question the nostalgia for empiricism that one can read in the work of both these artists as a symptom of the current desire for interactivity. What I am trying to understand here are the connections between different forms of *exploration* as they appear within an art historical context, an interdisciplinary frame, and — lest we should forget — a global field of art production.

At the ICA in London, the German artist John Bock presents an adventure-playground approach to art history that makes us crawl through plywood tunnels, up ladders, across wooden platforms and into areas that resemble segments of tree houses, hay barns, and make-shift storage spaces. As you move through his labyrinth you encounter numerous independent productions of art and pop from the 70s and early 80s. Videos of Robert Smith and The Cure resonate with photographs of the Viennese actionist Rudolf Schwarzkogler and his associate Gunther Brus. Elsewhere works by German artists Georg Baselitz, Joseph Beuys and Sigmar Polke speak to artists such as Heimo Zobernig, Sarah Lucas, and Elke Krystufek whose links to the older generation's work are undeniable. Various videos including documents of Bock's own actions and lectures are placed on shelves high up ladders or boxed into small viewing spaces. In addition to these individual pieces, references seep through the spatial design of Bock's show. We are reminded of staged settings by Mike Nelson, Gregor Schneider, Mike Kelley & Paul McCarthy, or even the recent hole that leads into the cube of Tobias Rehberger installed at the Whitechapel Art Gallery. Bock has borrowed and appropriated an impressive selection of works that signify his own conceptual trajectory but also a nearly mischievous wish on his part to debunk museographic displays, personalise art history and engage a younger generation in the mysteries of finding pertinent information. Bock takes you on a treasure hunt characterised by cryptology and the absurd. Sharply aware of the absence of wall documentation to guide the viewer through the exhibition, he plays on the initial confusion that this creates by literally hanging up safety blankets to protect one from obvious art historical references or cultural comparisons. On the first floor of the ICA, major pieces are shrouded in woollen rugs that distort our reliance on white partition walls and produce an emotive mix of homelessness and affectivity. Bock offers us a return to empiricism as a gesture on the part of the artist as historian, curator, and fan. In so doing, he manages to construct a circuit that gently runs against the educational precepts of exhibition organisation intended to teach art rather than initiate research into the boundaries of aesthetic practice, and heralded in Britain as part of public service commitment. Whilst viewing a recent show on video works at the Kunsthaus Graz, a colleague who had studied curating at Goldsmiths University in London told me how she felt lost and incapacitated without information panels to guide her reassuringly through the exhibition.

In Paris, the Swiss artist Thomas Hirschhorn, consummate in contemporary hagiography, manages to produce a gripping exegetical monument to Michel Foucault. A central key to the success of his exhibition at the Palais de Tokyo is its articulation of use value as a transient pedagogical exercise. Polyvalent and generative the situation he proposes can be invested into by all visitors whether these are adolescents searching for guiding thought structures or philosophers reliving the necessities of a past experience. With significant audio tapes from seminars, rare videos of television programmes and a multitude of books all installed in an ambience of audition, viewing, and duplication, we come close to excess in the drive to read and learn from the materials Hirschhorn provides. Significantly, the experience lasts no longer than 24hrs thereby increasing the sense of urgency that Foucault's politicised wisdom articulates. The Parisian public, ready to engage with the populism of the yearly Nuit Blanche, arrives in droves to listen to conferences that continue far into the early hours of the morning, drinking vodka for 1 Euro at the Foucault bar, and photocopying for free from the valuable publications that Hirschhorn has gathered together. In contrast to Bock, his show is framed by a condensed experience of time rather than a physical journey through space. This intensity transforms Hirschhorn's improvised cardboard architectonics with their ad hoc classroom, library, and auditorium into something far more intangible than the structures Bock deploys in his application of the principals of encounter, observation and learning. With Hirschhorn, the implication of the empiricism he proposes has all the potency of a future degree in the humanities transformed for a wider audience into a non-hierarchical, non-academic and essentially experiential data bank.

In quite different ways, both exhibitions play on the physical and conceptual discoveries undergone by visitors, and in both cases we are led away from the neutered approach of education departments within museums. Indeed, pasted up on the walls of Hirschhorn's environment are pages of erect dicks from gay magazines stuck alongside numerous portraits of the philosopher. This statement on heterodoxy would be hardly acceptable within the pedagogical conformism of the majority of publicly funded curatorial enterprises. Again it is the artist's ex-centric position as an intermediary and editor that enables him to emphasise the idiosyncrasies that characterise the very process through which one acquires knowledge between disciplines. Here he follows in the footsteps of Joseph Kosuth who once studied anthropology and whose Wittengstein show at the Secession in Vienna in the early 1990s was both a hommage to the philosopher and an exploration of transatlantic aesthetic and conceptual legacies. With John Bock's exhibition and Thomas Hirschhorn's '24h Foucault' we are invited to recall earlier live situations and periods in art practice when investigations were experiments and exhibitions were locations for research that was adventurous, open-ended, conjectural, and ultimately unrestrained by the rules of health and safety that increasingly regulate the mental spaces of art colleges and cultural buildings.

However, the ultimate dilemma between exploration and education emerges through contact with a global geo-aesthetic field of production. Unlike Bock's art-historical experience or Hirschhorn's interdisciplinary democracy, the process of travelling to other continents, to meet, learn, and relate this experience within the reflexive and necessarily subjectivist context of art is fraught with political and historical limitations. Even though Bronislav Malinowski's anthropological concept of participant observation has become a comfortable part of the paradigm of art practice understood as a relational, social situation, its disciplinary lineage has been erased for the benefit of the far less controversial approaches taken by cultural studies. This new discipline that extends deeply into curatorial work encourages education and access all too often by developing canons and references which accommodate rather than complexify interpretations of work produced in differing socio-aesthetic environments. This process of semantic foreshortening for which identity, urbanity, territory and race provide central organising principles takes place both through art critical publications, but also through event structures which include the on-going revivalism of the biennale and its relocation all over the world. Here the education game emerges in its most restrictive form, effectively cancelling out a sensibility of apprehension, patience, uncertainty and gradual reconnaissance that comes with risk and failure. A corollary is the growing inability today for art professionals to travel to unknown cities or locations without depending on the cultural and educational coding of catalogues or international manifestations in order to identify independent productions.

Yet internationalism has nothing more to do with where you come from or where you go to, or for that matter a plurality of nationals and their art works exhibited for all to see. In its least conformist expression, internationalism aligns itself increasingly with something akin to a gesture of exchange or hospitality with all the unforeseeable contingencies that this aesthetic of relation brings with it (cf. both Edouard Glissant and Jacques Derrida). This understanding suspends critically the reliance on physical difference, origin, nationality, and global location and suggests that what is at stake now is the formation of new working communities that mirror their aesthetic practices in fragile collective economies and sensitive systems of communication. Empiricism becomes redefined as vulnerability both within an institutional, intercultural, and interpersonal context and, in its most raw formulation as that which activates a form of education that is dissonant and anti-systemic yet imbued with the wish to forge new concepts and forms of inter-human currency.

FUTURES: EXPERIMENT AND THE TESTS OF TOMORROW

Eva Diaz

In 1999 Hans Ulrich Obrist and Barbara Vanderlinden organized the exhibition *Laboratorium* in Antwerp, Holland. Taking as its premise the frequent association between the artist's studio and the scientific laboratory as workplaces of invention, *Laboratorium* linked art and science in terms of a common zone of practice. Rather than merely replicating either space — laboratory or studio — the curators of *Laboratorium* self-reflexively posited the museum as the key venue of laboratory practice. [1] Within the exhibition sites, throughout talks, and on accompanying panels, they invited interdisciplinary collaborations between scientific researchers and contemporary artists. For example, the artist Luc Steels partnered with artificial intelligence researchers from Brussels and Paris to test robots' mimicry of human interactions in cyberspace. Also working in conjunction with scientists, artist Mark Bain wired nearby medical and chemical laboratories for hyper-sensitive sound recording, providing an alternative document of the activities of the research lab. [2]

So too did the subsequently published catalogue emphasize interdisciplinarity, interspersing theoretical and practical writings by artists and science scholars with an intentionally fragmented and open-ended compendium of documentation of projects in the exhibition. [3] With almost 100 contributors to the Bruce Mau design, the catalogue was itself an experiment in production, its creation process charted as

1.   That is to say that in doing a show about laboratories, the curators' felt they should adopt the methods of their object of inquiry in a self-reflexive move. Pierre Bourdieu theorized "reflexivity" as a necessary condition of any act of social commentary. According to Bourdieu, one cannot consider the social world as the object of one's analysis as one is inescapably, subjectively, and reflexively bound up with the presumed "object" of study. Reflexivity also points to the ways in which power flows unequally within knowledge claims — that the "object" of inquiry is often disadvantaged by a lack of access to the concepts and categories governing its representation. Please see Bourdieu and Loic J.D. Wacquant, *An Invitation to Reflexive Sociology*, (Chicago: University of Chicago Press, 1992).
2.   Not all artists collaborated with scientific practitioners. Rather, some artists used the exhibition as an opportunity to question the epistemological suppositions of science — particularly the overemphasis on empirical findings that encourages positivism — in much the same way that historians of science such as Paul Feyerabend and Thomas Kuhn have challenged the presumed methods of scientific discovery. For example, Francisco Varela's "Portable Laboratory" reduced the space of research to a small cushion on which the viewer was invited to sit. Radically reducing the accoutrements of science down to the human capacity for thought, viewers were encouraged to meditate on their conditions of experience and to note "the specific manifestations of the mind as if they were data." In Carsten Höller's "Laboratory of Doubt" the reliability of experimental "results" were questioned, with Höller speculating that results may cease to be experimental when they are represented as finished outcomes. Höller proposed instead experiments in stasis, in which the "aim is not to intervene" and to "do less."
3.   Hans Ulrich Obrist and Barbara Vanderlinden, eds., *Laboratorium*, exh. cat. (Provincial Museum of Photography, Antwerp, Belgium, 1999).

an ever-changing performance in the gallery. In typical Mau fashion, the typography and organization of the volume actively compete with the content. The latter half of the published catalogue, where artists' contributions are assembled, features pages cut into two halves, with identifying information and short project descriptions clustered in the upper section, overlaying images and artists' statements that continue through the bottom portion. Attempting to coordinate the pages to examine one project at a time requires beginning at the first entry and turning both top and bottom sections simultaneously, and continuing to do so for nearly 300 subsequent pages. Here it seems that the chaotic presentation of the laboratory "findings" emphasized processes of discovery that occur as works are juxtaposed — however difficult to read such incongruous contrasts are in practice — rather than an easily legible final product.

   Laboratorium continued what is Obrist's signature curatorial style — information-heavy projects that saturate a single, loose idea with a surfeit of visual information and scholarly resources. [4] Creating archives around particular nodes of inquiry — laboratory, utopia, "do it yourself" production — the accretion of great volumes of information substitutes for advancing a single argument. As the curators' statement of *Laboratorium* queried, "*Laboratorium* is the answer, what is the question?" [5] Yet with so many people from various disciplines contributing, how can one be sure that they are asking the same question(s)? By siting experimental practices in the museum rather than in the artist's studio or the scientist's laboratory, did the curators themselves intend to be the principal researchers or the creative producers? Pinning down an important concept often invoked in *Laboratorium* — "experiment" — can set these questions into better relief.

* * *

   A primary goal of *Laboratorium* was to use the idea of the experiment to rethink some underlying assumptions that position various disciplines into realms of discreet specialization. If the studio/laboratory are the sites of production, however dissimilar their physical

---

4.   For example, Obrist's continuing online exhibition "Do It" has had over 30 incarnations and currently consists of over 100 contributors exploring the notion of a viewer making a work on an artist's instruction. Obrist's "Utopia Station," a collaboration with Molly Nesbit and Rirkrit Tiravanija for the 2003 Venice Bienniale, archives 160 posters by an ever growing selection of contributors.
5.   Obrist and Vanderlinden, *Laboratorium*, 13-14.

incarnations, *experimentation* is taken to be the shared practice. In making this connection the curators were mining a deep vein. From Da Vinci's emphasis on experimental verification of the formal and structural constitution of nature, to Buckminster Fuller's proposal of a field of "comprehensive design" to reason inductively from "generalized principles into unique experimental control patterns," the notion of experiment as a procedure transcending seemingly disparate fields has long held attraction. [6] What these attempts to foster interdisciplinary connections argue against, of course, are notions about the total autonomy of certain fields of practice.

As I have written elsewhere, "experiment," whether it be in the context of science or art, has been generally treated as a generically positive appellation — as indeed it frequently was in *Laboratorium* — lumping diverse practices under a single category that comes unproblematically to signify intedisciplinarity, avant-gardism, cultural improvement, and often, political progressiveness. [7] Yet the concept of experiment to which *Laboratorium*'s curators and others appeal is in fact deeply contradictory. In large part this contradiction reflects the compound meaning of experiment, and its historically shifting relation to concepts such as innovation and tradition.

Experiment shares with *empirical* and *experience* a common root in the Latin *experiri*, "to try or to put to the test." Until the 18th century, "experience" and "experiment" were interchangeable in English usage, though subsequently *experience* came to indicate that which has been previously tested, a past accumulation of knowledge or skill — "lessons as against innovation or experiments" in the words of Raymond Williams. [8] Yet *experience* continued to carry a second meaning, that of a full and active consciousness or awareness, an experimenting with, testing, or trying out of something. The complexity in the definition of experience as either the past (tradition), or that which is freshly experienced (innovation), had the effect of splitting the meaning of experiment to include both "testing under controlled circumstances", and "innovative acts or procedures" more generally. Although exper-

6.   Buckminster Fuller in James Meller, ed., *The Buckminster Fuller Reader* (London: Jonathan Cape Ltd., 1970), 43.

7.   See my article "Experiment, Expression, and the Paradox of Black Mountain College," in *Starting at Zero: Black Mountain College, 1933–1957*, Caroline Collier and Michael Harrison, eds. (Bristol & Cambridge: Arnolfini and Kettle's Yard, 2005).

8.   Raymond Williams, Keywords: A Vocabulary of Culture and Society (New York: Oxford University Press, 1976 and 1983), 126.

iment is sometimes associated with systematic procedures such as the scientific method, which imply previously formulated hypotheses under test; experiment is also invoked in trials of new or different experience in which results are not forecast beforehand. Discussion of the degree of innovation or control inherent in, or permitted to, experimental practices as debated in art and science turns on this ambiguity in its etymology.

If experiment is posited as a methodology of practice shared by both art and science, undoubtedly certain distinctions undergird this comparison. Perhaps the most common is that science has an intrinsically empirical basis in contrast to the speculative nature of art. Yet just as often it seems, tests by artists inform understandings of the material constitution of reality, whereas science in heavily theoretical fields such as astrophysics often deals with empirically unverifiable postulates. A further distinction is between inductive and deductive practices; the former in which experimentally verified "facts" lead to theoretical conclusions or, conversely in the latter, hypothesized claims are empirically verified or refuted. Putting aside for the moment assumptions about the methods respective to art and science, the attribution of a common experimental basis to both fields stresses their shared desire to change present conditions. Experiment as testing the past or as moving toward fresh experiences is nevertheless a quest for new, more adequate understandings of the world. One would not experiment if the current state of affairs — the status quo — were satisfactory.

If we can think of the test through the range of meanings, from planned hypothesis to trials of experience more generally, it is indeed a fertile term. As this expanded definition of experiment is being rethought as a model of artistic practice that connects activities occurring in various disciplines, similar models are being generated connecting art practices to one other historically.

* * *

In a recent article in *October* Tim Clark set forth what he termed the two "central imaginings of modernity." The first aspiration was one of playful freedom, bodily pleasure, and consumerist abundance promised by spectacle culture, the second the physical comfort of a well-ordered, technologically rational and mechanized society. [9] According to Clark, the proposition of modernist art with respect to these dream-extremes was a putting to test those social desires through investigations of the form and material conditions of perception and representation. And as Hal Foster has noted of the conventionalization of the "testing" operation, "The purpose of the modernist work is to test the limits of its meanings and the understanding of its viewers over and over again." [10]

Invoking the test as the primary procedure of modernist art underscores the central role played by experimentation to, according to Foster, "ride the dialectic of modernization in a way that might keep these projects [of modernity] alive for the future." [11] Not necessarily rupturing or transgressing the symbolic order, rather the test forces the limits and adequacy of representation to depict or inform the conditions of society. [12] In this sense testing connects art to its public — and is a means of linking historical understandings of what has been and currently is intelligible as art to contemporary audiences. The test is also one of possibilities, of testing in material form what are frequently the most abstracted desires, for a different present and for a better future, thereby providing a concrete visualization with which to agree or argue.

Foster has recently isolated an "archival impulse" in recent art in which artists "seek to make historical information, often lost or displaced, physically present" by reorganizing bodies of "alternative knowledge or counter-memory." [13] The impetus is to galvanize the past in service of the present and future: "to probe a misplaced past, to collate its different signs... to ascertain what might remain for the present." [14] The artists he draws together, Thomas Hirschhorn, Tacita Dean, and Sam Durant, could be joined by a slightly earlier generation of artists whose interventions in museums involved a careful study of repressed or unrealized aspirations of the past. Fred Wilson, Mark Dion, and Andrea Fraser's projects in museums activate historical and archival materials in similarly

9.   T.J Clark, "Modernism, Postmodernism, and Steam," *October* 100 (Spring 2002). The formulation of bodily pleasure as opposed to physical comfort is also found in Susan Buck-Morss' *Dreamworld and Catastrophe* (Cambridge, Mass.: MIT Press, 2000).
10.   Hal Foster, *Design and Crime and other Diatribes* (London: Verso Press, 2002), 121.
11.   Ibid., 60.
12.   Or perhaps to test the manner in which appearance increasingly becomes the condition of society.
13.   Hal Foster, "An Archival Impulse," *October* 110 (Fall 2004), 4.
14.   Ibid., 21.

probing ways, testing the adequacy of representation to render into image the often abstract forces and relations of history.

If the archive is the object and outcome of study, then experimental research can be said to be the process. The experimental drive in art production is matched by a similar imperative on the part of curators and art historians. Much as *Laboratorium* sought to disrupt categories separating the work of artists and scientists, common ground between the work of artists, curators, and art historians can be found in the complex notion of experiment I am proposing. That is to say, if experiment can be understood as *both* a test of tradition and as a search for innovative outcomes more generally, we can begin to see the work of curators and art historians organized on an axis of practice, of which experiment is the hinge.

* * *

A rare pleasure is an art exhibition that mixes relatively recent and more historical work. Rare, that is, for how often has one visited a gallery in which the latest "emerging" art is stranded in an ahistorical present, silently crying out for dialogue with prior practices mining similar concerns? Conversely, too frequent is the historical exhibition in which current practices loom so large that their excision forecloses the possibility of thinking the historical in and through present practices. The greatest attribute of large survey exhibitions and biennials is the combination of the very recent with the recently past, but this is also their most arbitrary feature. The criteria for inclusion is less often the relation of works to one another, than loosely amalgamating a series of one person shows.

A key challenge facing a historically sensitive contemporary curatorial practice is the sometimes-distant relationship between curators and art historians — remote in terms of different professionalization tracks, and more importantly in terms of practice. [15] Art historical work is concerned largely with mapping a temporal, diachronic axis, one

15.   Of course, some of the confusion is due to the ambivalent associations of the word "contemporary". In debates that checker the last century and continue today, contemporary is often opposed to historical modernism, that is to say avant-garde art practices of the pre-WWII period that had a strong utopian and or political slant. Contemporary is often the catch-all category that denotes the present but also connotes a break with past practices. I am using contemporary to indicate artists from approximately 1960 to the present, that is to say living generations of artists currently practicing in the field.

in which the relations between works of art are positioned with respect to tradition and historical precedent. In contrast, curatorial practices are principally transacted on a synchronic axis of relations between socially coexistent, spatially synchronous practices. For a future practice that enriches both "camps," curatorial and art historical work cannot be viewed as differential, but as mutually informing and determining in their investigation of art practices.

In order to create speculative solutions about possibilities for a better society — solutions that can be activated strategically when opportunities arise — these solutions must be tested with a foreknowledge of both previous tests and those that are currently emerging. To mobilize for a future that is more informed, therefore, art historical work and curatorial work — diachronic and synchronic axes — must be constellated together in present practices. *Laboratorium's* arguments about experimentation and its relation to science and art can be pushed further, in order to understand experiment in its fuller meaning of testing the past in the present. In order to create conjectural solutions about possibilities for improving society, we must first develop settings for well-informed speculation. Applying an enriched concept of experiment facilitates this.

Experiment and the notion of the test describe a variety of practices in which artists engage, from the various research methods of the archive through the attempts to find common methodologies between artistic practices and other disciplines. As experimentation in artistic practice is inflected by both an emphasis on tradition *and* innovation, so too can art historians and curators relate it to their work. This sense of experiment, as a central way to organize thinking about the present and the future, yokes the projects of curators and art historians in a united pursuit: parlaying the knowledge of history into a better-informed horizon for the future.

CURATING WRONG PLACES... OR WHERE HAVE ALL THE PENGUINS GONE?

Claire Doherty

Berthold Lubetkin's 1930s penguin pool at London Zoo has been deserted by its inhabitants, in the interests of the penguins' strained muscles caused by the double helix structure. Potted plants, bark chippings, branches, murky water and pondweed have been substituted, effecting the site's transformation into an alligator pool. British archaeologist Andy Shapland remarks, "despite the best efforts of the Zoo keepers, this was a building in which 'penguiness' was produced." [1]

The rhetoric of "place" has become the rallying cry for the curator of the international scattered-site exhibition or biennial. In 2004, the "International" component of the Liverpool Biennial professed to "address and empower place as having value", commissioning some 48 artists to produce new works for the city. That same year, Donostia-San Sebastian was conceived as "a privileged social site and catalytic trigger" for Manifesta 5, whilst this year the Gwangju Biennale purports to provide "an impetus to the city of Gwangju to be reborn as a geographical metaphor". [2] Most notable of recent placed-based curatorial assertions was Charles Esche and Vasif Kortun's opening gambit for the 9th Istanbul Biennial in 2005, in which they proposed "an exhibition structure that folds out of and reveals its context — the city of Istanbul", by commissioning artists to respond both to the "urban location and the imaginative charge that this city represents for the world". [3]

Esche and Kortun's biennial signalled a pervasive shift in curatorial practice away from, what Declan McGonagle has termed, "wide and shallow [engagement] rather than narrow and deep — sightseeing rather than insight". [4] İstanbul emerged through a discursive process of short-term residencies and projects, which sought to embed visiting artists and artworks within the city. It created intersections between local and international, and eschewed locations which might endorse a nostalgic or exotic view of the city. Furthermore, with the integration of critical platforms

1.   Hicks, Dan. *"Days at the Zoo: Archaeological Perspectives on Context, Nostalgia and Site-Specificity."* 2005. Paper delivered at *The Wrong Place — Rethinking Context in Contemporary Art* Conference. Bristol. 5 February 2005
2.   Biggs, Lewis and Declan McGonagle. "Foreword." *International 04*. Ed. Paul Domela. Liverpool: Liverpool Biennial, 2004; "Manifesta 5 Press Release." *Manifesta*. 29 March 2004. www.manifesta.es/eng/prensa/notasdeprensa/manifesta5launchesitsprogram.htm; "Gwangju Biennale Exhibition Concept." *E-Flux*. 8 August 2005. www.e-flux.com/displayshow.php?file=message_1123518772.txt>.
3.   *Istanbul Biennial Press Release*. October 2004. www.iksv.org/bienal/bienal9/
4.   McGonagle, Declan. "Terrible Beauty." *International 04*. Ed. Paul Domela. Liverpool: Liverpool Biennial, 2004.

within the resulting exhibition — comprising the now ubiquitous biennial reading zones, workshops, talks series and home-grown journals — the curators established active participation as a key component of the public manifestation of the biennial, not just part of the research process.

Esche and Kortun's concept can be seen as a retort to the accusation that biennials operate merely as stopovers on the international circuit for the frequent-flyer tribe of artists and art *cognoscenti;* that biennials have little or no lasting impact on the inhabitants or cultural life of their host cities. Instead the co-curators of İstanbul posited engagement with the city as the primary motivating force for their exhibition (albeit still within the signifying system of the global art economy). İstanbul, they maintained, "as a metaphor, as a prediction, as a lived reality, and an inspiration has many stories to tell and the Biennial will attempt to tap directly into this rich history and possibility." [5]

The predominance of "place" as the subject for curatorial initiatives of this kind has emerged from the convergence of three commissioning models: the scattered-site international exhibition which preceded the recent swell of biennials, governed by the organising principle of place (from Tyne International and TSWA in the UK to Skulptur. Projekte Münster and the public art projects of Mary Jane Jacob in Charleston, Chicago and Atlanta); the research-based project programme (Locus+, Casco, Artangel) and the residency model with its concentration on engagement, process and encounter. Location seems to offer a suitably bounded space in which these commissioning models can come together and consequently meaning is produced through research-based projects and responsive programming in context. Over ten years ago, Bruce W. Ferguson, Reesa Greenberg and Sandy Nairne identified the harnessing of this curatorial strategy for a region's economic and political gain in their article "Mapping International Exhibitions",

The locale of an exhibition is embraced in its title as a rhetorical manoeuvre to appropriate cultural status, the meanings and the myths that attend the collective imagination attached to the city, region or country named... [6]

5.　"Exhibition Concept." 12 April 2006. www.iksv.org/bienal/bienal9/english/?Page=Concept>.
6.　This article was originally published in *On taking a normal situation and retranslating it into overlapping and multiple readings of conditions past and present.* Antwerp: MuHKA, 1993: 135–152. A revised version was published in Harding, Anna. Curating: *The Contemporary Art Museum and Beyond.* London: Art & Design, 1997.

Since the mid 1990s, the context-specific international exhibition has become allied to urban regeneration and cultural tourism, whereby the cultural event becomes an ideal cipher for the meeting of international and local — hence any thematic title tends to be superseded by the city's name followed by the word "biennial" or "international" and in some cases, as in İstanbul, are one and the same. The dilemmas of cultural tourism versus criticality notwithstanding, the promotion of place as both subject and site for international exhibitions also runs the risk of subjugating art to a notion of place that is out-of-date.

Considering the progressive notions of place advanced by geographers such as Doreen Massey and David Harvey in the early 1990s, how can curators support artistic engagements with places which can be seen to be "constructed out of a particular constellation of social relations"?[7] If we subscribe to a notion of place as an intersection of social, economic and political relations, rather than a bounded geographic location, where and how does artistic engagement with the context of the exhibition start? How do such works coalesce to form a meaningful "exhibition" for the biennial visitor when the experience of place itself is an event in progress? Does the emphasis on engagement lead to the privileging of process-based, participatory projects over materiality? And furthermore, how do context-specific projects and artworks become meaningful outside the signifying context of the exhibition?

To consider these questions, we might look to the etymology of the term "curator" and speculate that the same duty of care borne by the custodian of the collection, governs the curator of the context-specific international exhibition. Their responsibilities might be (rather schematically) broken down into two primary objectives: 1) To support the artist to produce a process, project or work that responds to place as a mutable concept, with due consideration to the context of the group dynamic; that is true to the artist's practice, but which moves beyond a replication of previous work; that eventually may also operate outside the originating context; 2) To support and engender encounters — recruiting participants, engaging viewers, interlocutors and collaborators to experience the projects and works as autonomous significations within the logic of an exhibition; provoking opportunities for new understandings and responses to context and initiating potential outcomes beyond the event-exhibition.

7.   Massey, Doreen. "A Global Sense of Place." Reading Human Geography. Eds. Trevor Barnes and Derek Gregory. London: Arnold, 1997: 315–325.

In contrast to the responsibilities of the curator-producer of the artist/concept-led solo project, the curator of the context-specific international exhibition has to engage with a progressive notion of place prior to the selection of artists. The components of the biennial — short-term residencies, research-based investigations, scattered sites and distribution mechanisms, interdisciplinary collaborations, urban interventions and critical platforms — ideally follow from a rigorous consideration of the basis of the invitation — place as an intersection of mapped location, urban mythology, power dynamics and social interaction.

One of the most useful and cogently argued new theorisations of place in relation to the commissioning and production of contemporary art is Miwon Kwon's *One Place After Another: Site-Specific Art and Locational Identity*. Kwon's study is particularly pertinent for a consideration of curatorial responsibility in place. She raises significant questions about the motivating factors for participatory projects, critiquing the essentialising of site and community in context-specific projects.

Kwon traces a genealogy of site-specificity through the 70s and 80s and suggests that, as artists and curators have become informed by a broader range of disciplines (including anthropology, sociology, literary criticism, psychology, natural and cultural histories, architecture and urbanism, political theory and philosophy), "so our understanding of site has shifted from a fixed, physical location to somewhere or something constituted through social, economic, cultural and political processes." [8] Given that the places of the biennial have been reconsidered as points of exchange and collision, remade through intersections of social, economic and political relations, it is not surprising that the predominant forms to emerge from these context-specific invitations are social, spatial and interdisciplinary.

Speculating on the impact of Gilles Deleuze and Félix Guattari's theories of deterritorialization and nomadism, Kwon argues that with increased pressure to conceive projects which engage locally but speak globally, comes a tendency to essentialize potential "communities" and to confine art to a set agenda. Kwon's argument is developed through a critique of New Genre Public Art in the 1990s (in particular Culture in Action), referring explicitly to Hal Foster's critical examination of the "Artist as Ethnographer". Foster critiques the pseudo-anthropological

8.   Kwon, Miwon. *One Place after Another: Site-Specific Art and Locational Identity*. Cambridge, Mass: MIT Press, 2002.

intent of engagements with the "ethnographic participant-observer" whereby, "the artist is typically an outsider who has the institutionally sanctioned authority to engage the locale in the production of their (self-) representation", and warns, "[s]uch mapping may thus confirm rather than contest the authority of mapper over site in a way that reduces the desired exchange of dialogical fieldwork". [9] Writing in the mid 1990s, Foster submits artists such as Clegg and Guttmann and curatorial projects such as Culture in Action, but we might well consider recent biennial projects such as Esko Männikkö's portraits of the residents of Altbridge Park in Liverpool (2004) or Bojan Sarcevic's *Workers* Favourite Clothes Worn While S/he Worked', an experiment in Berlin which gauged the behaviour of workers on and off duty (2004). The consideration here is not simply how the artists and commissioning biennials may have delimited the participants, but also how the nature of the collaborative relationship may have been predetermined.

Kwon's rejoinder is to suggest that community-based art might be approached as a "projective enterprise", rather than a descriptive one and that project should "unsettle", "activate" and "raise questions". [10] One might theorise the avant-garde struggle, she suggests, as a kind of spatial politics, "to pressure the definition and legitimation of art by locating it elsewhere, in places other than where it belongs". [11] Hence, the intention to uncover lost histories, to reveal what is unknown to a city's inhabitants, is essentially negated. Being situated, embedded, to feel that you belong or at least "know" a place is not necessarily of artistic merit. This aesthetics of the "wrong place" is close to the playful, psycho-geographical nature of the Situationist *dérive* and can be detected in recent biennial projects such as 'The Office of Alternative Urban Planning' in San Sebastian during Manifesta 5 and Nedko Solakov's *Art & Life (In My Part of the World)* in Istanbul. These are interventionist gestures, remedial actions and shifts in the status quo, which resist the representative/documentary tendency.

Kwon's argument has been developed recently by London-based art critic Claire Bishop (without specific reference to the biennial) who has suggested that "the social turn in contemporary art has prompted

9.   Foster, Hal. "The Artist as Ethnographer." *The Return of the Real*. Cambridge, Mass: MIT, 1996: 197
10.   Kwon, Miwon. "Public Art and Urban Identities." *Public Art Strategies: Public Art and Public Space*. Ed. Cheryl Younger. New York: New York University, 1998: 168.
11.   Kwon, Miwon. *One Place One Place after Another: Site-Specific Art and Locational Identity*. Cambridge, Mass: MIT Press, 2002: 165.

an ethical turn in art criticism". Citing Jeremy Deller and Phil Collins as exemplars, Bishop suggests,

> The best collaborative practices of the past ten years address the contradictory pull between autonomy and social intervention, and reflect on this antinomy both in the structure of the work and in the conditions of its reception. [12]

Grant H. Kester would argue that by pressing for work which resists (as Bishop suggests) "truthfulness and educational efficacy" in favour of "confronting darker, more painfully complicated considerations", we would miss the opportunity for art projects which engage in acts of solidarity. Kester argues for a dialogical or conversational art "which allows the viewer to 'speak back' to the artist in certain ways, and in which this reply becomes in effect a part of the work itself". [13]

Kester develops this argument and his response to Miwon Kwon's contribution in his book *Conversation Pieces: Community and Communication in Modern Art*. Here Kester suggests that perhaps artists can also work from a position of solidarity rather than simply as provocateurs, and that the effectiveness of this solidarity depends on their sensitivity to local political dynamics, histories and cultures and the possibility of a sustained relationship with participants. [14]

Thus, as participant, viewer, collaborator and client have become key roles for the audiences of the biennial, so the nature of engagement has become increasingly under scrutiny leading to a tension between the unsettling, provocative and interventionist and the complicit, strategic and collaborative. The unravelling of this debate in recent years (complicated somewhat by a pervasive misreading of Nicolas Bourriaud's "Relational Aesthetics" and the consequent confusion of "relational" with "social-engagement") has provided a platform for the critical appraisal of socially-engaged and participatory artworks in the context-specific biennial. Consequently, curatorial initiatives which seek to engender such interactions must begin to unpack the terminologies we use to distinguish one project from each other. For example, those artists who invite partici-

12.   Bishop, Claire. "The Social Turn: Collaboration and its Discontents." *Artforum* February 2006: 178–183.
13.   Kester, Grant, H. "Dialogical Aesthetics: A Critical Framework for Littoral Art." www.variant.randomstate.org/events_archive.html. 12 April 2006.
14.   Kester, Grant. H. *Conversation Pieces: Community and Communication in Modern Art*. Berkeley and Los Angeles: University of California Press, 2004.

pation, often through a complicit engagement with their subject, but who essentially remain the signatories of their work (Thomas Hirschhorn, Phil Collins, Santiago Sierra), from those who those embed themselves within the social fabric of a city through intervention (Francis Alÿs, Minerva Cuevas, Roman Ondák), from those who work collaboratively effecting a kind of 'social sculpture' (Superflex, Wochenklassur). So, to speak of context as a metaphor, prediction and lived reality necessitates less an emphasis on the ethics of artistic engagement than on a differentiation between types of engagement and the potential for resonance in the resulting exhibition beyond metaphor, prediction or lived reality.

And this leads us to consider the question of "quality and significance". The un-stated aim of any curatorial endeavour is to produce a situation like no other. Every biennial proposition can be seen as a response to its peers and its precedents. Significance is judged against cultural, political and economic agendas — claims are made for audience figures, sustainability, consumer targets, graduate retention, economic benefit, the list goes on... But what if we judge the resulting exhibitions and projects against the stated aims to "address and empower place as having value", to conceive the city "as a privileged social site and catalytic trigger", "to respond both to the urban location and the imaginative charge that this city represents for the world", how do the works which result from these ambitious, complex and sophisticated curatorial methodologies and structures actually respond to place and do they result in significant and surprising encounters?

Looking at the critical responses to the Liverpool Biennial in 2004 and İstanbul in 2005, it appears that İstanbul emerged as a critical success — though attracted fewer numbers of people. Critics heralded the latter for its "articulation of pleasure and politics, a confident world view and unpretentious sense of local place", whilst responses to the Liverpool Biennial were tempered by the alleged degree of "parochialism and a repetitive riffing (or even an unreflective capitalization) on certain politically or culturally charged episodes from the city's history." [15] Though the exhibitions diverged from one another in selected sites and accompanying programmes, both were developed through a dialogue between local and international curators. Artists in the Liverpool International 04 were selected by four curator-researchers — Sabine Breitwieser, Yu Yeon

15.   Polly Staple in Frieze. Issue 00. January — February, 2006: 113 and Tom Morton. "Liverpool Biennial 04." Frieze. Issue 87. November — December, 2004: 108

Kim, Cuauhtémoc Medina and Apinan Poshyananda — and supported to produce new artworks by a home team of curators at Tate Liverpool, FACT, Bluecoat and Open Eye Gallery; whilst Istanbul emerged from a dialogue between Eindhoven-based Esche and Istanbul-based Kortun.

What may distinguish critically-acclaimed biennials from the more quasi-anthropological is their capacity to allow projects to emerge over time in different guises in dialogue with existing works and contexts. If we were to consider some of the most significant art projects to respond to place of the past five years, among them Jeremy Deller's *The Battle of Orgreave* (2001), *When Faith Moves Mountains* (2002) by Francis Alÿs and Javier Tellez's *One Flew Over the Void* for Insite_05, we would see that they are multifaceted, temporary and durational; experiential and highly visual; interdisciplinary involving not only other art-forms, but other fields of knowledge and lastly, spectacularly engaging. [16] These projects effect a sense of the wrong place by shifting the status quo, by intervening in the bordered, prescribed spaces of location and consequently, when the films of all three projects have circulated through the art economy, these dislocations have been meaningful beyond the specifics of Lima, Orgreave and Tijuana/San Diego.

I remain somewhat suspicious about whether the international scattered site exhibition is the most appropriate context in which to consider place through the commissioning of new artworks. Recent history has shown that the curatorial emphasis on the city as research subject, interlocutor, social context and physical site may lead to exhibitions which are too interpretative, too quasi-anthropological in character. Most significant place-responsive or context-specific projects, whether they unsettle and provoke a sense of the wrong place or work collaboratively to effect social change, need flexible time-frames and tend to emerge from different kinds of motivation than a group exhibition rationale. That said the challenge to produce a situation in which such projects might occur in dialogue with one another, along with existing historical and contemporary works, in the context of the dynamic intersections of place, is still hard to resist.

16. 'The Battle of Orgreave' was a re-enactment of one of the most violent confrontations of the miners' strike in 1984, which took place on 17 June 2001. Francis Alÿs, 'Cuando la fé mueve montañas (When faith moves mountains)', 2002, in collaboration with Cuauhtémoc Medina and Rafael Ortega, Lima. Peru took place on 11 April 2002. 'One Flew Over the Void' a collaboration between Javier Tellez, the Baja California Mental Health Center in Mexico and human cannon ball David Smith took place in August 2005 as part of Insite_05. Smith was fired across the US-Mexican border — from Tijuana to a Border Field State Park in San Diego.

CURATING BEYOND
THE CANON

Okwui Enwezor Interviewed by Paul O'Neill

PAUL O'NEILL How do you think contemporary curatorial practice has evolved since the eighties when you began to organise exhibitions?

OKWUI ENWEZOR I wouldn't really say that what I was doing in the eighties was curating in the intellectual sense that I use for what I do today. These were my days of crude apprenticeship. I organized exhibitions not curating. I organized and curated poetry readings (before the slams drove me out of poetry completely). About the evolution of the contemporary art curator from the eighties, the way I see it, is like night and day. The eighties and before was the colonial, Jim Crow, and apartheid days put together. It was completely acceptable to the curators of the period that contemporary art did not happen in places like Africa, Asia, South America or the Middle East. While much credit is given to *Magiciens de la Terre, 1989* for breaking this hegemony, and I would concede its importance, the work of people like Rasheed Araeen, Gavin Jangtes are equally important. Put simply, globalization transformed the myopia that previously ruled the judgments of curators. When curators of my generation, began, against the better judgments of the gatekeepers, to show interest in a wide variety of artistic approaches and biennials began taking place in so-called peripheral cities the type of narcissism that previously dominated the art world had to come to an end. The insurgent discourse of postcolonial debate is another moment, and this remains vital for me in keeping sharp the distinctions amongst all of us working as curators today. The postcolonial is always my point of departure.

Obviously curators have to work out their ideas based on their interests. I like the fact that you are making a book about the history of curating because it is a way to ground it historically. I have often used a very simple notion: my role as a curator is as somebody who is intellectually interested in art and the meanings that it produces and how one can organise that within the limited context of the institutional space or the gallery space or the public space within which art is presented. Having said that it may sound pretentious, but it is an intellectual practice. I do think that the responsibility of the curator insofar as working with art and ideas that are made elsewhere, is an interpretive one, as well as performative. It is important to find curatorial devices to activate work that by virtue of its critical difference is resistant to easy translation. It is, I hope, not only about responsibility to the forms or ideas of the work but also responsiveness to the very historical conditions under which art of the present is being produced. Making an exhibition is a way to engender new ways of looking at the deep entanglements between art, society and its institutions and the ways in which all of the residues of the encounter between the public, artists, art, and institutions are registered in the context of historical narration. I think that a curator has to be alert to all these formidable edifices that impede our ability to be open to other types of work.

I want to go back to what is really instructive about the generation making exhibitions in the nineties: the fact that suddenly there was a larger awareness of the broader world and there was a greater degree of discourse and dialogue between people working in different contexts and locations, not only in cities but across continents. This trans-national context is fascinating and I think it is something quite productive. I say this because the previous generation of curators didn't really do this, they didn't really work in this way. Their area of focus was much more circumscribed by old models of modernity. Their work was much more related to the kind of social networks that the curators belonged to and of course the milieu of the artistic industry clustered in a limited art market in the Western Europe and North America. It was much more localised. When it was understood to be international it really was bilateral engagement between Europe and North America and there were economic and political reasons for that, for this lack of meeting points. The curator of this moment who is working with a broader awareness that art is made in all sorts of conditions and these conditions of production are as interesting a way to read the work, as a way to present the work, as the very context in which the work is being presented. We have very varied and diverse places of practice, people contributing to artistic discourse across a wide sphere of experience. There are obviously the informal and formal economies of contemporary art and I think it is really the role of the contemporary curator to constantly find a way to bridge these relationships. One other thing I want to add is the degree to which the contemporary curator really began to undo the power of the critic in this sense. That is really a story that still needs to be told in a way. We cannot possibly say clearly why it happened, but it did happen, but it appears to me that it came about as a reaction to the power of the critic as the arbiter of meaning. Think of Clement Greenberg and to a lesser extent the criticism that currently emanate from *October*. While in the past, it was difficult to ignore these authorities; today the insurgency of the curator of contemporary art has shifted the scope of the critic's power. This may partly owe to the fact that the contemporary curator was much more attentive to all the theoretical issues that came out of post-structuralism, postmodernism. As much as we want to deny that, all this has helped shape the very work of the contemporary curator and I believe that my work is part of this trajectory.

PO'N   There are now multiple, divergent and the multifarious models of curatorial practice since the late 1980s, do you think there are dominant forms that have emerged?

OE   The group/thematic exhibition is a dominant form. Though it may sometimes appear like a bazaar, it is a much more efficient way of taking the temperature of what is going on. And it remains to be seen what the impact of technology and the Internet as a different distribution system would have on curating. So far, it appears quite limited, partly because the process of dissociation that happens with media, with that of experience and engagement that happens in a gallery or museum have not been hospitable to so-called Web-based art and exhibition platforms. We have gone through different stages but it seems to me that the group exhibition model is very interesting because in a sense it works contra to the canonical model of the monographic presentation. It shows the vital and productive messiness of the contemporary, the inherent disarray within its forms, the indiscipline of the contemporary artist to adhere to a single rule. To bring a greater mix of people into an exhibition is as much a way of looking at the ruptures as they exist within the field of artistic practice — to set the emergence of new positions, and to understand the shifts in the tectonic plates that is the ground of culture. It is interesting to ask ourselves why the thematic group show has taken on such interesting possibilities, but within that we can begin to break it down. I would like to say that the work done by say alternative spaces in the seventies and the early eighties is really very important and formative for what came in the late eighties and early nineties, because they provided the possibility for addressing these other art economies, and the disarray I mentioned earlier. This includes having institutions, museums, galleries, criticism, media and the academy acknowledging such disparate interests as feminism, multiculturalism, identity, queerness, otherness, exoticism, etc., as genuine areas of art, not simply archipelagos that are allowed to drift away because they carry fugitive ideas that have incredible fragility, that cannot really survive otherwise in very traditional institutional contexts. I think the group exhibition has been the model for defining these multifarious ways of engagement. The one that has been very much critiqued is the geopolitical or the geographic group show, or context related art, like the Young British artist, the national model, which seems to be very problematic, very limited in terms of its perspective. I don't always agree that the national model in itself is a failure. It could be a bit tendentious.

PO'N   The exhibition *Magiciens de la Terre*, 1989 regardless of its flaws, was the place in which "contemporary African Art" made its first appearance in Europe. How significant an influence was this event upon later more integrated global exhibitions such as your own *Documenta11* in 2002?

OE   Throughout my career, *Magiciens de la Terre* has been the one exhibition that I have to contend with, to push off my back, but it has nothing to do with what I do or the way I think about the trans-national sphere that I mentioned. However, I think *Magiciens de la Terre* made a pragmatic impact in terms of the relations of exchange. If we were to see the exhibition space as a contact zone of culture, the way James Clifford talks about it, picking up on Mary Louise Pratt's more ethnographic reading of the contact zone, then Jean-Hubert Martin's project did indeed frame the problematic of transnational space of exhibition practice. I will say that *Magiciens* in a way opened up a space for really articulating the relationship between the works made in the West and non-West. However, the problem of *Magiciens* was that it was still very predicated on a very redundant view of who should be an artist in this "other" space. Many people say he [curator Jean-Hubert Martin] had an ethnographic eye. I don't think this was the problem with the show. It had a new colonialist eye and this manifested unwittingly for the curator a kind of curatorial bad faith, because what he couldn't deal with was an academicism that really was the dominant artistic paradigm in places like Africa and other places. It was ashamed of this academicism and therefore suppressed it. But it was not ashamed of it in the West, but it was ashamed of it in other places because the curator haughtily translated those academic art practices as really poor imitations. This is where the ethnographic authority comes in, in the search for authentic pasts, in the valorization of extreme otherness as way to generate a contrast between the primitive and modern. This for me represented the failure of *Magiciens*. So whatever way Jean Hubert Martin would put it, I think it was really intellectually very problematic in this sense. I would say that this is where the curatorial bad faith comes from. However, I must contradict myself by saying that I do in many ways have the highest regard for the boldness of Jean Hubert-Martin's statement. I am very grateful to him for making that attempt, because it gave us a tool, a possibility to argue vigorously about what is at stake in the shifting context of artistic production between the post-colony and the metropolis. So how do we reconcile the historical disentanglement of all these relationships, works of art that are not made to be viewed in a gallery context, but when presented there produce a new form of spectacle that could be quite clearly an engagement with art and so on? Here the curator becomes a different kind of actor which was an interesting idea posited by Jean Hubert-Martin. As far as *Documenta11* is concerned, I don't think *Documenta11* and *Magiciens* share anything at all in terms of methodology, in terms of curatorial interests, in terms of intellectual interests, in terms of historical questions, beyond the fact that we were really interested in the widest possible notion of where art is made and I think that is the case. I make no secret of the fact that I was very interested in the post-colonial dimension of *Documenta11*, and I mean the most expansive way that one could understand it. The post-colonial is not simply the elsewhere, over there, and over here means something else, but to see the entire global entanglement as post-colonial in its shape.

PO'N   One of the key questions you asked in preparation for *The Short Century: Independence and Liberation Movements in Africa 1945–1994*, at Museum Villa Stuck in Munich, 2001 was "How do you put together an exhibition about a continent?" is this a question that remains unanswered?

OE   It completely remains unanswered and I can say that I am very glad that we principally failed to address the entire continent. Even though there were seeds planted in the exhibition that made it possible to say ok, there is a trajectory that one can actually look at and say: "well it does make sense", but without completely totalising. I didn't set out to totalise in *The Short Century...* and I am very happy that even if I had tried that it was principally a very good failure.

PO'N   Would you say that *The Short Century...* was in part, a means of research or preparation for *Documenta11*?

OE   No it wasn't because it preceded my appointment as Director of *Documenta11*. I had already agreed to do this show before the appointment, but I must say that if it wasn't a preparation for that, it did make very clear what my larger historical and intellectual interests were, vis á vis art I wanted to show in *Documenta11*. I must say that I was fortunate that it was very complimentary in a way, even though I was focusing very much on Africa, even though it was not only African artists who were shown, we had people like Jean Rouch, French and American artists so it was not only just African artists, but I think that it prepared a ground for us to deal with the larger questions we wanted to pose with *Documenta11*, but it was not a research preparation for it.

PO'N   Are there particular past curatorial models, exhibitions, historical precedents, or precursors you have returned to again and again or that have been an influence your practice?

OE   I am really a type of autodidact in the sense of learning how to be a curator, I still don't think it is possible to teach people how to curate and so on. I really got into curating not looking into past examples, but obviously there are now examples that I admire incredibly and you can say that they are the usual suspects. I think of Pontius Hultén's practice for me is enormously satisfying, the bold initiatives he has taken. I like the fact that both Hultén's work as curator and a museum director and the interplay between these two positions, those two relationships and so on. It seems to me that he is first a thinker of artistic forms and their meaning and the practice of artists, and how to make that legible within an historical context, more so than before he is a "Museum Director." Ulli Beier, a German-emigre who worked in Nigeria during the 1950s and 1960s is enormously important. I obviously admire Harald Szeemann's

Documenta 5. I think that exhibition remains foundational and unsurpassed in terms of its ambition, energy, and adventurousness. I also admire people like Walter Hopps. I really admire Marcia Tucker who after the debacle at the Whitney in the late seventies went on and founded the New Museum in New York and the incomparable Susanne Ghez at the Renaissance Society in Chicago. I am a great admirer of some of my contemporaries like Catherine David. I also admire the work of Group Material and Marcel Broodthaers, not only because of its discursive nature, but because the work has a lot to give to curatorial history as well as the exhibitionary meaning that continues to come out of the work. Of my own generation, Hans Ulrich Obrist is enormously gifted.

PO'N   In *The Power of Display: A History of Exhibition Installation at the MoMA*, Mary Anne Staniszewski highlights a kind of art historical "amnesia" towards innovative exhibitionary display practices of the past, do you think this amnesia has affected the way we perceive contemporary curatorial practice?

OE   She is absolutely right on the side of art historians but not on the side of curators. One of the things that we fail to acknowledge is that the views we have of artistic practice have largely come through exhibitions, more specifically Modern art and art historians tend to deny that. They tend to deny how the curatorial energy of past exhibitions has really shaped the ways in which different movements emerged and were received. Whether it is the Fauvists or the Cubists and so on, those designations emerged out of exhibitions. She is absolutely correct. One other person I wanted to mention is the legacy of somebody like Kynaston McShine, in a much more institutional framework but non the less very formidable in the sense of his anticipating what is to come, whether it is through the exhibitions *Primary Structures* and *Information* in 1970 at MoMA and the Duchamp exhibition. Kynaston McShine needs to be known more in the curatorial world than he is. I think that *Information* remains unparalleled in terms of the effects that that exhibition has had in different curatorial practices. People may not actually know that exhibition, but somehow it has seeped into many of our sensibilities and the mixed economy of the exhibition space. The old Dada exhibitions are just as interesting to me and so on.

PO'N   How did being involved as a curator within a biennial context on many occasions such as *Documenta11* 2002, the 2nd *Johannesburg Biennale* 1996–97, alter the way your thinking about curating as a global and international practice?

OE   I don't know whether it has altered my view. One always has to look at these works in retrospect of course, but in the immediate period of making those exhibitions you leave not only drained and exhausted but also apprehensive, because obviously when you make large projects it is open season on the curator. What I will say is that it has made me aware of the fact that I am a great promoter of Biennials. I'm not the least dubious about them. There is a fashion of skepticism about Biennials. I am not skeptical simply because I have seen many of them, in so many different cultural and geographic contexts and very few are of the scale of say Johannesburg, Documenta or Venice. Most of them seem to be quite improvisatory, and most of them seem to be quite modest in what they intend to achieve. I am interested in how these Biennials have really infused a new sense of the contemporary in cultures that did not or do not have an institutional legacy to carry it forward. The kind of alternatives that they provide for the ideas of modernisation, modernity and the ways it opens up some institutional space for artists working on the local level. The principal lesson I have learnt is that Biennials have really exploded the myth of the lack of practice in very different parts of the world. It has forced curators to look more carefully. The careers of people like William Kentridge, or Anri Sala come to mind. Their work in the international circuit would not have been possible without these Biennials and they have really produced occasions to allow us to reflect on the very limits and the very limitations of the contemporary artistic sphere. I am quite resistant to the certain forms of critique of Biennials, more specifically because they are critiqued based on the fact that they are everywhere, that peripheral localities have acquired a taste for them. It is no longer small privileged places like Venice. Everyone does it, so it is not interesting anymore. I say, the more the merrier. No one says there are too may museums and there are.

PO'N   One of the common criticisms directed towards biennials often refer to duration and the insufficient time given to research process and it is often a small group of curators who are given the responsibility.

OE   That is true. That is less the problem of Biennials, but a problem of the organisers, who try to instrumentalise the Biennials for their own civic power. Because what you see in what you are mentioning doesn't seem any different to what you see with contemporary art museums all over the world, they are all the same. They all have the same Richter's, they all have Richard Long "spattered wall," they all have the same Carl Andre on the floor. I was just at the Tate the other day, and I thought my goodness, how terribly boring, how unimaginative, and how very mediocre in fact. It is like going to a catalogue and just simply buying your own version of modern and contemporary art. It hardly deviates. At least in Biennials there are mistakes that are visible and there is some energy. They are not always the same. Obviously there is a tendency to repeat the same artists, but they don't always repeat. I tend to

think that we should focus our attentions more on closing down
museums of contemporary art than Biennials. Museums of
contemporary art do absolutely the same things. I don't want to use
the notion of risk, because risk is not what museums are necessarily
about but I think that it has to have an imaginative vitality to strike out
in a different course and introduce ideas that is least expected from
the institution.

PO'N   As Artistic Director of *Documenta11*, you selected Carlos
Basualdo, Ute Meta Bauer, Susanne Ghez, Sarat Maharaj, Mark
Nash and Octavio Zaya to work with you on the overall curatorial
endeavour, was this a way of getting away from the more "single-
auteured" position associated with such large international
exhibitions?

OE   It was in a way. Obviously, it is very difficult to avoid the
position of being the auteur when you are being the Artistic Director.
You can bring in as many people as you want to sit at the table and
you still have this big question mark. But I wanted to emphatically
make it clear in the context of *Documenta11* that there was no single
author but a group of collaborators very much in tune with each
other's strength's and weaknesses. This was by far one of the most
transformative, energizing, and challenging group of people to work
with. What is the degree of the contribution by the group? We
wanted to address the context within which we were working and to
enter into a dialogue that we could make visible to a broader public
what was going on globally in contemporary art. And I deliberately
chose people who were not all curators by profession. I wanted to
have a mixture of intelligences, if you will, within the group and I
couldn't have been blessed with a better group of people. They are
smart, they are engaging, they are critical, and they are really very
tough people. It is not people whom you can overwhelm with a
singular, ungiving argument. I will say that I gained enormously from
working with them, but yes I wanted to get away from Documenta
being this thing of one singular voice. I wanted to have a kind of
"Think Tank" to elaborate some of the questions of Documenta.
I think it served the project immensely well. In Johannesburg
Biennale I attempted the same mechanism but a little bit differently.
I invited a number of curators to respond to my project, but they
were completely free to make their own exhibitions. When people
look at Venice in 2003, we did this already in Johannesburg. In 1997,
I worked with Hou Hanru, Yu Yeon Kim, Geraldo Mosquera, Colin
Richards, Octavio Zaya, Kellie Jones, and Mahen Bonetti curated the
film section. I think Johannesburg was far more experimental in this
sense. Number one, we say it was Johannesburg Biennale, but it was
not the Johannesburg Biennale alone. It took place simultaneously in
two cities; Cape Town and Johannesburg, amongst different
institutions in these two cities. This was a way to look for possible

contradictions in my own methodology. Kellie Jones for example thought that she wanted to make an exhibition of only women artists, which I completely abhorred, but I couldn't stop her from doing it. It's her prerogative, she did it, and it was a good exhibition. Colin Richards wanted to work only with South African artists. I said "oh my goodness that was precisely what I didn't want you to do". He said he wanted to do it and he did it and it really was very significant in a way. Hou Hanru wanted to use the end of the British colonialism in Hong Kong as a metaphor for the end of history. It really was very provocative and the wonderful thing was that we only had fourteen months to do the exhibition. Working with one's colleagues is really a way of opening up the process to new forms of accountability, to new ways of viewing the curatorial process, to multiple perspectives.

PO'N   Was *Documenta11*, as Ute Meta Bauer has suggested, a means of reconfiguring the art historical canon?

OE   It was in a number of ways, but it was also about where the canon was going to be read *from*. This has been one of Ute's preoccupations in her own work as well. This is one of the reasons why I chose her without even knowing that she was a candidate and one of the last two finalists with me for the Directorship of *Documenta11*. I had no idea she was. This was completely opportune and I thought it's great that we are doing this together. So already, for us the question was how do we read the map of contemporary art from Kassel and that meant that Kassel had to be connected to these vectors. That is how the "Platforms" emerged. Of course, this was the original idea that I had, that I presented to the nominating committee in 1998 in Berlin. We wanted to look at the notion of the canon. We wanted to look at different ways of working. We were very interested in documentary. It came out clearly and we were least interested in the short film genre or the mindless, numbing looped video. We wanted to use the medium length, or epic length like Jef Gey's 36-hour film or Ulrike Ottinger's 7 hours, or other artists whose films were 4-hours and so on.

PO'N   So playing with the impossibility of total viewership?

OE   Precisely. We wanted to confound that. We wanted to say that it is not possible to simple absorb everything as yet another fast food meal. We wanted to make it clear, that if the public were to insist on absorbing everything then the period of digestion must by necessity take much longer to digest the material. I think we run around these exhibitions thinking that you grasp it all, but that was precisely the point and it became not only a project of endurance. That wasn't the point. It was about impossibility of total consumption.

PO'N   Since the late 1980s it is through the predominantly "a-historical" and temporary art exhibition that the significance of an artwork has been determined by its assigned place amongst other works. Many of these exhibitions are very different in concept and selection of works and artists, but what they have in common the fact that they abandon the traditional chronological arrangement. Exhibitions such as Harald Szeemann's *A-Historische Klanken* at the Boijmans van Beuningen Museum in Rotterdam in 1988, and Jean-Hubert Martin's 1989 *Magiciens* at Centre George Pompidou, Paris, juxtaposed works from different times and cultures alongside each other. Such post-modern arrangements came under much critical assault for what curator Patrick Murphy, called "stay at home cultural tourism" — presenting art from other places as if other places are all the same, where artistic artefacts are paraded through the exhibition, the range of origins providing the meaning, a kind of polyglot regionalism. Since the late eighties we have had an increase in the number of Biennials, do you think that Murphy's claim is still evident today?

OE   I don't think it is evident at all. There is a striking provincialism in his statement, even though I can understand the perspective from which he is speaking. You can't know the content of artistic production just by mere display, there is a greater commitment one has to have, art historically and otherwise to be able to pull it off. I think he is correct on that level, but I think at the same time there is a kind of romanticism that people have that there will always be a misunderstanding when you take on the work of other cultures. Those do happen, but those misunderstandings can never be addressed unless you make an attempt and this is what is really productive about *Magiciens*. It provoked very important critical, historical as well as philosophical debate that has remained with us. That is why more than fifteen years after it happened it is still fascinating for us. It is still a touchstone, for or against ways of working. Maybe because Biennales have become so commonplace, we tend to ignore that these juxtaposition can produce visual incoherence. This visual incoherence in itself can be part of this excitement. The fact that you have to wade your way through this thicket of forms and meanings and ideas, and issues and subjects and so on, in order to emerge on the other side of some kind of intelligible distillation of what it is all about is not in itself unrewarding, even if its ultimately challenging. Many curators are using this as a method. If you look at *Cities on the Move* by Hans Ulrich Obrist and Hou Hanru, that is precisely the kind of maelstrom of things and so on, really the cacophony of the exhibition itself that becomes the meta-artwork in the exhibition if you will. It has had some positive consequences for how one makes exhibitions.

PO'N   Is it not a very western modernist notion of "otherness?"
When things are decontextualised from the social, economic and
cultural conditions within which the work has been made, it does
not necessarily quantify it as being unreadable?

OE   Absolutely. This is really the problem. Native cultures must
stay native in order to be properly understood and therefore they
are more authentic. This is really part of the problem. I think that the
chrysalis of this argument in and of itself does not quite do the job;
other models will have to emerge.

PO'N   What current curatorial projects or initiatives do you
think are breaking new ground? You have already mentioned
Hans Ulrich Obrist?

OE   I really thought that *Laboratorium*, which Hans Ulrich Obrist
and Barbara Vanderlinden organised in Antwerp was really engaging,
but I must say that right now I am very attracted to places like DIA
Beacon for the clarity and the partiality of that. There is a precision
to that institution, as frustrating as its deliberate exclusions might be.
I think we really have to find different forms and ways of playing with
making exhibitions. I love the Field Museum in Chicago because they
are really very funny as museums of material culture — time capsules.
But short of that I admired what Francesco Bonami tried to do in
Venice. I thought it was courageous on his part, in this setting to try
to unravel the relationship between the Director and the curator.
It was interesting. I must put in a word for the work of inIVA in
London. I think that is a great model. With this agency format Gilane
Tawadros has been able to do some very productive and important
historical stuff. The exhibitions they have organised in different
institutions since they were founded and also their publications have
been incredibly important. I really don't know of any comparable
institution of contemporary art really doing this kind of work. I like
the fact that inIVA has really been able to do these sorts of projects
and remain on significantly stable ground as they negotiate the
process of institutional discourse, artistic discourse. I am really
surprised it is not taken as seriously as it should be. It really is a
significant institution. I like the agency model.

PO'N   In an interview with Carol Becker for *Art Journal* in 2002,
you said that you wanted to "make distinctions between curating
within the canon and curating within culture." What are these
distinctions and how were they explored in your projects?

OE   I have always tried to work outside of the canon and to do
it within culture. This is not to say that the canon is bad but the
canon already has a highly circumscribed notion of what artistic
practice could be. I think this is already embedded within a very

large historical determination that is in many ways very much set. It is un-giving. I am really interested in curating within culture, even when I am drawing from the canon in order to unsettle the kind of methodological issues that have become so situated in one place. To curate within culture is to take a space of culture in the present as an open place of working and that means that you have a greater mobility in terms of bringing in procedures of making art that may not yet have a place in the broader context of contemporary art. I suppose this is the realm within which most curators work, except when their ambitions change and they want to make an exhibition of Andy Warhol. What could be more generic? When their ambitions change, when they want to become more institutionalised, they want to prove their commitment to the canon. This is what usually happens, it is more strategic. You can see immediately the intellectual poverty of some of those gestures and I completely understand what you see when the move happens. The curators have already reached a threshold when they want to have a permanent job.

PO'N   Is this also what you mean when you say that you are "looking historically at the present"?

OE   Precisely. It doesn't mean giving up the canon, but I think to find a way to re-jig the canon and to make work that obviously, in the broader cultural context, can have the possibility of opening up a different kind of dialogue.

PO'N   Do you think postgraduate curating courses and institutionally led curatorial training programmes have impacted upon the increasing professionalisation of curatorial practice? Do you think the role of the curator has usurped that of the critic?

OE   Obviously, this is really a consequence of the proliferation of museums, blockbuster exhibitions, biennials, but also the proliferation of other forms of mega exhibitions. Exhibitions have become legitimate mediums for art as the novel has been for fiction. Some one has to look after these things and the connections they help us make in negotiating the relationship between art and society, institutions and the public. Just like you have tons of writing programmes for aspiring playwrights and novelist, the curatorial training programmes are going to grow to meet the demands of exhibition-making systems, all of which derive from the total absorption of life into various formats of display. We live in an exhibitionary context at the moment. We are each in different ways always embedded in a potential exhibition, from the mall to the high street. We either want to be seen or to look. So here it makes perfect sense that curatorial training programmes can be developed according to this logic of increasing diffusion of life into display. My doubt however is whether it is possible to train people in such a one-dimensional way, in which curating is only what they learn how to do. What is very significant in terms of the curator supplanting the role of the critic is that a lot of works of criticism today, of course is for a generalised public and are almost like press releases in service of either the economic interest of the commercial art world or the ideological purposes of the public museum. Curator's writing is mainly understood by a specialised public, who happen to read exhibition catalogues. That is because attempts by institutions to foreground their own memory has really led to the uses of skills of curators as honest tools of propaganda. At most curators operating under these conditions become reduced to mere cheerleaders of artists. I don't know the way out of this dilemma.

PO'N   Can we or should we evaluate what good or bad curating is? Is there such a thing as a "good" curated art exhibition?

OE   I wouldn't even begin to touch that. I think it is possible with any form of criticism, but I can't quite tell you what good or bad curating is. I just don't know. I really have to think about it. It is a provocative question. To do so one has to really do a comparative analysis of curating and it is only within a comparative context that one can begin to sort that out. I mean there are exhibitions, which are deliberately bad, what ever that means, but that is part of their statement so how can that be bad. Exhibitions have been like laboratories of incredible investigations and I would really like to take away these absolute judgments like good and bad as a value, as a way of describing what people are trying to do, whether they hang it low, whether they put it on the floor, whether they take it off the wall. It's like good or bad art, we can make those judgments but I tend to reserve them for my own personal experience than something that has any kind of intellectual efficacy.

This interview was recorded in Bristol on 04.02.2005

FOR A... FUNCTIONAL UTOPIA? A REVIEW OF A POSITION

Liam Gillick

"Utopia Station" is complicated. Writing about the project produces a necessarily partial and fragmented account due to the mass of meetings and discussions, both formal and informal that have surrounded its various manifestations. In relation to the decision to avoid personal projects in this book, things are further problematised by my involvement in "Utopia Station", which means that this text should exclude itself from consideration from publication. Yet the implicated role of the artist within the curatorial structure and vice versa, combined with the peculiar nature of "Utopia Station", as an extremely inclusive and promiscuous event means that hopefully it should be considered a special case here. I also find it difficult to accept the validity of approaching a book such as this without addressing the involved role of the artist in something concrete yet still soft, where people are unsure of their roles and their level of authorship, especially when the approach to the project has been marked by scepticism and enthusiasm at all stages, even from those at the centre of the discussion. For "Utopia Station", organised by Hans Ulrich Obrist, Molly Nesbit and Rirkrit Tiravanija, was not a singular event nor did it develop as a precisely realisable concept. Here I will outline the origins of the project, reproduce an edited version of my sceptical intervention in the first formal discussions around the exercise and follow up with a review of the potential of "Utopia Station" as something "in progress" and dislocated — from the multiple moments of inception to the final intense semi-private arguments surrounding the idea to take the project to the World Social Forum in Porto Alegre in 2005. These discussions arguably became the most productive aspect of the whole project for me up to that point. While I will not go into detail about the various manifestations of the project at the 50th Venice Biennale and the Haus de Kunst in Munich as these have been described and written about extensively elsewhere with all the usual misattributions and misunderstandings it is crucial to understand these key moments as the enabling structures that could lead to such productive follow-up dispute and potential. I will use this opportunity to broadly outline the genealogy of the project from a partial and personal perspective and combine this with critical comments coming from a position of both insider and outsider simultaneously. Hopefully, in the future, this will be joined by further narratives around "Utopia Station", that will inevitably offer some complete inversions of the account here. For it is the following-up aspect of the project that renders it special in relation to the tendency for the culture to produce "re-makes" rather than "episodic" approaches to structures whether they be the Venice Biennale or an improvised project in Brooklyn. With "Utopia Station" we return to the construction again and again. The problems and questions circulate and dissolve, condense and re-emerge. It is easier to organise projects that have one moment of exposure and no developed sense of post-production reassessment. It is the ongoing reassessment of "Utopia Station" built into its structure that renders it relevant for consideration here.

While most exhibition/curated structures embody a sense of hierarchy which is open to challenge from all "sides" (curator, artist, audiences, participants, critical communities) the way "Utopia Station" came together was often contingent upon who happened to be around at certain times, by invitation or accident. Many people, especially theorists and writers were central to the project without appearing to be part of the structure. They often thought they were commenting on an aspect of the manifestation of "Utopia Station" whereas they were forming the structure as they spoke. Others thought they were defining and pinning down an implicated strategy only to find that the project had already shifted shape and moved along without them. Additionally, as with many projects organised by Hans Ulrich Obrist, a large number of artists were always listed as involved in the "Utopia Station" without contributing a great deal beyond a single poster or their presence at a given event, so we shouldn't look to artist lists for guidance. They often simply formed a particular new kind of implicated "audience" for the multiple events. Bearing this in mind, this text is an attempt to bypass many of the apparently visible participants and look elsewhere for tension and engagement. Many people just happened to be around during a dinner or discussion and limited their role to that one night of confusion or clarity. It is these moments that I am most interested in and that will form the crux of my argument that "Utopia Station" is best considered a site of ideas "in progress" rather than a sequence of moments of discourse or presentation. It is a series of events that are productive and in mid-flow only.

The issue here is not to propose a new exhibition or curatorial structure but to use this opportunity to provide a parallel history of "Utopia Station" and examine something that claims to have no official end point — in other words to look at an ongoing project while it remains ongoing. Through this it might be possible to record the potential of a project not limited to a simple discussion of the relationships between the artist and the curator or the structure and the institution but to unpack the conflicting impulses at the heart of a project marked by a desire to engage and disengage simultaneously from a slippery yet over-determined underlying concept. This is a project where the significant moments have proved hard to express within the mediation of the structure for they are not manifest during the moments of the "Utopia Stations" themselves. This is a text that should reveal the potential of discourse in relation to a distracted structure, which has lent itself to the formation of multiple narratives around the increasing absence of the excessive abstraction at its core. As such this should be seen as one of those narratives and will bypass those that were only reported, as I did not attend the extensive discussions in Frankfurt, Berlin and elsewhere.

The central body of this text was presented as a contribution to a symposium held at Vassar College in Poughkeepsie, New York, around the time of the development phase of the project "Utopia Station" during 2002/2003. At that point only the discursive nature of the project had been defined in concrete terms. However, "Utopia Station" had emerged via a wide-ranging invitation from Andrew Brown, commissioning editor at Thames & Hudson, to a number of artists, curators and critics to consider developing books that could function as quasi-exhibitions with no "show". Using as a conceptual base a sequence of parallelities — the body, urbanism, artist's collectives — and so on. Molly Nesbit and Hans Ulrich Obrist had initially outlined the idea of addressing "utopia". These specific invitations from Andrew Brown have produced more than books. Some titles have been developed, such as "Art Works: Place" by Tacita Dean and Jeremy Millar ("Art Works" is the series title), a large number of duos were activated by the process and began initial discussions around possible subjects for publication without actually producing a book for Thames and Hudson. An example would be my own project with Maria Lind provisionally titled "Collectives" which produced a great deal of discussion yet no concrete results. While there was an understandable scepticism from many about the "theory-of-everything-expressed-in-small-chunks" quality of the overall project, most people just sublimated the art part of the equation into freethinking about the potential of its double.

In relation to large exhibition structures, the working methodology of Hans Ulrich Obrist can be loosely described as content-creation heavy. He has brought a uniquely energetic and complex approach to curating over the last fifteen years. In many cases he has reconfigured the hierarchies of exhibitions by drawing a relatively un-premeditated set of content providers into a loose mix that will inevitably generate content and lead to the establishment of a book machine that will somewhat configure itself via discussion and discourse rather than through classical models of over-determined planning. Of course such an approach is what has led, in the past, to accusations of relativistic bricolage from some who would prefer things to remain more fixed and less mutable — effect and process being the primary providers of meaning within the exhibition structure rather than the presentation of discrete artworks. It is a promiscuous approach that has mutated recently, possibly in the light of the "Utopia Station" experience, and been affected by his recent series of monographic exhibitions for the ARC in Paris and his ongoing interest in producing texts and projects with individual artists.

Molly Nesbit is primarily a theorist and critic teaching at Vassar College in upstate New York and a contributing editor to Artforum. Her extensive knowledge of twentieth century avant-garde practice and her relative inexperience in relation to large contemporary exhibition structures ensured that she offered a level of precision and pacing that is normally considered out of sync with the increasingly blur of exhibition making. The dominant structures that surround cultural production have tended to over-emphasise Nesbit's position as an art historian and therefore underplay her role as an equal curator of the "Utopia Station". Her position throughout has been complex yet at the centre of all developments around the project.

Rirkrit Tiravanija's work is often incorrectly described as involving the presentation of undirected or content free places for the encouragement of open discourse. Anyone familiar with his work or with a passing knowledge of any of his projects in the last fifteen years will know that there are always structured intellectual backdrops to his projects — films, texts, subjects, teaching projects — that form a critical vortex at the centre of each work that are there to be engaged with or not in a manner that rigorously attempts to avoid didactic or dogmatic mirroring within the work of aspects of the society which are already known to the dominant discourse. The "Utopia Station"s in Venice and Munich were little different, apart from the open inclusion of multiple parasitical projects around the central core, which functioned as plug-ins in relation to the quasi-architectures at the centre and periphery of the events.

Hans Ulrich Obrist, Molly Nesbit and Rirkrit Tiravanija adapted the initial concept of a project related to the notion of utopia and in light of their perception that many other artists and curators had also some interest in the conflicting discourses around the notion of idealised progressive models, started a process of bringing together critics, theorists, philosophers, artists and hybrid figures for a sequence of discussions leading to the creation of a content heavy ultra discourse that would begin to find some distribution form at the Venice Biennale in 2003 and continue to mutate and develop during an unspecified number of future projects, locations and events.

Hans Ulrich Obrist had been invited by Director Francesco Bonami to contribute a curated section of the 50th Venice Biennale. Obrist suggested continuing the development of the Utopia project alongside Molly Nesbit, so the combination of a potential book and a potential exhibition structure were fundamental to the development of "Utopia Station" as a semi-functional project. In 2002 Rirkrit Tiravanija had also been asked to contribute a curated project to the Biennale. Having recently worked on a number of "stations" for exhibition structures (literally station-like neo-architecture) it was decided to combine the utopia project with a new "station" for Venice. A sequence of meetings took place in early 2003 in Berlin at which I too was invited to contribute ideas to the overall physical design of the Venice space along with a number of other people.

The project finally presented in Venice included a large basic "station" structure that was designed by Rirkrit Tiravanija, seating adjacent to the station designed by myself. Various parasitical semi-autonomous projects such as the Guarana Bar by Superflex, Martha Rosler's work with her Scandinavian students, Christoph Schlingensief's "Church of Fear" and Radio Arte Mobile organised by the Zerynthia group. The manifestation of the project also included a series of posters, each by a different contributor to the discussion and in many cases posters designed by various contributors as their sole offering to the project. This poster project became the central core of "Utopia Station" and the only aspect common to further manifestations in the Haus der Kunst in Munich and in Porto Alegre during the World Social Forum. The text that follows was presented before the "Utopia Station" project had become completely clarified and the conference during which it was presented was marked by the conflicting desires to sustain an open-ended discourse on one hand and to know more about the precise details of the planned manifestation of the "Utopia Station" project in Venice that was clearly already forming in the minds of the curators.

THE UTOPIAN IMPULSE IN THINKING IS ALL THE STRONGER, THE LESS IT OBJECTIFIES ITSELF AS UTOPIA — A FURTHER FORM OF REGRESSION — WHEREBY IT SABOTAGES ITS OWN REALISATION. OPEN THINKING POINTS BEYOND ITSELF. FOR ITS PART, SUCH THINKING TAKES A POSITION AS A FIGURATION OF PRAXIS WHICH IS MORE CLOSELY RELATED TO A PRAXIS TRULY INVOLVED IN CHANGE THAN IN A POSITION OF MERE OBEDIENCE FOR THE SAKE OF PRAXIS. BEYOND ALL SPECIALISED AND PARTICULAR CONTENT, THINKING IS ACTUALLY AND ABOVE ALL THE FORCE OF RESISTANCE, ALIENATED FROM RESISTANCE ONLY WITH GREAT EFFORT.

(Adorno, Resignation, 1991)

Over the last few years I have avoided a number of exhibition structures that have used the word "Utopia" as part of their underlying concept. The reason for this is connected to my resistance to the misreading of some work now as being solely part of some semi-effectual quasi-utopian project or at best a commentary upon a particularly Anglo-Saxon misreading of post-modernism predicated upon an ironic focus on the failure of modernism which renders all progressive thinking as Utopian by default. My interest is far more grounded and potentially complicating than this. And could be described as an ongoing investigation into how the middle ground of social and economic activity leaves traces in our current environment. For if we agree that we live in a post-consensus sequence of moments, you might also agree that we live in a post-utopian environment that requires analysis. Throughout, of course, I am glossing over the notion of the rogue individual, the visionary and the baroque dream-scapers. Their apparent "visions" are retrogressive and not utopian in quality as they are not part of an effective critique of contemporary social models. So, if we are working in a post-utopian situation, how are things still agreed, planned and developed and who controls these processes? And if the situation is effectively post-utopian in terms of the absence of functional alternative visions, does the word Utopian only exist as an accusatory for cultural workers now? If it is true that there are no functional utopias describable today, what kind of alternative vision can be proposed to the dominant ideologies that control and alienate our relationships and circumstances? The reason for avoiding these prior utopia structures has been connected to my rejection of the assumption that any progressive movement is somehow utopian. My frequent use of the term "post-utopian" in writing and in relation to my work is an attempt to break free from the application of the word utopia to any old (modernist) alternative structure that happens to have existed.

The modern left has always been multiple and essentially fractured, the nature of its developed arguments never consolidated or singular. So one question might be — is it necessary to resurrect the notion of a functional utopia in order to provide a set of rhetorical tools that might help us out of the currently reactive situation we find on the progressive left, or should we keep with a relativist form of multiple interest development that remains mutable, fluctuating, responsive and inclusive?

My last short book was titled "Literally No Place: Communes, Bars and Greenrooms". It attempted to outline certain narrative structures that might expose the conditions under which we might find ethical and moral traces that resist commodification within our current situation. It is a text that is more focused on the relationship between the urban and rural as it continues to develop under the same cultural conditions — the connection between personal relationship structures within broad battles to control the images that they create and an attempt to look at the particular American development of forms of functional communality in place of the suppression of the legacy and potential of communism and truly alternative structures at an organised and general level. Of course these undercurrents remain deeply embedded within a sequence of narrative texts that present some environments where such play and negotiation might take place. The commune, the bar and the greenroom.

So why would someone change their mind? Why suddenly shift into an association with the word utopia in an art context. If I understand this potential structure — as a participant rather than an organiser — "Utopia Station" appears to be working towards a temporary, if rather visible, marker of a sequence of "becoming utopias" or "in relation to the application of the accusation of utopias" rather than a reflection of work that appears to reference a set of aesthetic tools that have been deemed dysfunctional and rendered as ironic failures by the dominant culture's desire to corrupt and prevent through the accusation of hypocrisy and lack of economic realism, yet are still used and passed around as a sad reminder of how good things could have been. A "Utopia Station", on the other hand, might be an ongoing arrival and departure framed by waiting at an in-between space that has been designated by the organisers. All this combined with something to look at and to pass the time with before moving back into the islands of art and art-like production that are always presented by the Venice Biennale. Rather than a reflection of flawed social models, it could be a refutation of the accusation of utopia, which is merely one stage, or station in the development of any progressive idea. In order to bypass a simplistic application and ongoing corruption of the applied meanings of the word Utopia, the "Utopia Station" might be a call to question whether we are happy with a situation where certain politically engaged art remains characterised by the phrase: "it's all very interesting but..."

This "becomingness" rather than "aboutness" is combined with a way of reconfiguring and reassessing the activities of certain artists, critics and curators whose position is hopefully shifting and shimmering under the umbrella of the project. Ironically this "Utopia Station" emerges at a time when the worst predictions from the recent past are playing out. The warnings from those who chose to continue the analysis of social and political conditions in the face of emergent globalisation and the rise of relativism have come true. The apparent utopists were working in the realm of documentary rather than fiction after all. The quasi-rationalisations of neo-liberal thinking are, right now, in full flow. Once again confronting us with a non-choice wrapped in a perversion of moral positioning that renders things binary, unsophisticated and potentially deadly. Anyone opposing both the leaden thinking that emanates from the governments of the US and UK and the too-late manoeuvring and poorly articulated positions of the French, German and Russian governments might be called a fool or worse, a Utopian thinker. The use of a baseball bat to destroy a hornets' nest is not a perfect technique at any point, but the fundamental opposition to the entire matrix of value systems that has generated the current international situation, whether in favour or against a war scenario, is generally viewed as an operational system that should be analysed with utopistic tools at best and suppression at worst.

The problem here is linked to the wide-ranging use of the term Utopia — the literally no place — in our current language. It is a common enough word so we don't think twice about using it. We tend also to associate it with art and architecture or withdrawal and communality. The developed sense of a word that was originally used to title a book that was intended as a localised critique of a particular historical circumstance has little relation to its original meaning. The question is; how does any consideration of such a term avoid the micro-fascistic traps that lie in wait for anyone who is not convinced that things are the way they could be? As I have said, in the hands of neo-liberal pragmatists Utopia has come to describe any art movement, architectural moment, political system or communal proposition that doesn't operate within the terms of global capital. Utopian is the term that refers to the desire for something that is impractical, because it levels and implies harmony, while sidestepping the generalised, lurching linearity of the dominant system. The thinking goes that the attempted application of utopian systems has had to be forced onto people whenever it has been attempted. There has always been a suppression of "human nature" in order to temporarily experience something more enlightening and less guilt or repression ridden. The strange thing is that the current international tension is between two sets of people who veil their true interests with a faked set of socio-economic anxieties. The religious underpinnings, and therefore essentially truly utopian, value systems of the ongoing Middle-Eastern crisis are dragging us into mire. The question for us, is do we leave this utopian question to these people to fight over and, or do we reclaim it through the use of analytical tools that are more rigorous at identifying the way things work. The question is, can there be a Marxist analysis of utopia that has any functional role within our range of interests. But it is not as simple as this. Moments in the recent past when people have found their own functional utopias have been suppressed and broken down. Power is most vigilant when mini-utopistic structures emerge and make every effort to point out the apparent hypocrisy in their set ups so as to hasten their demise.

So why use such a flawed dysfunctional, accusational tool for an exhibition title? The question is linked to how to proceed when you are not convinced by current conditions. Working in a relativist, parallel fashion appears to be sufficient at various moments, yet with a continuing proliferation and appropriation of models of radicality by others, it becomes more and more difficult to divine the differences between one named structure and another. It is possible that there is some kind of irony at the heart of its use here. An acknowledgment that the activities of the artists concerned has reached a point of perfect irrelevance. It is arguable that the notion of utopia within the cultural sphere is most attractive to those who have no ongoing interest in making productive change. Instead they create a sequence of mirage visions of how things could be if they were everything/anything/something other than the way they are now. I would argue that the greatest strength of "Utopia Station" would be derived from its becoming a functional utopia. A model of a more discursive and contingent exhibition structure that could cut free from the generalised experience of its hosts and retain a utopistic becomingness throughout the time of any exhibition or display moment. Scooping up and re-spreading a layer of ethical traces from a sequence of suppressed attempts to actually create a better place and actually have a better time, rather than just providing soothing images of experi-mental architecture and a mish-mash of interactive structures, however temporarily interesting they might be.

How could an exhibition like the one in Venice perform tasks of refusal in relation to the utopistic legacy while retaining some reconsti-tuted sense of how things could be? In other words, how could it become a free-floating non-defined sequence of propositions that wander in and out of focus and avoid being lodged within the consumable world of the singular concept.

* * *

It is worth taking a moment to reflect upon the physical and tempo-ral quality of the "Utopia Station" project that subsequently developed. In Venice and at the Haus der Kunst in Munich the work inserted itself into established contemporary art structures that have a precise history and programmation. In both locations it appeared alongside other exhibi-tions. In Venice it was an entire mix of parallel exhibitions while at the Haus de Kunst, a large Rem Koolhaas exhibition opened in the other spaces of the institution shortly after "Utopia Station" began. A third potential location emerged around the time of the Haus der Kunst station. Extensive discussions in Poughkeepsie, Venice and Munich frequently circulated around the idea that the "Utopia Station" approach could lend itself to operating within or alongside other structures that might demonstrate a differently engaged relation to the complexity of contem-porary Leftist discourse. This was partly in response to a perceived over-reliance on the art context in the initial phases of the project devel-opment. Particular enthusiasm for creating an alliance with the World Social Forum came from Molly Nesbit, Liz Linden, Immanuel Wallerstein and the Raqs Media Collective who attended the Mumbai World Social Forum in 2004, returning with detailed reports and video of the event. Immanuel Wallerstein had also presented a paper in Poughkeepsie that made attendance at such an event appear valid. Yet, the moment of decision to attend the 2005 World Social Forum in Porto Alegre is hard to identify. A meeting at the TAT (originally the Theater am Turm) in Frankfurt in 2004 further addressed some of the possibilities suggested by potential involvement with the World Social Forum. Flagged on its e-flux communiqué, the TAT meeting circled around the question of implicated and directly engaged future manifestations of "Utopia Station".

While it could be argued that the Haus der Kunst stage of the project was essentially closed off by the boundary role of the institution, the World Social Forum emerged as a potential, non-resolved experiment in establishing relations to organised activism. Rirkrit Tiravanija and Molly Nesbit travelled to Brazil to meet the cultural group of the World Social Forum in November 2004. At this point a great deal of discussion took place about how and in what form a developed presence could be made manifest at the event.

Following these developments, participation in the World Social Forum was presented as something of a fait d'accompli and a desire by some before and during discussion about the relevance of the project to the event and the event to the project. Using the assumption that the World Social Forum might be a natural ally and co-conspirator in the establishment of what we might call "functional relativism" within the context of "Utopia Station", it was implied that group attendance might be an assumption as well as a matter for discussion or dispute. Certainly there was precise interest in attending from many after material brought back from Mumbai had been circulated. But clearly faced by scepticism and confusion from some who had been involved in the first two episodes of "Utopia Station", Molly Nesbit arranged a series of meetings in New York City which were open to anyone involved in "Utopia Station" and were presented as opportunities to establish the terms of reference and multiple languages that might be employed in the event that a group of people felt it to be possible to join the non-aligned multi-faceted collection of interest groups, pressure groups and non-specific alliances that make up the World Social Forum.

The follow-up discussions leading up to Porto Alegre proved the most dynamic, complex and tense of my involvement in the entire project. Generally taking place in New York City, they were marked by the absence of Hans Ulrich Obrist and Rirkrit Tiravanija, although they were constantly in touch by telephone and for the central role taken in the discussion by Molly Nesbit. It was the moment when Nesbit's pedagogical experience could start to function in terms of creating an interface between the participants in small group environments where people could speak freely without appearing to break down the collective multiplicity of the project. They were also notable events for bringing together an inter-generational discussion from a progressive perspective that did not lead to agreement but helped to define difference and conflict in terms of the artist's relationship to the project as a whole.

Martha Rosler, Lawrence Weiner, Anton Vidokle, Pierre Huyghe, Julieta Aranda, Hans Haacke and myself being common figures, engaged in an ongoing, non-recorded, non-transcribed follow-up series of discussions about how to approach a concrete potential engagement with the World Social Forum. The differences of opinion represented in relation to Porto Alegre are worth simplifying for the sake of this text. Broadly Molly Nesbit and Liz Linden spoke alongside the absent participants who believed that it was a social obligation to introduce a real and critical art presence into the World Social Forum without much requirement for further discussion other than in what form a participation should take; Martha Rosler appeared to view it as another possible place to work, little different from any other venue and absolutely different at the same time; Lawrence Weiner expressed that artists are critically engaged with the culture anyway so the approach should not be any different to any other exhibition structure. I agreed with him but added warnings about cultural imperialism and the potential that any art projects at the World Social Forum could become another part of the global trail of art biennales and merely introduce aspects to the World Social Forum which would distract from its core functions. Hans Haacke, Lawrence Weiner and myself also expressed scepticism at the idea of the World Social Forum from the perspective of a classical leftist critique of relativism leading to wilful marginalisation. Anton Vidokle viewed the exercise as one with critical documentary potential. Pierre Huyghe appeared concerned about the relationship between the curators of the project and the artist in terms of the suppression of the artist's critical voice in relation to the event. Many of us were concerned that we would merely appear to be some kind of pressure group among many, but a particularly privileged and well-established one. It was therefore suggested that we either: a) sublimate the authorship of work to the broader structure of the station which would mean posters, video screenings and literature/handouts (Nesbit, Hans Ulrich Obrist, Rirkrit Tiravanija); b) continue our normal artwork which is supposed to be critical anyway and failings within it may be highlighted in a loaded situation (Huyghe, Gillick, Weiner); c) Not go at all (Gillick, Haacke); d) Go and witness/document and listen rather than present or exhibit (Gillick, Vidokle, Weiner). At no time was there any consensus on any of these issues and it was only at the point when a few of those involved in the discussion actually arrived in Porto Alegre that the final manifestation of the project there was articulated and formulated. This group did not include Hans Haacke or myself as we had decided that the

World Social Forum could not be treated as a viable place for the ongoing continuation of the "Utopia Station" project at that time.

There have been various misunderstandings generated around the "Utopia Station" project. The primary one being that it was and is somehow connected to an open-ended exhibition structure with the emphasis on structured events. In fact, as became clear via the Porto Alegre disagreements and discussions converging from the multiple starting points, it is primarily a discursive set up that only has meaning in the midst of its function. As a potential it demonstrates tensions between possibility and realisation expressed in the middle of its function rather than before or after the fact. As a reported event it generally appears as a semi-alternative exhibition structure alone. However, the project should be understood as a series of "Utopia Stations" rather than "The Utopia Station" — a point of temporary stasis within a distracted excess of context. As the few who went to Porto Alegre set up their projections close to a bar outside the official border of the World Social Forum and showed films to locals and participants alike, the echo of the absent complexity of the discourse generated around the project was once again muted by context and pointed towards future obligations to revise the project. A "Utopia Station" is not predicated on a conceit but on the presence of a sequence of discussions that fail to find form within the presentation of the event itself.

The question might be, how to reconfigure a project such as this and redirect focus to an inverted exhibition structure that emphasises the ongoing tensions provided by the context rather than adopting a notionally egalitarian exhibition format where each participant "sets out their stall" within a broad and apparently inclusive set-up. If "Utopia Station" is to have any future role it will be via the careful assessment of the relationship between its presented self and the reintroduction of the ideas produced alongside and within it into new forms of exhibition production unrecognisable from its first pell-mell manifestations in Venice and Munich. Dropping the word "Utopia" could be the first step in reaching towards a structure that could actually point towards the activation of better conditions now that the talk around the abstraction has revealed the necessity for active work. By not going to Porto Alegre, certain people were not aligning themselves with the art-world over the world-world but asserting the discursive nature of the project over replacing one relativistic parent structure with another.

A CERTAIN TENDENCY
OF CURATING

Jens Hoffmann

The title of this essay derives from François Truffaut's landmark text "A Certain Tendency of the French Cinema", published in 1954. [1] Truffaut's essay introduced the influential theory of the *auteur* and described a transformation that was happening in cinema at that time, whereby film directors sought to be perceived on the same creative level as literary authors. Truffaut's text, closely linked to the films of the *Nouvelle Vague* and French cinema of the 1950s, originated as a response to the traditional forms of filmmaking in France and the Hollywood studio system. In this short text I plan to connect Truffaut's theory of the *auteur* to the practice and conditions of recent exhibition making and to analyze the concept of the curator as a creator or, in fact, author rather than a facilitator or administrator of exhibitions.

What do I mean by the author-curator or exhibition author? The term author is used here in a manner similar to how it was used in relation to film directors during the 1950s to draw a parallel between the author-director and the creative writers of that period. The characteristics of an author-director include thematic consistency of production, a strong creative sensibility in regard to how the director interprets a script, and an apparent artistic development through her/his career from film to film. All of which are attributes that one could apply to some of the curators working today. Despite the differences in curatorial methodology and their related ideologies one can connect the work of curators such as Hans Ulrich Obrist, Maria Lind, Eric Troncy, Sabine Breitweiser, Ute Meta Bauer, Thelma Golden, and Hou Hanru, to name just a few, on the basis of their individual creativity as well as their integration of intellectual and theoretical models. A clear paradigm shift in curating took place over the last 15 years as a result of these curators' work. It is still too early to analyze the effects this change has had on the overall development of curating and art making and what results it will have on the formats of exhibitions and the programs of art institutions but it can be said that curating has clearly reinvented itself to a degree that it is unlikely to return to the situation in which the curator is perceived as facilitator or caretaker.

Interestingly, the author theory in filmmaking, as defined by Truffaut, was a critical reaction toward the Hollywood studio cinema and what was seen as traditional filmmaking in Europe at that time, for which

1.   François Truffaut, "A Certain Tendency of the French Cinema" in *Movies and Methods*, Ed. Bill Nichols (Berkeley and Los Angeles: University of California Press, 1976)

directors simply provided images for a pre-existing script. Transferring this argument into the context of today's visual art world, the US studios could be compared with the large museums or Biennials, all of which form part of the so called culture industry, and traditional filmmaking could be perceived as comparable to curating a museum collection in a standard chronological manner.

One cannot talk about the idea of the author as expressed by Truffaut without looking at one of the most important intellectual currents contributing to a critique of author theory: post-structuralism. Particularly Roland Barthes formulated a rejection of author theory in his essay "The Death of the Author" [2] arguing against the belief that the author is a unifying and sole creative source for the meaning and value of a unified work of art. This criticism has been widely accepted today and the manner in which I use the idea of the author here fully takes this into consideration and follows the idea of authorship as "a certain functional principal by which, in our culture, one limits, excludes and chooses" as defined by Michel Foucault in his essay "What is an Author?" [3] The result of this selection process could be what we might call a unique and novel creation and, the creative act being the transformation of chaos into order or in other words the act of selecting against an infinite number of possibilities which is ultimately how we would describe what a curator is, someone who limits, excludes, creates meaning with existing signs, codes and materials. This means within the process of making an exhibition the curator is as a result decentered, only a part of a larger structure, a subject position, and not the core.

Not surprisingly, many of the curators responsible for a new under-standing of curating worked predominantly independent of institutions or with large independence overseeing smaller more flexible institutions. The advantages and disadvantages of working as an independent curator versus working as a curator in an institution have been discussed at length over the last few years. Having made that transition fairly recently I feel that it might be worthwhile to reflect, once again, on this issue here as it is integral for understanding the development of curating.

2.   Roland Barthes, "The Death of the Author" in *Image, Music, Text*, Ed. Stephen Heath (New York: Hill, 1977).
3.   Michel Foucault, "What is an Author?" in *Language, Counter-Memory, Practice*, Ed. Donald F. Bouchard (Ithaca: Cornell University Press, 1977).

Firstly, what is supposedly a very attractive profession, the independent curator, is in reality far from a congenial occupation. There are only a handful of independent curators that can make a living from their earnings. Most independent curators are indeed independent simply because they cannot find a position in an institution and not because they believe in the idea of independence, in the true sense of the word, or for political principals. And who can blame them? Jobs and opportunities are rare and it is not financially rewarding in any conceivable way.

Secondly, there is a problematic tendency, inside and outside the art world, to generalize approaches to curating that emerge outside of the mainstream that explore different formats and ways of organizing exhibitions. While there are affinities and connections between these curators, there are also substantial disparities. By and large, the work of non-institutionally based curators has been viewed as a generalised project — to be affirmed or dismissed depending on one's viewpoint — a result of the sudden increase in those working outside of the museum in the early 1990s and their association with a particular group of artists. However, for those working in this context it was clearly apparent that Hans Ulrich Obrist and Nicholas Bourriaud, to take just one comparison, have fairly diverging practices. This brings us back to Truffaut's text and the generalisation that no doubt was applied to French cinema at that time: Truffaut = Godard = Chabrol. Not that I am claiming a similar cultural significance for these curators, but it is a useful analogy to pursue.

So what has happened to the role of the independent curator in recent years? The main shift that took place over the last few years is that many independent curators have moved into institutional positions resulting in a form of "new institutionalism". [4] It is possible that the emancipation of curating reached its peak with Francesco Bonami's Venice Biennial in 2003; in retrospect, this was the grande finale of the independent curator of the 1990s. While it was a celebration of diversity in curating (and one of the few occasions perhaps when the differences of these approaches was made clearly apparent), one unfortunate result was that audiences began to grow tired of the curatorial premise and as a result, larger and more experimental group exhibitions became less popular as they were perceived, in part, as too specialized for a regular audience.

4.   Jonas Ekeberg, Ed., *New Institutionalism* (Olso: Office for Contemporary Art Norway, 2003).

Is there any site then that remains for alternative approaches in curating? At this point in time no major museum dares to present such controversial and inspiring group exhibitions such as *Black Male* (1991), curated by Thelma Golden, *Cities on the Move* (1997), curated by Hou Hanru and Hans Ulrich Obrist, *Places with a Past* (1993), curated by Mary Jane Jacob, *This is a Show and the Show is Many Things* (1994), curated by Bart de Bare. Intellectually and politically ambitious exhibitions have been moved out of the major museums and are more at home in smaller institutions such as Contemporary Art Center, Vilius; Generali Foundation, Vienna; Witte de With, Rotterdam; Le Consortium, Dijon — among several others. It is now common knowledge that museums have become the arena for blockbuster exhibitions and that a separation between the various forms of curating and programming is becoming increasingly visible, dividing the art world into various, almost unrelated camps.

Smaller institutions have profited from this change, because it has made opportune the move of creative curators into such sites while they remain representative of high professional and intellectual standards despite an open and experimental character. The change is in fact advantageous from both sides having occurred at a time when curators themselves have moved away from the notion of independent curating as it was developed in the 1990s and are seeking positions as directors and curators of institutions. Positions that can provide not only more responsibility, but provide the challenge to engage in a much more profound way with their audiences.

Even the most conservative institutions have by now understood that curating has changed, and many of them are inviting curators to organise exhibitions. While one can make a career in a large institution as a creative curator it is only by accepting compromises as the major museum will frequently demand experimentalism in a palatable form using the curator as an alibi in order to claim a form of experimental programming. We all know the priorities of most museums, audience figures and fund raising, and it will not come as a surprise that exhibitions, therefore, can rarely hope to be that radical. As a curator in a large institution one often has no say in what I understand to be quintessential parts of the profession: titles, book covers, press images, exhibition schedules, and even content, which are often decided by the PR and marketing departments. Maybe curators need to emancipate themselves again from the anonymity of the institution after having made apparent that curating is more than just displaying works from the collection in an anachronistic, orderly fashion.

But then there remains the question of where to go from here? Is the idea of returning to independent curating, away from the institution, away from the pressures of audience figures and recognisable or momentarily fashionable names, really that desirable? Undoubtedly, if one is interested in exhibitions as the manifestation and result of a personal creative vision, there are necessary conditions such as control over the overall creative process. But there is yet no system in place that would allow this to happen from a financial perspective. Biennials and so on are similarly controlled by their own net of complexities in regard to the politics of funding, audience figures, and so on.

There is seemingly no "free zone" for creative curating. Exhibition making in smaller public institutions is not a profit-making venture as it is in general directed towards a niche audience of art insiders. As long as this remains the case independent/author exhibition making will stay a problematic business for curators. The goal must be, it would seem, to create what one could describe as "intelligent shows with mass appeal." It needs a system that would allow independent curators to find producers for their curatorial endeavours, inside and outside of institutions, in a manner similar to the author directors of the 1950s as well as a way to bring this product to a wider audience. If communicated in the right manner specialized exhibitions might be an appealing experience for a wider public but it will be a long time until we get there.

TO BE READ
(ONCE EVERY TWO YEARS)

Robert Nickas

Do Biennials still make sense?

If you are a city that hosts one of them, the mayor of that city, its travel and tourism director, the owner of a hotel, a sauna, or sex shop, the answer is yes. Biennials make a lot of sense. Dollars and cents.
The population of Kassel, Germany is largest every ten years. In between the massive Documenta exhibitions, is anyone making a special trip to Kassel for the many no-star restaurants? For a pizza almost as bad as the ones you find in Venice?

In their defense, the average visitor to these big art shows is not an art specialist. Just look at the numbers. There can't be that many critics, curators, collectors, artists, and dealers in the world. Many visitors to biennials are simply people interested in art. We forget about them, don't we? You often see families, although the children look like they would rather be almost anywhere else. (A child, like much of the art produced today, is another portable object in a world filled to the brim.) Let's not forget that these big shows have a function for people interested in art who may not otherwise have the opportunity to see as much as you or I over the course of two years. Or even one. Maybe biennials are a way for art lovers to catch up with the so-called art world. We are not so much a world as we are many small satellites in orbit around one another. And around us, as biennials often serve as a reminder, there are many shooting stars.

So as a critic and curator, how do you answer the question:
"Do biennials still make sense?"

The answer would have to be no. Any critic or curator who thinks differ-ently is a traitor to the cause. Biennials are about business and politics first. Art will always come in a close second or even third. And why should it be otherwise? The entire world is organized along lines of commerce and power. Art institutions and their wardens (to use Robert Smithson's term), not to mention quote/unquote independents, are not immune from a perverse fascination with the game and how it is played. Are they merely drunk with power? Order another Mimosa at Harry's Bar and try not to fall in the canal. You can always save your doubts for another day ... So why don't biennials make sense anymore? Because art is not in charge.

Art should be in charge. I second that emotion. Of course prizes are at the center of this issue. Let's not forget that by the end of the 60s, in the midst of global unrest and the war in Vietnam, the idea of prizes came under fire, and many were suspended. Imagine being given a medal for Best Pavilion in a time of war. How could you possibly accept? But today these awards are back in favor, and others have been newly minted. Rewards are in place precisely for those in control to maintain their power and influence, as well as to alienate artists from one another. This idea of competition brings up another question. Can we tolerate a show with national pavilions and prizes?

In a word: no. Nationalism has always gotten us into trouble and, at times, dead. Who's representing Germany at the Venice Biennale this year? My vote: Kippenberger. Der Tod in Vendig. The idea of a prize is beyond anachronistic. Ancient, a thing of the past. Art is not a prize fight, or a science fair in high school. There are even little statues for them now, as if a prize for an artist was like an Academy Award for an actor. The Academy Award is generally considered to be a glorified popularity contest linked directly to the box office, to how much money the movie made. Maybe prizes in art should be based on auction results. Give the artists a little statuette, let them make a speech, and applaud politely. In England you have the Turner Prize. In France there's the Duchamp Prize. Would those artists have even been given awards in their lifetime?

Why the Americans don't have a prize of their own remains a mystery.

Maybe they can't decide who it should be named after. How about the Warhol? After all, he is at the same time one of the central figures in the art of the twentieth century and a complete sell-out. A commercial artist who became a fine artist in love with commerce. One day he pretended he didn't know what to paint so he could wrangle more ideas from his entourage. One suggestion that was made was obviously taken: "You should paint what you love. What do you love?" Warhol went on to paint money and, in effect, continued to paint it for the rest of his life.

Biennials are often saddled with overwhelming themes. How can an artist be expected to honestly produce a work for an exhibition called the Plateau of Mankind?

How about a pile of bodies? Maybe from Rwanda. Or have the show there. Pump up the local economy. The Rwanda Triennial. Of course there are other places to choose from these days. The Chechan International? How about the Beijing Biennale? The cost of building the pavilions would be almost nothing. Thousands of Chinese workers would be delighted to take part in a new cultural revolution. The catalogs, T-shirts, and souvenirs could all be produced right there in China, and certainly cheaper than almost anywhere else in the free world.

And how do women feel about the grandiose idea of Mankind? Just look at any biennial list. 70% men, 80% men… This is a plateau to which women rarely ascend. With biennials frequently organized by committee, compromise is less the exception than the rule, and even when women are among those on the selection committee the final list of artists in the show, more often than not, is heavily male. Compromise ultimately transcends gender.

Think of a curator choosing artists for big biennials as someone at the racetrack picking a horse. It's a bet and you want to go home a winner. Is art all that different? Art in our time is too easily about winning and losing. How often have you heard collectors ask: "This is a young artist, just starting out. Where do you think he'll be in five years?" It seems an innocent question on the face of it, but really what they are asking for is a prediction. What they want to hear is that in five years' time the work will be worth five times what they originally paid. That, and the artist will end up in the Whitney Biennial…

With biennials, we always inherit a structure which seems stronger than its content. Manifesta, for example, is the biennial for young European art. The curators have to tour all over Europe in order to make their selection. The problem is that they meet the same people who met their colleagues two years before. And each time they have to go one step younger.

Maybe the choice should be made from women artists who are pregnant?

Now you're being ridiculous.

Well, all this biennial talk can't help but degenerate into the absurd.

I mean, consider the central point: when did biennials become giant art fairs? How ridiculous is that? An art fair is a trade show. You always expect it to be commercial and a not a little bit repugnant. Any other response is completely disingenuous. You shouldn't have the same kind of queasy experience in a museum or a biennial. But sometimes you do.

These days, museums look more and more like art fairs, and art fairs look more like museums. Visit any major art museum on the weekend: the idea of the Sunday painter has been replaced by the reality of the Sunday audience. Families, young couples on dates, babies in strollers… it looks like the crowd at the shopping mall. And this is not so far from the truth. In recent years, the trend has been for museums to move their gift shops front and center. You often have to pass through aisles of merchandise to get to the show. But as much as we are all amused by the perversity of a Jackson Pollock painting turned into a one-thousand piece jigsaw puzzle, wouldn't you rather see the painting before you buy it in novelty form? Museums now also keep score. Almost ruthlessly. A show is ultimately judged as successful based on how many paying visitors come through the gate. The quality of the show itself almost never enters the picture. The numbers are the quality of the show. The numbers are the picture.

What was produced by biennials over the years? What is our memory of them? Who are the artists we discovered in these events? What are the pieces we liked?

David Hammons is one artist who famously refuses every invitation to a biennial. Having never seen a David Hammons piece in a block-buster show that I didn't love, you have to respect the integrity of that strategy.

Can't you even pretend to be serious?

That was an honest response. But you seem to want a "greatest hit." How about this. The premiere of Rodney Graham's "Vexation Island" at the Venice Biennale. Who doesn't remember that? The idea of being shipwrecked, a castaway, lost at sea… how absolutely perfect that the piece was presented there. Venice, the art world's own Vexation Island.

This text was written in response to questions from Christophe Cherix.

A PROTEST AGAINST FORGETTING

Hans Ulrich Obrist interviews Jean Leering

"Tutto, tutto, tutto é memoria"
Giuseppe Ungaretti

The following interview with Jean Leering is part of a series of interviews with curatorial pioneers that I have been recording since 1997, which will be gathered together as a book in 2008 and so far includes: Johannes Cladders, Anne d'Harnoncourt, Werner Hoffman, Walter Hopps, Pontus Hultén, Kasper König, Jean Leering, Franz Meyer, Suzanne Pagé, Seth Siegelaub, Harald Szeemann, Walter Zanini.

This project has to do with what Eric Hobsbawm calls a "protest against forgetting." In a BBC breakfast interview with David Frost, Hobsbawm said: "I mean our society is geared to make us forget. It's about today when we enjoy what we ought to; its about tomorow when we have more things to buy, which are different; it's about today when yesterday's news is in the dustbin. But human beings don't want to forget. Its built into them."

* * *

HANS ULRICH OBRIST   Let's begin with the beginnings: how did you become a curator? What kind of studies did you undertake?

JEAN LEERING   I didn't study art history or anything like that. I studied architecture, in Delft. Even if I was on the way to become an architectural engineer, at that time I was already organising exhibitions. My first exhibition, which I organised in the Museum Het Prinsenhof in Delft, was about religious art of the last century.

HUO   When was this?

JL   1958. So from 1956 to 1958 I was working on this exhibition, which took place in the first month of that year. After I completed my studies in architecture and became an engineer, I had to do my military service (1963). Before that, in 1962, I did another exhibition with some friends, in the same museum, which was about autonomous architecture.

HUO   Who were the architects or what types of projects were included in this exhibition?

JL   Architecture was the greatest part, starting with Piranesi, followed by Boullée and Ledoux, and reaching recent architecture through the work of American architects like F.L Wright and Louis Kahn. The smaller part was devoted to works of art, by people like Van Doesburg and the then actual Zero-movement.

HUO   Was it about the relations between architecture and utopia?

JL   Well, if you take, for instance, Boullée who lived at the time of the French Revolution, he made very few buildings, and so what remain of his work are mostly just beautiful prints. He made some large drawings, painting them with black and white only, in shades. Then there were Ledoux, Loos, De Stijl, architecture from Utrecht, and the latest architecture of that time. Because I had these experiences of making exhibitions, friends of mine told me to apply to the Van Abbemuseum in Eindhoven, because they were looking for a new director. I did, and unexpectedly, after the selection I was the only one who remained! [Laughs]

HUO   So you went from being an architectural engineer to the director of an art museum. Chris Dercon insisted during our discussion that this is certainly one of the reasons your curatorial work has influenced so many people and is now so important for a younger generation of curators. The notion of the interdisciplinary is at the core of your practice. How did you handle this as the director at the Van Abbemuseum?

JL   Yes, that's true. Since the beginning these crossovers have been the main point of interest. My latest book [*Beeldarchitectuur en Kunst: Het Samengaan van Architectuur en Beeldende Kunst*, 2001] treats this. It's about the relations between images, architectures and art. I went back to the years of Ancient Egypt and examined those forms of relations until 1990.

HUO   When you suddenly became director of the Van Abbemuseum, what type of ideas or projects did your have in mind?

JL   As soon as I got this position, my interest in the inter-disciplinary was already taking shape. I was very interested in artists of De Stijl that I had already studied for that previous exhibition in Delft. I was also very fond of El Lissitzky. But my first exhibition there was about art and theatre and it was made to coincide with the opening of the new theatre in Eindhoven. I organized the first exhibition on that occasion; it was September/October 1964.

HUO   Were there curators that influenced your practice, such as Willem Sandberg?

JL   Yes. I knew Sandberg already; he even wrote in favour of my nomination to Eindhoven. He was a fantastic man. And in a certain way the younger generation knew of the reputation that he had abroad. Although there were many critics who did not approve of his policies, I admired him. He was a fantastic worker; he slept only a few hours a day. Often he went to bed after dinner for an hour or an hour and a half and he would work until the morning; then he would sleep again for an hour, then he would go into the museum. He had a strong regime, he didn't eat very much, he liked to drink but not too much and he had a lot of self-control.

HUO   And like you, he wasn't an art historian, he came with a graphic designer background, and maybe this interdisciplinary characteristic also explains why he was so important.

JL   Yes. Another example of this kind is Edy de Wilde, my predecessor at the Van Abbemuseum, who studied law.

HUO   Like Franz Meyer.

JL   I think that it's important to say that at that time very few museums were paying attention to architecture. And because that was my background and profession, I took a lot of interest in subjects coming from the architectural field. So I did an exhibition of Adolf Loos. And then there were three exhibitions in a row in 1965: an exhibition of Duchamp and an important show of El Lissitzky, which led to the purchase of a whole bunch of his drawings and watercolours for the collection of the Van Abbemuseum. In 1967, I organised a show of Moholy-Nagy, another of Picabia and Van't Hoff and in 1968 I organised an exhibition of Theo Van Doesburg. Later on came Tatlin… As you can see I paid quite a lot of attention to the art of the 1920s and early 30s. A very important moment also in terms of what was going on in the arts was the exhibition organized in 1967; it was a series of shows called *Kompass*. One was about New York, and in 1969 I organized a show about Los Angeles and San Francisco, called *Kompass West Coast*. Those were very important exhibitions for me. In between there were exhibitions on architecture and then in '69 I also organised an exhibition, which I found quite important for civic development, called *City Plan*. In fact the exhibition presented a new plan for Eindhoven. Unfortunately, the plan has never been realised on the 1:1 scale for the city, but it was beautiful. For the exhibition, there were four rooms and I built a model of a part of the plan, which filled all the rooms, 8 by 12 metres. It was on a scale of 1:20, and it was built in such a way that you could walk through it, through the streets, and get a real sense of the design.

HUO   So you had to work with an architect for this?

JL   Yes, with Van den Broek and Bakema. Van den Broek was the person with whom I completed my studies and Bakema was his collaborator. Bakema was very much in charge at that moment of the real city plan for Eindhoven, so it was all the more interesting to collaborate with him to make the model.

HUO   To come back for a moment to your exhibitions about the artists and architects of the 1920s, how this interest in the convergence of the realms of architecture, art and design in the work of Lissitzky or Van Doesburg for instance was received at that time in Netherlands?

JL   Lissitzky was a man who was both an architect and an artist. And so was Van Doesburg; he was an artist who started in the 1920s with architecture. But it's true this exhibition was a tactical one because at that time, in the early 1960s, Van Doesburg was mostly seen as the organiser of the De Stijl movement, and not so much as an artist per se. My wife is the niece of Nelly van Doesburg and so because I had this connection, I had the possibility to exhibit some of his works for the exhibition in Delft in 1962. And when I was nominated in Eindhoven I knew that I would make a larger exhibition of Van Doesburg. I wanted to open the eyes of the art colleges. About Van Doesburg people said that he just followed Mondrian. Well, yes, he did, but he made something new out of it. He connected art with the field of architecture, he did things like rebuilding the restaurant-cabaret l'Aubette in Strasbourg and he also built this house in Meudon-Val-Fleury. Although I didn't know it at the time, my wife was the sole inheritor of Nelly van Doesburg, and so later we decided to give all the works that were still there to the State of the Netherlands. The house was given on the basis that young artists would be able to stay there for a year.

HUO   Like a residency... Thinking of the 1920s, the first curator that comes to mind is Alexander Dorner, the director of the Hannover Museum. Was he another influence?

JL   Yes, very much. In my new book I quote him often. I organised the exhibition of El Lissitzky with the Museum in Hannover, and I also met the widow of Dorner.

HUO   So Dorner's legacy was very present for you?

JL   Yes, we can say that.

HUO   For me the *Yellow Book* was some kind of bible because I found it as a student and read it many times ever since.

JL   I also read it as a student. His ideas were quite familiar to people at the time I started in Eindhoven. I have a lot of respect not only for his book but also for him as a person. He left Hanover and went to America, where for a short time he was again a museum director before becoming an art history professor.

HUO   Both Sandberg and Dorner defended the idea of the museum as a laboratory. Johannes Cladders also insisted on this idea of the museum as a space in which one should take risks, a space that should be used as a means to build bridges between various disciplines. Do you also find this idea of the museum as a laboratory relevant?

JL   Yes. In a sense that the exhibition *City Plan* in 1972 lead to an even bigger exhibition that was called *The Street: A Form of Living Together*. The idea behind that exhibition was to investigate ways of living together. Why an exhibition about streets? Well it goes back to the show *City Plan* in 1969 when I had the idea that it would be very interesting to see that the experiments that were made in the 1960s — environments or happenings — were very connected to the idea of the city. Eindhoven was the nucleus of that exhibition, but it became so wide that at a certain moment I decided to dedicate a whole exhibition to the plan of Eindhoven. The people from the municipality of Eindhoven said that they were very interested in following up the original idea, and that became *The Street* exhibition. So to get back to your question about laboratories, as you can see, there was an experimental aspect to it, but if you want the public of the museum to be interested in art, you should not only bring in art, but you should ask what the people are interested in. The street is made not only by architects, urbanists and planners; the people themselves, the people who use them, make the real streets. What they do in the streets and the significance they attach to the streets each day — the market day for example gives a different significance (and outlook) to the street than a Sunday.

HUO   How did you resolve this problematic? Did you bring in artists and non-artists? Was it well received by people not so familiar with the exhibition realm?

JL   Well it was one of the best-attended exhibitions we ever did. I was quite keen to develop this kind of exhibition even further, but then the mayor of Eindhoven died from a tumour and the local authorities were not so interested in following that line. Finally I discovered that it would be very difficult to develop the museum further here, so I moved to Amsterdam. I got the directorship of the Tropenmuseum there and after two years I discovered that they were very pleased to have me there, but they were not comfortable with the changes I wished to bring to the museum. So I left the museum and pursued in other ways: I worked for the ministry and I became professor of art history at the University of Technology in Eindhoven.

HUO   What you're describing here is how the "laboratory years" of the Dutch museum world were suddenly interrupted in the 1970's. This also happened in the United States as Mary Ann Staniszewski remarkably demonstrates in *The Power of Display*, her book about the transformations of the MoMA in New York. Do you think it's possible to speak of a global context disrupting the experimental modes of curatorial practice of the 1970s?

JL   Yes, take Cladders, for instance; he somehow had to build his own new museum. And his decision to do this in a little town (Mönchengladbach), which became famous only because of this museum, was not an innocent one. In September/October 67, he organised the opening exhibition of the museum, which was then located in an old villa. This exhibition was experimental, and convinced me of the value and importance of the work of Joseph Beuys. So I took over this exhibition, which opened in February 1968 in Eindhoven.

HUO   Was it the first collaboration between you and Cladders? Did you know him from before?

JL   That was not the first time. Earlier on he was an assistant to Paul Wember, who was director of the museum in Krefeld, and with whom I had been working since 1964.

HUO   Was Wember also interesting? Because he's not mentioned much these days...

JL   Yes he was. He made the first large museum exhibition of Yves Klein and he was a fantastic museum director. He was also the first German museum director that Sandberg visited after the war because of his daring policy. It was a small museum but with a beautiful collection. There are the Museum Haus Hermann Lange in Krefeld, and the Haus Esters, two houses designed by Mies van der Rohe. Wember became the director of the Museum Haus Lange at that time.

HUO   Are there other people who have been important for you?

JL   Harald Szeemann of course. And Pontus Hultén...

HUO   I would like to come back to this idea of the laboratory years and to this question: what went wrong in the 1970s? I have never quite understood why one could find all these models for

new museums in the 1960's — your model, Sandberg's model,
Cladders' model — and then nothing in the 1970s.

> JL   Well I think it was connected to a kind of revolution, of the youth
> in particular, but also a sexual revolution. I think that many people
> were afraid, especially those in the government. I already mentioned
> this mayor whose ideas about the museum corresponded with mine,
> but most of his peers were afraid. I remember that at that time also,
> in Eindhoven there was a theatre group, which was very forward-
> looking, very avant-garde. They were strongly criticised by the older
> generation in Eindhoven, especially by a man who was in charge of
> the art foundation in Eindhoven who wrote a very critical article in
> the local newspaper about this group. A week later I attacked him in
> the same newspaper. This was not appreciated [laughs]. I thought
> this theatre group was doing very well, exploring new educational
> programmes with school classes and so on. These reactions were
> for me a sign that further development was not possible. They chose
> more classical persons for successors. My successor, Rudi Fuchs,
> cut out many of the things I had set up.

HUO   One could also think that it has a lot to do with fear — a fear of
the interdisciplinary, a fear of pooling knowledge. And so perhaps it
was also a fear of vested interests.

> JL   Yes, and also the sexual revolution that accompanied the
> laboratory idea. There was a new form of commitment between
> people.

HUO   You also made a link to urbanism. At the time, in the late
1950s and early 60s there was a lot of interest in self-organisation.
Was this tendency — and I'm thinking here of Constant's *New
Babylon* in particular — important for you?

> JL   Yes, during my studies, once a week on Wednesday
> afternoons, my professor, Van den Broek, opened discussions on
> these ideas. There were lectures about things such as Constant and
> his *New Babylon*, which were followed by discussions with the
> audience. I remember being caught in vigorous discussions with
> Constant and yes; I got to know him very well then. We were
> examining the slides that had been made from the models of *New
> Babylon* and I pointed out to him that the influence of Schwitters'
> collages was so detectable in the slides it was striking. Aldo van Eyck
> was also connected with these discussions and with the exhibition
> about the autonomous architecture that I mentioned earlier.

HUO   How was Van Eyck involved?

JL   There was a group of fifteen students for which Van Eyck
was somehow the spiritual mentor of that group. In fact, we had
asked him to be involved in such a way, and so did he. Later on,
we proposed him to become Professor in Delft, which he accepted
around 1965.

HUO   *The Street* exhibition of 1972 brought this idea of the experimental show a step further, by bringing real life into the museum.
It reminds me of Allan Kaprow, and of his desire to blur art and life.
And then you said that you wanted to push this idea further, but it
was halted by politicians. Had it not been, what would you have liked
to do with the museum?

JL   As the director of the museum I thought it important to try to
make the art museum into an anthropological museum. Therefore
I went to the Tropenmuseum in Amsterdam. What I mean is that
human interests should always be at the centre of your policy as a
museum director. Your job as a director was to interest people in
art, to consider the correspondences between their interests and
art, and then to use these interests as a starting point.

HUO   Another link or connection that you established was this time
the one between art and anthropology. This is an idea, as well as the
practice, which derived from it, that have inspired Kasper König. What
were the first exhibitions that you organised at the Tropenmuseum?

JL   We did an exhibition about world population. This might be
a beautiful example of my handling of the theme. Population in the
third world and the underdeveloped world is a big problem, in
part because sexual life is lived in different ways there than in our
part of the world. I wanted to confront these gaps between ideas of
population, procreation and children and to show how it is in the
West through comparison. A sculpture by Di Andrea had been
accepted for Documenta in Kassel; it was a sculpture on the ground
of a young man and a young lady who were having a sexual
relationship, in very realistic style... I thought we should have that
piece in our exhibition about population in order to create a kind of
shock, but also in order to get people to ask themselves what was
the meaning of the presence of this piece in the exhibition, and
enable them to discover something about their sexual lives in
comparison to sexual lives in underdeveloped countries. In a certain
way, art was being "used" to get people to think and be aware of
their own situations. This was the idea, along with addressing how
such a message can be achieved in an exhibition. Then, there was
another exhibition about the situation of women both here in the
West and in the underdeveloped countries. I tried to use the classical
methods of the anthropological museum, such as showing the

difference between an axe and the tool with which rice is stamped, and underlining the fact that the axe has a very streamlined design.

HUO   I interviewed Jean Rouch some time ago and he told me a lot about the beginnings of the Musée de L'Homme, about Rivet, Rivière, Griaule, Leiris, Metraux... Do you consider the Musée du Trocadero and the Musée de l'Homme as two important institutions of the first half of the 20th century?

JL   Yes, probably. I also knew Georges-Henri Rivière, who was associate director of the Musée de l'Homme in 1937 and who directed the Musée des Arts et Traditions Populaires in Paris afterwards.

HUO   Can you tell me about an unrealised project of yours, about a project that for a number of reasons has never reach completion?

JL   Well, I think that the ambition I had for the Tropenmuseum is an unrealized one. My idea of the anthropological museum, the Tropenmuseum in Amsterdam, was to have a museum liked by ordinary people. And while I had ideas about how to arrange that, there was then the problem of how to connect what I see in art and about the benefits of art in human life with the ordinary interests of ordinary people. I don't necessarily think that everybody should go to the museum, but I do think that art could play a larger role than it does if the museum evolves in that direction. I wrote an article in 1999 on how the museum could learn from the public library. The public library asks the users of the library about what they are interested in, which is already a lot more than what museums do. It is professional in that way. It is not the public taste that determines the content of the library; it needs to be done thoroughly by professionals. But the public knows that the library is there for its use. I tried to reshape the Tropenmuseum to a new kind of anthropological museum based on this idea. If you compare the history of the public library with the history of museums, it is evident that museums have come far more from the third layer of the population (the leading layer after the French Revolution), than from the idea that we have to educate the fourth layer.

HUO   So you think the museum can learn from the public library. And isn't the issue of time also significant here, because people spend a lot of time in the library, far more than in museums...? And certainly, people feel less excluded there; the threshold of the library, as Adorno would say, is easier to pass...

JL   Yes, that's right. I think that the average level of the public library is somewhat broader than people who come to the museum.

Yes, and that was one of the main ideas of Sandberg. At a certain moment there was a reconstruction of the road outside the museum, and Sandberg created an exhibition in which people could see the exhibition from outside by standing on the scaffolding. I thought that was wonderful idea.

HUO   What about the specificities of the catalogue? Sandberg is very famous for his catalogues, Johannes Cladders always made these boxes and Pontus Hultén was also always very interested in the idea of playing with publications, what about you?

JL   I must say I haven't concentrated so much on the renewal of the catalogue; my main focus was on the renewal of the exhibition process. I think that catalogues should follow; they shouldn't be the primary feature.

HUO   How do you understand the notion of museum now, in the third millennium? How do you see the future of the museum? Are you optimistic? Undoubtedly, there are some reasons to be pessimistic in the sense that as contexts become more and more neo-liberal, the museum becomes a token of neo-liberal politics or of the market economy. As a consequence, it is increasingly losing its experimental possibilities. There is clearly a homogenisation, especially in all the packaged exhibitions and at the same time some optimistic models are popping up. What do you think; are there any museums in the world that you think are still interesting?

JL   The future is a big question mark. As you said things have regressed since the mid-seventies. I have lectured and published a lot about museums and I hope that somehow there is some interest in these ideas that I have exposed to you I hope that they will be picked up and that things will go in the direction I have worked on for all these years. But really I can't think of any museum doing it right now. Maybe you know some museums that are picking up on these ideas.

This interview was conducted in Amsterdam, 2002.
It has been translated into English for its first publication here.

159 – 173

A POLITICS OF INTERPRETATION

Sarah Pierce

> The new panorama for today's artists is truly complex, difficult and yet, fascinating. [1]

Jorge Oteiza

> New York has never learned the art of growing old by playing on all its pasts. Its present invents itself, from hour to hour, in the act of throwing away its previous accomplishments and challenging the future. [2]

Michel de Certeau

> I am not a fortune teller. [3]

Catherine David

Perhaps in considering the future of curating we can begin by rephrasing three questions: Who curates? For whom is the curating being done? In what circumstances? [4] When posed, these questions and their answers form a 'politics of interpretation', revealed in present moments, which in turn imply future modalities. Within a system that draws boundaries around specific manifestations of professionalized output (who does what, where, and when) the parameters that define curating do more than simply describe work. Professional boundaries legitimise positions, validate expertise, and ultimately stake claims that are as territorial as they are economic. If we look, for example, at the ongoing debate about blurring the boundaries between art and curating — we can see that different manifestations of curating imply certain modes of representation, from the 'artist/curator' to the 'artist-curator', to the 'artist and curator'. Each variation subtly conditions how we read one person's work in relation to another's.

1.   Jorge Oteiza in a letter to Jose Antonio Sistiaga, reprinted in *With All Due Intent*, (Manifesta 5/Centro Internacional de Cultura Contemporanea, S.A., 2004), pp. 81.

2.   Michel de Certeau, *The Practice of Everyday Life* (Berkeley, University of California Press, 1984) as quoted in *Object to be Destroyed* by Pamela Lee, (MIT press, 2001) pp. 90.

3.   Catherine David in an interview with Rob Hamelijnck and Nienke Terpsma in *Fucking Good Art #10*, (Rotterdam, July 2005).

4.   Edward Said first posed the questions, "Who writes? For whom is the writing being done? In what circumstances?" in his text, "Opponents, Audiences, Constituencies and Community," originally published in *Critical Inquiry 9* (Sept.,1982) and reprinted in *The Anti-Aesthetic Essays on Postmodernism*, edited by Hal Foster (Bay Press, Seattle, 1983).

Besides re-establishing normative behaviours, current debates around curating often ignore the role locality plays in how people work. Work happens through slippages between collective outputs and individual projects, between authorship and incorporated identities, and despite at times obscure patterns of communication, every situation begins with an invitation. Associations outside our locality are often a means of working locally. Although this might sound contradictory, it acknowledges that the 'local' is played out through strong, ongoing connections to other places. A little over three years ago, I decided that instead of differentiating between the work I did as an artist and work I did as a curator, instead of distinguishing between projects or making discrete 'pieces', I would name it all the 'Metropolitan Complex' [5]. For me, The Metropolitan Complex helps describe my work through its associations and its organisation, and acknowledges relationships between individual and collaborative work that arise along the way. As a way to play with the hang-ups (read 'complex' in the Freudian sense) of a particular place, The Metropolitan Complex negotiates some of the recurring questions asked by artists, institutions, and curators that indicate a shared neurosis. Who curates? For whom is the curating being done? In what circumstances? While the questions themselves are not particular to a given place, their answers are.

Three questions. For the sake of returning some answers, I would like to describe three projects: *D.A.E.* in Donostia-San Sebastián, *Orchard* in New York, and *Fucking Good Art* in Rotterdam. As structural responses they risk some of the conditions that have come to define curating today by rethinking the role of the artist in institutional (ised) practices. Each organises amidst specific circumstances, against particular histories, and gives rise to different sets of relationships. The purpose here is not to align these projects ideologically, nor to promote them as models within a larger context of alternative frameworks. The aim here is to consider them as examples of collective ways of working. [6] Here, the criticality and precision that a certain situation calls for *is* the local.

5.   Based in Dublin, The Metropolitan Complex taps into locality through a variety of established discourses such as talks, papers, exhibitions, and archives — often opening up these structures to the personal and the incidental.
6.   I am borrowing from Annie Fletcher in a talk at the Lewis Glucksman Gallery, Cork (February 16, 2006), where she explained the need to particularise the local through *the example*. Expounding on this idea, we can distinguish the model, which is general and widely applicable, from *the example*, which is particular in a given situation.

A Proximate Past

In 1999, Donostiako Arte Ekinbideak[7] (D.A.E.) began as an independent art structure based in the Basque city of Donostia-San Sebastián. In 2002, it reorganised and since then, the curatorial team of Peio Aguirre and Leire Vergara have together carried out D.A.E.'s activities, which include exhibitions, artists' talks, presentations, screenings and commissioned projects.

D.A.E. is not attached to a specific space; rather it works as a decentralised unit that generates individual collaborations with different institutions in the city. In this way, its activities assume a parallel discourse to other cultural programmes in San Sebastián, proposed as a constant re-formulation of site, production, community and collaboration. In inviting people into this context, Aguirre and Vergara take into account a certain discontinuity in the work process by developing projects across different time frames and by promoting art as activity that involves crossing-over discourses and disciplines. Here, we might relate discontinuity to a notion of 'permissiveness' developed by Charles Esche in describing the temporariness of certain contemporary curatorial and institutional projects. Esche evokes what he identifies as an increasing 'permissiveness', even promiscuity, in art's ability to take on activities that fall out of other categories, "a movement that runs counter to the increasing specialization of society in other fields." In laying out a proposition for the future Esche concludes, "Our task in terms of alternative strategies is then, to create the institutions and devices that can respond to this permissiveness, physically creating those places, times and meetings of possibility that the art and the society of today seem urgently to require." [8] It follows that art's permissiveness relies on permissive structures that facilitate less obvious choices and less predictable combinations of people. Expanding on this, it is important to differentiate between the vagaries of practices where 'anything goes' and the precision of tapping into other fields of knowledge as a means of forming a critical position.

The response that Esche calls for forms a pragmatics — a laying out of institutional practices and structures, which in turn forms a political

7.   D.A.E. in English translates to Contemporary Art Activities in San Sebastián.
8.   Charles Esche, "Temporariness, Possibility, and Institutional Change," *In the Place of the Public Sphere?*, edited by Simon Sheikh (B_books and OE, Berlin, 2005), pp. 138

proposal: Permissiveness is a position. Through permissiveness the subjects of cultural history, philosophy, and language emerge as open-ended energies, where established methods of representation collapse in favour of more experimental conditions. Permissiveness includes revisiting the past, but in ways that resist reclaiming historic movements in order to secure 'currency' in the present. Instead, we can call upon the past as a means of 'cutting-through' the present by disrupting recurrent claims on aesthetics and collective representation, and by restaging defining experiments *through* their defining politics.

A poignant example of the cut-away (to use filmic terminology) as a rupture in the present is the project *Film ideal siempre* (Film ideal forever), produced by D.A.E. for their participation in 2004's Manifesta 5, which took place in San Sebastián. With this project, permissiveness and discontinuity are the means through which past subjectivities draw us towards a historical 'future.' That is, discontinuity in the case of *Film ideal siempre,* looks to the past to form associations in the present; a present *in anticipation of time yet to come.*

From the moment the International Manifesta Foundation announced the exhibition's impending decent upon the city, the potential for this moment to 'represent' was both a source of excitement, and a deeply problematic prospect in the face of ongoing national and European cultural/political agendas. It is clear that Manifesta 5 became a platform for those working in an official capacity to pronounce their relationship to culture in the Basque Country. The catalogue's opening text by the Deputy General of Gipuzkoa (where San Sebastián is located) asserts in the first line, "It is no accident that Donostia-San Sebastián was chosen to host Manifesta 5 or that it should take place in the Basque Country, a country with a strong political and cultural identity and a clear commitment to opening up and engaging with other cultures and identities." [9] As the only Basque group invited to participate in Manifesta 5 (out of 54 artistic contributions), Aguirre and Vergara's status as 'locals' risked being incorporated into the exhibition's externalised politics, or worse, being tokenistic within the exhibition itself. Without fixating on the local, Aguirre and Vergara excavated a particular moment in the cinematic avant-garde of the Basque Country, without using the exhibition to

9.   Joxe Juan Gonzalez de Txabarri, "It is no accident" in *With All Due Intent*, pp. 9 Statements similar to this one, poignantly political in every sense, peppered the speeches given by local officials and cultural representatives throughout the Manifesta 5 programme.

parade the spectacle of Basque culture (which literally made up Jeremy Deller's contribution to Manifesta 5 — a parade through the city of various clubs and associations in San Sebastián).

The film *Operación H* was commissioned in 1963 by Juan Huarte, and directed by the Basque artist Néstor Basterretxea. There are several ways we come to know the conditions surrounding these origins. A short essay in the exhibition catalogue by Aguirre and Vergara includes pertinent historical information, including references to an interview with Basterretxea (who is still alive). Huarte invited Basterretxea along with Jorge Oteiza to make a short film about the various industries with which he was involved, asking each artist to present him with a finished script. He chose one as the basis of a singular commission, deciding in favour of Basterretxea's treatment — the 'H' in the film's title refers to its commis-sioner's surname. In tracing these origins, Aguirre and Vergara note that Oteiza, who won the Major International Prize for Sculpture at the IV Bienal Internacional de Sao Paulo a number of years before (in 1957), used the phrase 'Operacion H' to describe himself "in military language as if it were a wartime engagement — to refer to the 'operation' of staking everything in the biennial at a moment of closure when he had definitively abandoned his practice as a sculptor as an experimental conclusion." [10] Basterretxea framed Huarte's factories, in black-and-white, concen-trating on the formal structures and lines of exteriors and interiors. The floors, the equipment, and the factories' architectures appear sculptural, sculpted, with gleaming contours and intense shadows. It is a celebration of industry, but also of art and architecture. It is a modernist celebration, optimistic in its imagery and in its richness of sounds. Viewing the film forty years later, Basterretxea remarked he had forgotten the ending, which in his memory was a colour image of children running through a field of poppies. [11]

As though toying with the idea of Manifesta as "the European Biennial of Contemporary Art", *Film ideal siempre* opens up the proximate past as a way of self-consciously examining a present moment. Yet it does so fully aware of the direct and indirect conditions surrounding the original film's production and distribution, and without revision or distillation,

10.   Peio Aguirre and Leire Vergara, "Donostiako Arte Ekinbideak" in *With All Due Intent*, pp. 151
11.   Peio Aguirre and Leire Vergara, "Excerpts from an interview with Néstor Basterretxea" *With All Due Intent*, pp. 396

it links these to a politics of representation inherent in Manifesta. [12] Again, as a means of cutting through the exhibition as a 'manifestation' of national representations, *Film ideal siempre* taps into the collectivism of cultural identity. Partly due to the political circumstances surrounding the film's creation and its use as a promotional tool (primarily as an in-house document for Huarte's group of companies) *Operación H* never really gained consideration as a work of art. In part, by including *Operación H* in Manifesta, D.A.E. attempts to recover its political agency, not only as an historical document, but also as work of art. To re-present the film, Aguirre and Vergara collaborated with Xabier Salaberria and Gorka Eizagirre to design a context for the installation. Set up in the Casa Ciriza, the film screened for small fluid audiences throughout the course of Manifesta 5. To supplement the screenings, D.A.E. included a text related to *Film ideal siempre,* which situates their gesture as *una propuesta* or proposal, obtainable through the original film, and revealed through an aesthetic language specific to the Basque context of the 1960s. What *Operación H* suggests is a working situation that permits artistic freedom with regard to official policies (policies which subjected all cultural activities to censorship, especially those associated with Basque and Catalonian identities). In turn, what *Film ideal siempre* proposes is that this way of working relates to other projects initiated during the same time, and which when considered together constitute "a particular aesthetic tradition" and "a catalyst of the collective unconscious" [13] that, despite historical brackets around the period of Franco's dictatorship, is potentially available today. *Film ideal siempre* incites collectivity as a way of organizing one's own relationship to history and to politics as a 'continuing' or 'constant' aesthetic gesture.

In the spirit of permissiveness, Aguirre and Vergara published a letter in the Manifesta 5 catalogue to coincide with the installation of *Film ideal siempre*, written by Oteiza to an artist named Jose Antonio Sistiaga. It contains the conceptual foundations for a new art gallery that was about to open in San Sebastián in 1965. In Oteiza's words, "It will develop and manifest itself in the first experiences resulting in the revision in the organization of the art gallery in form and direction.

12.   The MACBA museum in Barcelona bought *Operacion H* for its collection shortly after Manifesta 5, further complicating the terms of politics and representation inherent in *Film ideal siempre.*
13.   Pelo Aguirre and Leire Vergara, "Donostioko Arte Ekinbideak" in *With All Due Intent*, pp. 151

To speak about the nature of these experiences is to announce the nature of the organization and structure of these new galleries. We should try to anticipate a possible first idea to define amongst ourselves such a gallery focused on the immediate worldwide future." [14] As a space it didn't last for very long, but it related to the artist group GAUR (Basque for "Today"), which Oteiza, Basterretxea, and Sistiaga formed with five other artists in Gipuzkoa around the same period.

Going back to 2001, to a project commissioned by D.A.E. that became the matrix of many future connections and relations, and the first indicator of a curatorial structure, German artist Tilo Schulz set up a project in Donostia-San Sebastián that asked the question, "What is the future of the exhibition?" [15] Four individuals — Charles Esche, Carles Guerra, Rebecca Gordon Nesbitt and Lisette Smits — responded with texts that were subsequently reprinted as posters and circulated throughout the city. Perhaps the publication of Oteiza's letter for Manifesta 5 is a fifth response, a tentative gesture on the part of D.A.E. that looks to past futures. We enter D.A.E. at a particular juncture, and this is precisely where it exacts meaning as a source of speculation, redefinition, and above all critical intervention. It is relevant that *Film ideal siempre* is one of the last of D.A.E.'s projects, at least in relation to this curatorial structure.

Forms of Separation

It is fitting that D.A.E.'s reflections on a proximate past bring us to a notion of the art gallery. Oteiza writes in anticipation of "the industrialization through which art will evolve creatively, pedagogically, politically, and culturally to the people." [16] His letter is interesting not only because it presupposes alternative commercial arrangements that will affect experiments in production, but also because it expresses more subtle attitudes towards collaboration, collectivism, organising, and exhibiting as played out through the gallery as a formative, localised network. In the spring of 2005, a new gallery called Orchard opened in New York, founded by twelve individuals and named for its street location on Manhattan's

14.   Jorge Oteiza, "For a new functional approach to an art gallery" in *With All Due Intent*, pp. 81
15.   "The Return of Display: What does Exhibiting Mean in 2030?" — A project by artist Tilo Schulz, commissioned by Peio Aguirre at D.A.E in 2001.
16.   Oteiza, *With All Due Intent*, pp. 80 — 81

Lower East Side. Its partners include artists, filmmakers, critics, art historians and curators with various associations with the "New York experimental film and video scenes, late 80s and early 90s institutional critique, 90s 'non-yBa' UK practices, and the South American political conceptualist tradition." [17] The information surrounding the gallery openly expresses the relationship of practice to programming, making it clear that the diversity of its members' interests filter into exhibitions and other events occurring in and through the gallery.

Mostly formed around exhibitions, Orchard's programme favours group shows, and also incorporates other events such as book launches, performances and screenings. Speaking about the gallery in an interview with Christine Würmell in *Neue Review*, Andrea Fraser, one of Orchard's founding partners, describes the basis for programming decisions:

> Orchard is 'programmatic' in the sense that all of our activities intend to make an argument and articulate, enact or support a position. What that position is, however, is not singular or fixed but the subject of on-going debate and dialog among the partners of the LLC. This is not the case because of any political or philosophical adherence to a principle of dialogism or heterotopia, etc., but because the cohort is composed of individuals with different backgrounds, interests, projects, programs, politics and philosophies. Those differences, however, as well as some commonality amongst us, do serve as a basis for what has emerged as our 'program.' While that program is largely driven by the initiative of individual partners, our group-process seeks to involve as many members as possible in each initiative. [18]

In this paragraph, we witness the full range of machinations inherent in Orchard's structural politics: from the insistence that its programme has a position but is not fulfilling a 'singular' or 'fixed' imperative, to a self-conscious distancing from a manner of working or theorising that might be read as an affirmation of 'difference' for the sake of it, to a reinstatement of the collective. Fraser continues:

17.   This list of associations, found on Orchard's website, makes a direct relationship between these legacies and the practices of Orchard's founding members: Rhea Anastas, Moyra Davey, Andrea Fraser, Nicolás Guagnini, Gareth James, Christian Philipp-Müller, Jeff Preiss, R.H. Quaytman, Karin Schneider, Jason Simon, and John Yancy, Jr.
18.   "Das Orchard-Galerieprojekt" by Andrea Fraser and Christine Würmell in *Neue Review #12*, January 2006.

This process has produced a program that is rooted in our diverse engagements with the legacies of minimalism, conceptualism, neo-concretism, performance and experimental film; our diverse backgrounds in the United States, Europe, and Latin America; trans-generational networks in which we are involved; and a sense of alienation from the dominance of the market in the contemporary art world and conservative politics in American society. Other principles of general consensus include a commitment to historically based artistic criteria (as opposed to market criteria) in our programming and a preference for conceptually, politically or thematically driven group exhibitions or projects (as opposed to solo exhibitions). [19]

What might sound to many readers like an overly-burdened portrayal of quite an ordinary undertaking (opening a gallery), it is through these rhetorical moments that we come to recognise Orchard as a 'local' response to a 'local' situation. By suggesting this, I do not mean to minimize Orchard's *actual* structure or to circumscribe its connections to an 'international' art world. On the contrary, as a localised response Orchard takes into consideration a complex set of circumstances, which include locally-specific discussions of funding, hundreds of other New York-based galleries and not-for-profit arts organisations, and a legacy of art practices embedded in New York's cultural history.

To begin, Orchard exists currently as a three-year project, set up as a limited liability corporation, meaning that it is a 'for-profit' organisation and that its founders have invested their own income into its organisation. As Fraser explains, "Commissions on sales are divided so as to repay major investments while also providing percentages for all partners involved in a sale in any way..." [20] More than simply adopting the gallery as an economic model, Orchard figures new economies into the gallery's financial structure that reflect the gallery's social systems. This social framework includes a role for the artist as part owner, part-director, part-curator, and part-exhibitor. Often self-described as 'alternative', there is a tendency for artist-run enterprises to position themselves against the art market. However, with Orchard there is the acknowledgement that 'alternative' does not necessarily guarantee a critique of market values, especially in New York where both commercial and not-for-profit spaces determine art's market value. Like Woody Allen who observes, "I won't

19.   Ibid.
20.   Ibid.

achieve immortality through my work. I will achieve it by not dying," simply deciding to be against the market is not enough to avoid it. By working in a way that remains collective without undermining the potential for diverging individual positions, Orchard bases its commercial structure within the market, without being 'market driven'.

In addition to reanalysing a mythology of claims around group work, collectivism, and inter-disciplinarity, Orchard's economic structure can be read as pragmatics, but only with an understanding of how pragmatics particularise certain ideological interfaces connected to cultural values. Firstly, within a matrix of private and public funding Orchard's status as an LLC allows it to avoid applying for grants as a tax-exempt organisation. While this may seem like a misunderstanding of pragmatics, in New York this choice means circumventing a host of foundations, trusts, councils, and funds that represents a highly-professionalised, capital-driven infrastructure for administrating art. For many people working in the arts, aligning with the not-for-profit sector is a political position, one that keenly opposes a right wing, conservative agenda. However, this position is not as clear-cut as it may have once been. Despite what might seem like Orchard's abandonment of the not-for-profit sector, the more radical position right now in the U.S., especially in relation to delivering 'cultural value', is to forego the moral pledge of public money and to rethink the economics of for-profit versus not-for-profit work.

Secondly, in explaining how sales will happen through Orchard we are told a percentage of the commission will repay 'major investments' and a percentage will go to any member(s) who facilitated in the transaction. Certainly, this is not anything new in terms of gallery practice; however, it infers that Orchard will not turn over high revenue profits. Again, this arrangement might seem economically imprudent (why not take more), but it is expedient. After the decision in the 1980s by the National Endowment for the Arts to stop making grants to individual artists, not-for-profit organisations became a way to legally, albeit indirectly, siphon federal money to artists, usually through small grants and almost never through the purchase of work except on the level of a national museum. Orchard simply bypasses the bureaucracy, paying artists directly and covering the cost of exhibitions.

Perhaps we can already see where pragmatics moves into critique. In setting up as a for-profit venture Orchard does not return rigid art world divisions predicated on a relationship to the art market (inside/outside, commercial/not-for-profit). As an organised response *to* the market, Orchard takes responsibility for relationships *within* the market. Pragmatics is not just about getting work done. This practical and realistic attitude towards selling work and supporting artists, means that people are paid for their work, whether that work is art-making, curating, or administrating. Alterity here is positioned from inside, which posits a more radical and more profound critique of the systems that determine how artworks circulate.

Finally, as part of a comprehensive answer to the questions: *How is Orchard different from other alternative-spaces? How is it different from other commercial galleries?* In the interview with Würmell, Fraser responds that Orchard's for-profit status arises (among other reasons) from a desire "to critically engage the economic relations and conditions of value in the art market and attempt to construct functional alternatives; [...] and to develop a structure of financial support for positions, works and practices that are not being supported by the art market." [21] This statement, in conjunction with one from the website, "The production of a social relation is central to Orchard's project, and is posed against the forms of separation explicit and implicit to the conventions of commercial galleries," [22] reveals that in many ways Orchard organises along the lines of institutional critique. I am not suggesting that Orchard is a performative exercise (or an artwork), or that it involves only one type of inquiry. How we do things (and with whom we do them) involves sticking to our guns idealistically in ways that many 'alternative' projects have forgotten. Lest we take for granted terrain that has been hard fought for, it is more important than ever to take seriously what it means to contest the values and histories that determine the economic, social, cultural and political arena we participate in as artists, curators and publics. By doing just this Orchard prepares us for new systems of value, which bring new economies.

In Selfless Service of Our Community

Fucking Good Art is an art magazine. It is sometimes described as a 'zine'. To be a zine is to be a lot of things. Typically it means being a publication, something that circulates in print, whether that means physically or over the Internet (or in the case of FGA, both). Zine culture is part

21.   Ibid.
22.   www.orchard47.org

of an ongoing history of alternative movements arising predominantly out of the underground music scene. Most zines relate to the do-it-yourself ethics/aesthetics of punk, are non-professional, distributed locally or through localised, non-geographic communities, and are of minority interest. An historical look traces zines back to specialised publications made in the 1950s for science fiction fan clubs, thus the term 'fanzine', which derives from combining the words 'fandom' and 'magazine'. The 1980s and 90s saw an influx of 'artzines' coming out of cities in the U.S., of which *Fucking Good Art* is one example. Although it started in Rotterdam in 2003, the title comes from a zine out of Chicago, which no longer exists, and which has been replicated in other cities in the U.S. (Hamelijnck and Terpsma attribute their zine's title to its Chicago roots.) In approach and design *FGA-Rotterdam* is different from its Chicago counterpart; the Chicago paper was more underground, perhaps more contentious. The fact that both arise from a 'zine tradition' exemplifies that zines function locally in different ways in relation to a mainstream.

FGA-Rotterdam circulates freely throughout the city, mostly through distribution in arts venues, artist-run spaces and collective studios. Less about an underground network, socially or economically, than it is about functioning for a specific community as a complement to the plethora of art world periodicals, in the words of FGA's editors, "We try to radicalise positive art criticism and look at it as meta art. We are not critics, we are artists writing about and reflecting on art, inviting friends and other artists and film makers." [23] This editorial position suggests a role for both art and criticism in forming a local scene, not by reinstating professional territories, but through a social network that reveals itself in each issue. Articles are written in Dutch and in English, most in first person and in a casual tone. An example is a text by Steven Rushton, entitled "Great Dead Artist Makes Bad Work Shock". The author relays his horror upon attending a screening of films by Gordon Matta-Clark at the Boijmans museum in Rotterdam: "this isn't the Gordon Matta-Clark that we know from the densely packed pages of October magazine, this isn't Mr. Institutional Critique at all!" [24] Despite his sardonic tone, ironically Rushton seems to desire *that* Matta-Clark, the one he knows from the pages of art criticism — a sentiment he confirms with his ending quip, "And, if you happen to be a crap artist you can take some comfort

23.   www.fuckinggoodart.nl
24.   *FGA #11*

in the knowledge that, sometimes, even the greats are just like you."
While casual, informal, and personal writing are valuable points of entry
into critical discourse, there is a potential to sound glib, and thereby
undermine what is actually stake in radicalising how we talk about art.
In any attempt to 'radicalise' art criticism, we need to be clear that *all*
language is contestable, situated, and fallible (not just the language of
critics). Anti-intellectualism, as *FGA*'s editors well understand, is often
more about conservatism than access, especially in a Dutch context.

An important edition of *FGA-Rotterdam* came out in the summer
of 2005. As it was the zine's tenth issue, the editors chose a book format
in place of *FGA*'s usual A3 broadsheet. Given changes in the city of
Rotterdam particularly in relation to recent turnover in several highly held
positions at various cultural institutions, *FGA #10* includes successive
interviews with key players in these decisions, including old post-holders
and their replacements. Among these is an interview with Catherine David,
former director of Witte de With, which took place on her last day as
director and chief curator. A fair amount of local controversy surrounded
her three-year tenure, including ongoing battles with city officials and a
local art community that accused her of exclusivity, (although these are
not the interview's only focus).

Paradoxically, the claims of exclusivity directed at David arose
mostly as a reaction to the seminars, publications and talks that drove
Witte de With's exhibition programme during David's directorship. As
chief curator at Witte de With, David insisted upon developing her long-
term project Contemporary Arab Representations. What does it mean
when using exhibitions to dig deeper, to push politics, and to exact difficult
answers is considered too critical, too intellectual for a local audience?
The implications for curatorial practice and its relationship to a cultural
industry that wants it to move closer towards entertainment (an area that
typically asks 'soft' questions and delivers 'soft' answers) seem to revert
to political correctness as a means of silencing. Calling upon her own
strong interests and connections to other places, without tuning them to
her local situation, meant David was cast in the Netherlands (by the press
anyway) as the aloof outsider, the non-Dutch (speaking) Frenchwoman.

For her part, when asked by Hamelijnck, "What will be the future
of our artistic practice in the West?" David brings us directly to a notion
of politics, "The values we are dealing with are not just about money,
quantity, speed. It is about creating value. You can't say how much it costs.
Cultural value has more to do with why you are alive, why you are dying,

and not: 'How much?'" [25] It is David's attitude towards complexity that I would argue all three of our examples share, from D.A.E., to Orchard, to *Fucking Good Art*. If speculating on the future is to be more than superficial posturing, or sheer narcissism, then we need to assess honestly the terms in which we are operating. When governments of the world bandy about democracy as an automated excuse for violence, when a notion of transparency is more rhetorical than actual, it is perhaps time to reexamine the terms that surround alterity.

Who curates? For whom is the curating being done? In what circumstances? We live in an age of mega-curators and major exhibitions. The visibility of certain projects over others in an ever-increasing field of internationalised outlets is often how we come to know certain places. This alone makes it worthwhile to rethink what constitutes a localised response, and to ask what conditions, politics, and power relations construct a collective future. To presume that 'bigness' equals oversimplification or is about destruction, and that the local restores authenticity, is too facile a response to real challenges. With an acute awareness that the local is no longer read only from a local perspective, D.A.E., Orchard, and *Fucking Good Art* identify platforms that accumulate in a local scene, but that involve simultaneous and connected outputs elsewhere.

Rather than assessing projects according to current parameters around curating, perhaps we can declare different lines of inquiry, analysis, and ways of organizing (temporally, spatially, socially, institutionally) as fundamentally available. And without subsuming entire practices into a 'new relational', we can seriously consider a range of entry points, including unofficial, informal, personal, incidental and radical inputs that happen along the way. What we learn from D.A.E. is that a collective situation/location can draw on a proximate past, and that when we pay attention to different speeds and different times, the political and cultural relevance of our work is not so easily confined. In Orchard, there is not one point of view, but there is a position. To allow collective work to appear through analysis and co-operation, and to risk the conditions that regulate how work happens is more than pragmatics. It is politics. And finally, with *Fucking Good Art* every issue delivers a short by-line that reads, *"In selfless service of our community."* As far as a future goes, perhaps that is an answer.

25.   "Last Day in Rotterdam," Catherine David in an interview with Rob Hamelijnck and Nienke Terpsma in *Fucking Good Art #10*, (FGA, Rotterdam, 2005), pp. 43

CONSTITUTIVE EFFECTS: THE TECHNIQUES OF THE CURATOR

Simon Sheikh

In contemporary art a great deal of attention is given to the activity of exhibitions. Exhibitions are one of the primary vehicles for artistic production. However, this activity of exhibiting and exhibition making is largely predictable and repetitious, involved in specific circuits and structures, as well as economies (both symbolic and real). Perhaps we could even speak of a typology of exhibitions — specific modes of address meant to produce certain meanings and audiences, and we could discuss these modes of address according to history, contingency and potentiality. In the following, I shall try to do so according to the three premises outlined in this book: the past, the present and the future.

Past:
Historically, exhibition making has been closely related to strategies of discipline and enlightenment ideals, not as a contradiction or dialectic, but rather as a simultaneous move in the making of the 'new' bourgeois subject of reason in 19th century Europe. Exhibition making marked not only a displ ay and division of knowledge, power and spectatorship, it also marked a production of a public. By making museum collections open to the public and by staging temporary exhibitions in the salons, a specific viewing public was imagined and configured. What we would now call curating, in effect this organizing of displays and publics, had constitutive effects on its subjects and objects alike.

The collection and display of specific objects and artifacts according to certain curatorial techniques, represented not only the writing of specific colonial and national histories, but also crucially, the circulation of certain values and ideals. The emerging bourgeois class was simultaneously positioning and assessing itself, and thus extending its world-view onto objects — things present in the world, both historically and currently — and therefore onto the world. But this dominant, or hegemonic, gaze was not to be seen nor visualized as a sovereign dictum, or dictatorship, but rather through a rationalist approach, through a subject of reason. The bourgeois class attempted to universalize its views and visions through rational argument rather than by decree. The bourgeois museum and its curatorial techniques could not articulate its power (only) through forms of discipline, it also had to have employ an educational and pedagogical approach, present in the articulations of tho artworks, the models of display of the objects, the spatial layout and the overall architecture. It had to situate a viewing subject that not only felt subjected to knowledge, but was also represented through the mode of address involved in the curatorial technique. In order for the mode of address to be effectively constitutive of its subjects, the exhibition and museum had to address *and* represent at the same time.

The cultural theorist Tony Bennett has aptly termed these spatial and discursive curatorial techniques, 'the exhibitionary complex' as a means of describing the complex assemblage of architecture, display, collections and publicness that characterize the field of institutions, exhibition making and curating. In his article of the same name, Bennett has analyzed the historical genesis of the (bourgeois) museum, and its production of relations of power and knowledge through its dual role, or double articulation, of simultaneously being a disciplinary and educational space:

The exhibitionary complex was also a response to the problem of order, but one which worked differently in seeking to transform that problem into one of culture – a question of the winning of hearts as well as the disciplining and training of individual subjects. As such, its constituent institutions reversed the orientations of the disciplinary apparatuses in seeking to render the forces and principles of order visible to the populace – transformed, here, into a people, a citizenry – rather than vice versa. They sought not to map the social body in order to know the populace by rendering it visible to power. Instead, through the provision of object lessons in power – the power to command and arrange things and bodies for public display – they sought to allow the people, and *en masse* rather than individually, to know rather than to be known, to become subjects rather than the objects of knowledge. Yet, ideally, they sought also to allow people to know and thence to regulate themselves; to become, in seeing themselves from the position of power, both as the subjects and objects of knowledge, knowing both power and what power knows, and knowing themselves as (ideally) known by power, interiorizing its gaze as a principle of self-surveillance and, hence, self-regulation. [1]

Whereas the 'strictly' disciplinary institutions (in a Foucaultian sense), such as schools, prisons, factories and so on, tried to manage the population through direct inflictions of order onto the actual bodies

1.   Tony Bennett, 'The Exhibitionary Complex', in R. Greenberg, B. Ferguson, S. Nairne (Eds.), *Thinking About Exhibitions*, London: Routledge, 1996, p. 84.

and thus behavior, the exhibitionary complex added persuasion to coercion. Exhibitions were meant to please as well as to teach, and as such needed to involve the spectator in an economy of desire as well as in relations of power and knowledge. In a sense, the exhibitionary complex was also meant to be empowering, in that you could identify with the histories on display and act accordingly. In this way, exhibition making was directly connected to the construction of a national body, and as such it was involved in identitarian as well as territorial politics of representation. The knowledge that became available to the subject was a means of inscribing that subject within a given nation-state, of cultivating the populace into exactly that: a people, a nation.

Access to knowledge then also involved an acceptance of certain histories and ways of understanding them. The exhibitionary complex not only curated histories and power-knowledge relations, but also indicated ways of seeing and behaving. Hence the specific rules of conduct in the museum: slow-paced walking, lowered speech, no physical contact with the objects on display, a general discretion. In this way, regulation gets added to representation, interpellation is coupled with identification, and the bourgeois subject of reason becomes both subject and object of power in a complex relation of knowledge. In fact, representation of your values and histories goes hand in hand with proper behavior — relations of power and knowledge become internalized through behavior and empowerment: *self*-regulation and *self*-representation. You must behave properly in order to be (allowed) in the museum. Not touching the objects indicates not only respect towards them and their status, but also an acceptance of the rules, of given prohibitions and, more crucially, an intimate knowledge of your own position: that one is in the know, capable of watching, of being cultivated, in both the active and passive sense of being. And thus the importance of the art opening, the *vernissage*, as a bourgeois ritual of initiation and cultivation: one is not merely the first to watch (and, in some cases, buy) but also to be watched: to be visible *as* the cultivated bourgeois subject of reason, in the right place and *in* your place.

Present:
In an attempt to describe how this history has also conditioned present day exhibition making and institutional foundations, as well as its critique, Frazer Ward has described the museum as 'haunted'. This

has to do with certain histories and contingencies, and how the museum continues to construct a specific subject, not only individually, but also collectively as a public:

> The museum contributed to the self-representation of and self-authorization of the new bourgeois subject of reason. More accurately, this subject, this *"fictitious identity"* of property owner and human being pure and simple, was itself an interlinked process of self-representation and self-authorization. That is, it was intimately bound to its cultural self-representation *as a public*. [2]

The modes of address in exhibition making can thus be viewed as attempts to at once represent and constitute a specific (class-based) collective subject. This also means that a double notion of representation is at play, at once the narrations and sensations of the displayed artworks themselves — the aspect most commonly referred to in both curatorial discourse and criticism — and the representation of a certain public (as spectator), being represented, authorized and constituted through the very mode of address. Making things public is also an attempt to make a public. A public only exists 'by virtue of being addressed', and is thus "constituted through mere attention" as Michael Warner puts it in his recent book *Publics and Counterpublics*. [3] What is significant here is the notion of a public as being constituted through participation and presence on the one hand, and articulation and imagination on the other. In other words, a public is an imaginary endeavor with real effects: an audience, a community, a group, an adversary or a constituency is imagining, and imagined through a specific mode of address that is supposed to produce, actualize or even activate this imagined entity, 'the public'. This is of course crucial to exhibition making, to the techniques of the curator.

However, as Frazer Ward points out, the spaces in which such exhibitions are produced and received are conditioned by certain histories, by certain residues of imagination, behaviour and reception. It is not my point to endlessly repeat a project of institutional critique, but rather to point out how the construction of a certain site was complicit with a certain subject, what Ward called 'the bourgeois subject of reason', and how this

2.   Frazer Ward, Frazer Ward, 'The Haunted Museum: Institutional Critique and Publicity', *October* 73, 1995, p. 74.
3.   Michael Warner, *Publics and Counterpublics,* New York: Zone Books, 2002.

has produced the plethora of strategies and responses we see in contemporary exhibition making. Within the history of institutional critique, art institutions are mainly seen as the instruments of the bourgeoisie, and as a machine that can include and thus neutralize any critical form through its exhibitionary techniques, such as the infamous 'white cube' of the gallery space. This is a process also known as cooptation, indicating that the institution needs, even desires, critique in order to strengthen itself and its neutralizing gaze. But this needs to be examined more carefully, and in the context of the historical appearance of museums, salons and galleries during the bourgeois revolutions, where the exhibition place functioned as a space for cultivated discussion, for self-representation and self-authorization through a rational-critical discourse. In other words, the discourse (including criticism) was rational and the objects (and to some extent the artist subject behind them) were irrational. The objects had to be irrational in order to be rationalized, which, in turn, produced the rational-critical subject whose values and judgments were represented by the exhibition. Exhibition making then became the staging of this discourse, of this debate, making curators caterers of taste and the artists as much objects of the gaze as the artworks. Seen in this light, so-called institutionally critical artworks were allowed into the institutions by default, as products of more or less rational artist-subjects, as mere contingency.

We are thus resting on the pillars of tradition in more than one sense, and in a sense of articulation and representation not always reflected in contemporary exhibition making. If the historical role of exhibition making was to educate, authorize and represent a certain social group, class or caste, who is being represented today? Arguably, the bourgeois class formation of the 19th century cannot be directly transferred to today's modular societies, neither as the goal for representation nor for critique or counter articulation(s). So which groups — imagined as real — are being catered to by contemporary exhibition making and institutional policies? And what modes of address would be required and desired to represent or criticize these formations? Answering this question directly will, partly, require a turn to the futuristic section, and partly a reversal: to ask what spectators can be said to be represented by the current strategies of exhibition making, whether reflected or not by the exhibition makers, since these strategies can be analyzed as modes of address, and thus as operating through specific articulations and imaginaries. This will require, though, a certain typology of exhibitions.

As mentioned in the beginning, the exhibition format is the main vehicle for the presentation of contemporary art, but this does not mean that the exhibition is a singular format with a given public and circulation of discourse. Rather, the format of the exhibition should be pluralized; obviously different types of exhibitions are speaking from different locations and positions, with different audiences and circulations, be it the self-organized group show in a small alternative space or the large scale international biennial. What they do share is a sense of a double public: the local, physically present (if only potentially) audience as well as the art world public (if only potentially). Exhibitions find themselves placed within an ecosystem as well as a hierarchy of exhibitions (and exhibition venues). This can, naturally, be employed strategically and cynically, but the important issue here is how — within the given exhibition format — to reflect upon its placement and potentiality in order to stretch it, circumvent it, sabotage it, or, if you will, affirm it, which happens to be the most common usage of a given exhibition format these days. The notion of 'alternative', for example, is infused with a large degree of symbolic capital within the arts, and is potentially transferable into real capital, thus making 'the alternative' into a stage within artistic-economic development, into a sphere placed on a time line rather than on a parallel track.

Exhibitions often seem tiresome, their use-value given and predictable in an endless repetition of the same formats and intentions. We find this in the very fixed format of historical museum exhibitions, retrospectives of either: 1) a specific period (always a 'golden' age), 2) a specific movement (preferably a clearly definable painterly style) or 3) a specific artist (the monographic exhibition of the artist as genius). Such exhibitions exist in more or less luxurious variants, usually curated by museum experts rather than freelancers, and feature some sort of art historical research. According to the prestige of the institution or theme/artist, a catalogue book of some substance accompanies this exhibition type: the prestige and importance can be directly measured in the volume of the publication. One is often led to believe that such exhibitions have the most un-reconstructed notion of their publicness, expressing a discrete charm of the tradition, but actually this format has proven extremely adaptable to changes in the public sphere from the bourgeois model of enlightenment to the current culture, or even entertainment, industry. Such exhibitions offer a feeling reminiscent of bourgeois rationality and taste in the form of light entertainment for the family; spending a couple of hours in the museum, with its gift shop and café, as an alternative to a trip to the mall.

Although exhibitions of contemporary art are not always popular, populism is as present within such exhibitions as it is in the retrospective museum shows. Again and again, we are offered the 'new' — the generational show being an ever-popular and career-building move, just as we constantly are subjected to the most retrograde exhibition format of all, the national show, regularly combined with the generational, producing 'new' miracles in the discovery of new happening scenes. Not only do such shows fit seamlessly into the demands for new trends and products of the art markets, but they will very likely also receive assured funding from national cultural agencies, making them a perfect example of the currently ever-so desirable merger between corporate and public funds. If such shows do not guarantee large numbers of visitors the way certain retrospective shows do, they tend to privilege that other imagined public, the art world, and give access to the strange circuit of magazines, discourses, word-of-mouth, curatorial attention, teaching jobs, galleries and money.

A merger between funds, economies, national interests and the production of art world trends are also at issue in the most international of all formats, the ever-growing biennials. It would not be difficult to be critical, even dismissive, of the biennial circuit and its relationship to market and capital, and lack of reflection on 'local' audience — indeed such a critique is almost commonplace among art professionals, often in a cynical form of fatigue (it must be the jetlag...), but this would be overlooking the potential these biennials actually offer for a reflection of the double notion of publicness, for creating new public formations that are not bound to the nation-state or the art world. By being perennial events, both locally placed and part of a circuit, they have the potential for creating a more transnational public sphere, with both difference and repetition in the applied mode of address and implied notion of spectatorship and public participation.

Future:
In order to alter the script of the existing formats, we need more rather than less reflection on the conception of publics, and the contingencies and histories of various modes of address. As I have tried to argue, all exhibition making is the making of a public, the imagination of a

world. It is therefore not a question of art for art's sake or art for society, of poetics or politics, but rather a matter of understanding the politics of aesthetics and the aesthetic dimension of politics. Or, put in another way, it is the mode of address that produces the public, and if one tries to imagine different publics, different notions of stranger relationality, one must also (re)consider the mode of address, or, if you will, the formats of exhibition making.

There not only exist public spheres (and ideals thereof), but also *counterpublics.* According to Michael Warner, counterpublics can be understood as particular parallel formations of a minor or even subordinate character where other or oppositional discourses and practices can be formulated and circulated. Counterpublics have many of the same characteristics as normative or dominant publics — existing as imaginary address, a specific discourse and/or location, and involving circularity and reflexivity — and are therefore always already as much *relational* as they are *oppositional.* A counterpublic is a conscious mirroring of the modalities and institutions of the normative public, all be it in an effort to address other subjects and indeed other imaginaries. Where the classic bourgeois notion of the public sphere claimed universality and rationality, counterpublics often claim the opposite, and in concrete terms this often entails a reversal of existing spaces into other identities and practices, a queering of space. This has indeed been the model of contemporary feminist (and other) project exhibitions that use the art institution as a space for a different notion of spectatorship and collective articulation that runs counter to the art space's historical self-articulations and legitimations, what Marion von Osten has described as 'exhibition making as a counter-public strategy'. [4]

An exhibition must imagine a public in order to produce it, and to produce a world around it — a horizon. So, if we are satisfied with the world we have now, we should continue to make exhibitions as always, and repeat the formats and circulations. If, on the other hand, we are not happy with the world we are in, both in terms of the art world and in a broader geopolitical sense, we will have to produce other exhibitions: other subjectivities and other imaginaries. The great division of our times is not between various fundamentalisms, since they all ascribe to the same script (albeit with a different idea of who shall win in the end...),

4.   Marion von Osten, 'A Question of Attitude — Changing Methods, Shifting Discourses, Producing Publics, Organizing Exhibitions', Simon Sheikh (Ed.), *In the Place of the Public Sphere?*, Berlin: b_books, 2005.

but between those who accept and thus actively maintain the dominant imaginary of society, subjectivity and possibility and those who reject and instead partake in other imaginaries, as Cornelius Castoriadis once formulated it. For Castoriadis, society is an imaginary ensemble of institutions, practices, beliefs and truths, that we all subscribe to and thus constantly (re)produce. Society and its institutions are as much fictional as functional. Institutions are part of symbolic networks, and as such they are not fixed or stable, but constantly articulated through projection and praxis. But by focusing on its imaginary character, he obviously also suggests that other social organizations and interactions can be imagined:

[The] supersession [of present society] – which we are aiming at *because we will it* and because we know that others will it as well, not because such are the laws of history, the interests of the proletariat or the destiny of being – the bringing about of a history in which society not only knows itself, but *makes itself* as explicitly self-instituting, implies a radical destruction of the known institution of society, in its most unsuspected nooks and crannies, which can exist only as positing/creating not only new institutions, but a new *mode* of instituting and a new relation of society and of individuals to the institution. [5]

It is thus not only a question of changing institutions, but of changing how we institute; how subjectivity and imagination can be instituted in a different way. This can be done by altering the existing formats and narratives, as in the queering of space and the (re)writing of histories — that is, through deconstructive as well as reconstructive projects, *and* by constructing new formats, by rethinking the structure and event of the exhibition altogether. Either way, I would suggest that curating in the future should center around three key notions: *Articulation*, *Imagination* and *Continuity*.

By *articulation* we shall mean the positioning of the project, of its narratives and artworks, and its reflection of its dual public and placement both in and out of the art world. An exhibition is always a statement about the state of the world, not just the state of the arts, and as such it is always already engaged in particular imaginaries, whether or

5.   Cornelius Castoriadis, *The Imaginary Institution of Society*, London: Polity Press, 1987, p. 373. (French original published 1975).

not it claims to be so engaged. A work of art is, at best, an articulation of something as much as it is a representation of someone: it is a proposal for how things could be seen, an offering, but not a handout. Articulation is the formulation of your position and politics, where you are and where you want to go, as well as a concept of companionship: you can come along, or not. In cultural production, there is no separation possible between form and content, between means and ends: modes of address articulate and situate subject positions, and where you want to go and how you get there are one and the same question. Thus, the more clearly the articulatory element is stressed, the more productive it will be in partaking in other imaginaries and subject positioning.

By *imagination*, we shall take our cue from the thinking of Castoriadis, and his analysis of society as self-created, as existing through institutions. It is, as stated, a question of imagining another world, and thus instituting other ways of being instituted and imagining, so to speak. To say that other worlds are indeed possible. For our present situation, we can also say: another art world is possible (if we want it). Secondly, the imaginary, as articulation, naturally has to do with the processes and potentialities of artistic production itself: to offer other imaginaries, ways of seeing and thus changing the world. An artwork can indeed be seen as new modes of instituting, of producing and projecting other worlds and the possibility for the self-transformation of the world: An institutionalization that is produced through subjectivity rather than producing subjectivity. It can, quite bluntly, offer a place from which *to see* (and to see differently, other imaginaries).

By *continuity*, we shall refer to the very work processes of curating itself, and how it can appear as lost in repetitions and trends. Rather than feeding the market, repetition could be transformed into continuity, literally doing the same in order to produce something different, not in the products, but in the imagination. I propose not only working in the same field or theme as a researcher, but actually radicalizing this aspect, as well as the resistance to the market, by working on a long-term plan. Not a five-year plan, but rather a ten-year plan; constantly doing the very same exhibition with the same artists. Imagine this: constantly asking the same artists to contribute to the same thematic exhibition, thus going into the depths of the matter rather than surfing the surface. Indeed, going off the deep end as it were, by refusing the demands for newness, for constantly new (re)territorializations — 'painting now!', 'the return of the political', 'new British art show', etc. — and insisting on working on the very same show, whether it is traveling or within the same institution or city. Now, one could argue that this is what a lot of curators are already doing, regardless of the fact that they might change topics, scenes and generations regularly; but rather than dismissing or hiding this fact, I would suggest articulating it, and through this self-imposed and self-transformative continuity, going deeper into the artists' production and thinking, as the artists then would with the curator's thinking and methods, as well as developing — quite literally, and for better or for worse — long-term relationships with one's imagined audience, constituency and/or community. Producing a public is making a world. It is also making other ones possible...

GRAND ILLUSIONS: THE "NEW" MUSEUM OF MODERN ART

Mary Anne Staniszewski

The art world is in ecstasy. One of its crown jewels, the Museum of Modern Art has re-opened in a glorious new building with acres more exhibition space. After being handicapped in cramped quarters for decades, the museum can finally fully realize its mission to show the art of our time and to be truly "modern." Crowds are pouring in and reviewers are giddily gorging themselves on the treasures to behold.

Bucking the trend of building museums that are at war with the art — or just steal the show — it seems as if Yoshio Taniguchi has performed magic. The architect has, to repeat his now famous line, made the building "disappear."

But has the building really vanished? And how new, how "modern" is the "New MoMA?"

Yes, in a sense, something new *has* happened at MoMA. The museum, previously an "ivory tower," has visually become one with the city. The lobby doubles as a passageway, with entrances on 53rd and 54th streets. Approaching from 54th, the glass grid of galleries with floor to ceiling windows rises above the sculpture garden wall and lets any passerby see what's inside. Most eye-catching is the bright-red sports car parked on the third floor next to a New York subway sign. Throughout the museum vistas frame galleries, the garden, and the city outside. Judging from the architectural experience, you might think the great divide that has haunted the modern museum — the separation of art from life — has dissolved. But does the art match what appears to be the timeliness of the architecture?

Upon entering the lobby from 54th Street, the first thing you see is an Ellsworth Kelly color spectrum painting. Straight ahead is a Roy Lichtenstein, to your left a Joan Miro, to your right, a David Smith. The sculpture garden is studded with the likes of a Pablo Picasso, a Claes Oldenburg, a Donald Judd. This prelude is a clue to the entire enterprise, and limited perspective, of the "new" Museum of Modern Art. Too many of MoMA's galleries have no artworks by women. When they do appear, the representation is miniscule. I can understand low numbers pre-1960s, but since the 1970s women artists have been a part of the art world and working at full force. Even in what I call the multicultural gallery (on the second floor) — where there are not only artworks by women, but by the art stars of color — of nineteen, only six are by women. With the recent exception of the Lee Bontecou show, the Modern, like most major Manhattan museums, almost never gives women their due. So in terms of the status of the "second" sex — nothing much is new.

The heart of the museum, the massive airy atrium, dramatically reaches five stories and is the featured panorama throughout the building. Expanses of white wall open up around you, overwhelming several lackluster paintings from the 1980s and 1990s? a passive Willem De Kooning, a grey nothing by Jasper Johns, a mild Brice Marden. The selection is astounding in its dullness, and is testimony to MoMA's failure to present the most vital art of the past few decades. On the third wall, presiding as the great ancestor, is Monet's "Water Lilies." At the old MoMA, this series was installed in its own semi-circular gallery, creating one of the most pleasurable, priceless, and immersive of museum displays. Now the "Lilies" are flattened, floating on an ocean of white. At the atrium's center, like some satiric joke, stands Barnet Newman's *Broken Obelisk* (1963–69). Are the curatorial powers-that-be blind to the fantastically Freudian symbolism of this twenty-six-foot steel phallus?

The symbolism next-door in the "multicultural gallery" is also loaded. Stacked with work ostensibly engaged with issues of color, there is almost the total absence of any. In this bright-white, twenty-foot high space pretty much all you see is beige and black. A banishment of color predominates in MoMA's contemporary installations and is evidence of sanitized curatorial selections. Mathew Barney, notorious for his inter-sex, inter-species imagery, is represented by *The Cabinet of Bay Fay La Foe* (2000), a beige and black wax table with a top hat. Kiki Smith — who has portrayed the body in abject, fanciful, and downright shocking ways — has twelve tasteful silvered-glass jugs, her *Untitled*, 1987–1990. If MoMA has done its best to drain the lifeblood out of so much contemporary art, they've completely missed the technological revolutions. Seven works stand-in for all the film, video, digital, and multi-media installations produced during the past several decades.

While problems like the lack of female presence are not remedied in the third floor Architecture and Design galleries, the displays of furniture, fabrics, and familiar household items provide an oasis of color, texture and connections to everyday life. But if you want to experience the creative spectrum of chaos and calm that characterizes modern art, head for the fifth floor. At the entrance, you finally confront a timely reference for citizens of a nation at war — José Clemente Orozco's 1940 mural, *Dive Bomber and Tank*. In these smaller, more human-scale galleries you find the ecstatic colors of a Vassily Kandinsky, the surreal sexuality of a Salvador Dali, and Soviet-style experiments that revolutionized graphic design. The oldest acquisitions of the Modern remain the most new.

MoMA's apex, the stadium-scale sixth floor gallery, is awarded to the work of three artists. Michael Wesely's time-based photographs of the museum's exterior renovation face each other on the two smaller walls at and opposite the entrance. James Rosenquist's famous *F-111* (1964–65) — which should wrap around the insides of a small room, as was done at his Guggenheim retrospective — is flattened on the humungous right wall, making it more picture perfect for the PR paraphernalia. Installed in such an escapist context, even I, who knows this artist's work so well, forgot that *F-111* was originally an anti-war painting. And last, but certainly not least, a monumental Ellsworth Kelly relief is given the wall on the left. At MoMA, the universe begins and ends with Kelly — certainly a respectable artist, but a producer of rationalized abstractions, the kind of work favored by corporate collections, and lacking any reference to politics, emotion, war, sex, love, insanity, wisdom, and the revelations of the commonplace.

Of all the failures of the new MoMA, the absence of women's work is most arrogantly shocking. Like the massive bronzed obelisk lording like an idol in a temple for the exclusively male, so many of the curatorial choices seem to have been made by those oblivious to all kinds of symbolisms and meanings, most glaringly, the mono-gender myopia. When a small cluster women's pieces is finally found in surrealist galleries, they are all the tiniest of works and "caged" in a wall vitrine. This is most conspicuously seen a painting by an artist not known for her miniatures: In small self portrait, Frida Kahlo is shown with hair shorn, sitting in a chair, dressed in a man's suit, holding scissors, with her former long locks of strewn on her body, the chair and floor around her. For a woman artist to have her work included in MoMA's permanent collection, you have to a least portray yourself as a man. As one visitor said to me, this "just says it all."

A more subtle masculine masquerade parades throughout the collection. Complex, idiosyncratic, and diverse artistic visions are edited so that rationalist abstraction reigns. Traditionally, and symbolically, this "way of seeing" has been associated with a patriarchal positivism. This is especially the case in the painting and sculpture galleries where the oppressive presence of these puritanical prejudices preside.

When a Georgia O'Keeffe is permitted to appear — albeit in a corridor near the escalators — it is an almost colorless, almost abstract, rectangular image titled *Lake George Window* (1929). Banished is the artist's signature vegetal eroticism rendered in lurid hues.

Mondrian's "discovery" of abstraction was founded on his devotion to mysticism, most specifically theosophy. But all traces of these "icky," "new age" passions — the early figures and flowers circled by auras, for example — are effaced. Mondrian's "classics" of primarily the twenties and thirties are instead informed by later works that have links to more empirical, urban, and "worldly" sources, like his 1943 Broadway Boogie Woogie (1942–1943), which is a literal grid, mapping Manhattan's syncopated city streets. These later paintings are the antithesis of Mondrian's groundbreaking quest to paint the impossible, the essential, the spiritual.

The detachment and "strained" neutrality of so much of the permanent collection can been seen in choices like Rachael Whiteread's, *Untitled*, 1993. Revealingly different from most of the artist's other sculptures, Whiteread's mold was not taken from any room, any specific site, or any place on this earth. Rather, it is an "abstraction," that is, a sculpture of a non-existent generic room.

The history that the museum of modern art has written within and on its walls offers only a single point in the spectrum of possibilities for modern art. What we see at the Museum is "modernism" in its most specific and limited sense, that is, art that is supposed to be autonomous, supercedingly aesthetic, and separate from everyday life. The counterpoints would be what so many of us call the "avant-garde," practices engaged not only with aesthetics, but with politics, popular culture, and all things that may pose vital and provocative challenges to such exclusively "modernist" institutions like MoMA. Of course, most art is neither "pure modernism," nor a melding-into-everything-else avant-garde. And often the latter, becomes the former when subject to the institutional processes of museums, markets, and art history.

MoMA's simplistic version of modern art as modernism still dominates so much of the art world in the States. It is the legacy of Clement Greenberg, and others, who have argued that to prevent art's authenticity, criticality, and life force from becoming one with advertising, propaganda, and the maw of capitalist consumerism, you need to keep art separate, pure, and involved with questions of its proscribed disciplines. Such a strategy would preserve fine art. The current MoMA regime embodies this heritage and makes the complex experiments of art in the modern era much smaller than they need to be. So despite the thrill of seeing so many masterworks in one place, a visit to the Museum of Modern Art short-changes its visitors. In so doing, the Museum fails in its grand mission as a cultural public trust.

MoMA's inaugural extravaganza — from the building to the works within it — is an exercise in collective blindness.

The isolationist art that exemplifies curatorial selections is enhanced by MoMA's installations and architecture. Far from being invisible, Taniguchi's environments are the most aggressive aspect of the new museum. They add a dynamism to the current fashion for "extreme" galleries, where the walls are whiter, bigger, and more overpowering.

Most visitors do not perceive that isolating works in neutral interiors provides settings both for the art, *and* for those who view them. Invented for the modern art museum, these sites have a subtle but powerful affect, enhancing our identification with ideals of independence and autonomy while obliterating references to the world outside. Despite seductive glimpses of the streets and skies beyond the Museum, the scale, size, color, and predominance of the white walls at MoMA has increased.

But these "support systems" not only enhance the artworks' segregation, they foreground the structure of the institution itself. This is an omnipresent phenomenon that has been increasing since the middle of the 20th century: the visibility and preeminence of "systems," "frame-works," "networks" supercede the elements within it. The Museum of Modern Art continues to deny this dimension of its authority — what I have described as the "power of display." [1]

Amidst the hallucinatory inaugural publicity, it has perhaps been difficult to see that the new MoMA is isolationist, apolitical, sterile, segregated, oppressively rationalist, and dehumanized-in-scale. If museums, like the works within them, are mirrors of ourselves, then a much truer portrait of who we are now needs to be rendered at MoMA.

Postscript, one year later:

The dominant — domineering? — impression of the permanent collection? It remains mostly male. Gestures like adding William Tucker's *Gymnast II* (1984) to the already male-artists-only sculpture garden, seems like a slap in the face to all women sculptors. This is just one of many similar examples that could be cited.

1.   This was a key element of the thesis of my book, *The Power of Display: A History of Exhibitions at the Museum of Modern Art* (Cambridge, Massachusetts. MIT Press, 1998).

There has been an improvement in the atrium. Even the most euphoric reviewers of the new MoMA complained about the pathetic placement of Monet's "Water Lilies." And this mistake has been ameliorated somewhat by moving them to a more hospitable location in fifth floor galleries. But rather than hanging paintings on the three walls surrounding the Newman, one has been left blank. Startling in its massiveness, this field of whiteness underscores the sovereignty of the building that was so striking to me a year ago.

Different from all the galleries housing the earlier decades of the painting and sculpture collection, the contemporary galleries have twice been completely rehung with thematic shows, which therefore count in my book as "temporary exhibitions."

The first was a public relations disaster *Contemporary Voices: Works from the UBS Art Collection*. Devised by the Museum "to celebrate the donation of works of contemporary art to the Museum by the financial services firm UBS," the UBS collection was described by *The New York Times* as the 30-year passion of chairman of UBS American and vice chairman of MoMA's board, Donald B. Marron. [2] Forty-three of the 74 works are gifts to the Museum. [3] The brand of bland corporate neutrality and abstraction that haunted the inaugural selections became ever more evident by beginning the new MoMA's programming with a corporate patronage exhibition.

But since then, there have been some signs of hope.

The second exhibition in the contemporary galleries, *Take Two. World Views: Contemporary Art from the Collection*, is a mix of both internationalist and inter-media work. Produced by Klaus Biesenbach, Chief Curator of P.S.1 (the alternative space that "merged" with MoMA in 1999) [4] and Curator of MoMA's Department of Film and Media and Roxana Marcoci, Associate Curator of the Museum's Department of

2.   "The Museum of Modern Art Presents *Contemporary Voices: Works from the UBS Art Collection*," Department of Communications, The Museum of Modern Art, n.d., 1. Roberta Smith, "Corporate Taste in Art, And the Art of Donation," *The New York Times*, February 4, 2005, E35. As MoMA's press release recounts: "Works in this exhibition are drawn from the former PaineWebber Art Collection, which was assembled under the leadership of former PaineWebber Chairman and Chief Executive Officer Donald B. Marron, a longtime Trustee, former President and current Voice Chairman of MoMA, as well as a member of the UBS Art Collection Advisory Board. The PaineWebber Art collection became the core of the UBS Art Collection in 2001 when UBS acquired Paine Webber." "The Museum of Modern Art to Presents *Contemporary Voices: Works from the UBS Art Collection*," 1.
3.   Ibid.
4.   "Two Leading Art Institutions Join Forces," Press Release, P.S. 1, www.ps1.org/cut/press/Mrgrel2.html (January 8, 2006).

Photography, this show does not shy away from a diversity of "identities" and media, and has broken many boundaries routinely left intact at MoMA

Another surprise is the retrospective of Elizabeth Murray's paintings. This combined with the recent Lee Bontcou show sets a new precedent for frequency of one-person shows for artists of the female gender.

Finally, there is the tellingly titled *Safe: Design Takes on Risk*, curated by the Department of Design and Architecture Curator Paola Antonelli and Curatorial Assistant Patricia Juncosa. This smart, provocative, and timely exhibition is one of the first acknowledgements by the Manhattan museum establishment that we are fighting a "War on Terror," a phrase that has often come to replace "The War on Terrorism," suggesting a phantom enemy that is a never-ending emotional state.

Jammed, packed with all sorts of unusual inventions, artistic creations, and objects of the commonplace that make us feel more safe, the show includes a refugee shelter, a first-aid bag, a "civil disobedience suit," a pacemaker, and crowd control barriers. The exhibition gathers together an array of eloquently designed "equipment" for citizens programmed for fear. This is a brilliant portrait of ourselves and "our world" as manifest in our design objects. On the more modernist level, I can't help but see *Safe* as more than a report on our societal state of mind. It doubles as a comment on what has been — for too long — the condition of curatorial vision and courage at the Museum of Modern Art.

Please note the author toured the Museum galleries in early December 2004.
The description of works in the galleries match what was installed at that time.

MAKING NEW

Andrew Wilson

Although there has been much discussion of the shift in the activity, position, status and role of the contemporary art curator over the last 30 or so years, there has been little discussion about the curator's relationship with and position concerning history. The viewpoint adopted by the curator both reflects on how the products of a certain activity can take their place within an evolving sense of history, but more directly also impacts on the ways in which history is itself dealt with, understood and presented. The curator's relationship to history, understood in these ways, is as much complicated as it can be contentious, but that it has been so little remarked on is also rather surprising. Writing here as a critic of contemporary art, a historian of 20th-century art and a sometime curator of exhibitions and events, my different activities have dealt with and used history to different ends and rather than feel conflicted about the contradictions that are often thrown up by this situation, I believe that the often paradoxical way in which my different activities sit provides positive sites of slippage. Indeed, most significant for me are those projects, which explicitly use the slippages in definitions of history as the basic material for an activity, which recognise Michel Foucault's dictum that 'A new form of modernity has always appeared each time our relationship to the present found itself drastically changed by history.' [1]

All writing about art is to an extent about storytelling and as such is subject not only to the particular peculiarities of each authorial voice, but also to the deployment of different narrative or structural devices. Much the same, of course, also holds true for making exhibitions. For most historical exhibitions the curator's voice is close to that which used to be called a keeper — the histories embodied by the exhibited works were presented to its audience as a form of largely unproblematic transcription in which a past significance becomes reconfigured according to a narrative

1.   This remark was also used by M/M Paris for its exhibition, 'Translation', of works selected from the Dakis Joannou Collection and shown at the Palais de Tokyo, Paris, June 23 September 18, 2005. M/M's proposal was to find the answer to the question 'What would be the current form of "modern" in art today in the age of globalization, that gigantic movement that is calling into question all that we know?' that was suggested to them by Foucault's statement. 'Translation' asked 'Are we about to see a new Modernism appear, one founded on a resistance to the standardization of culture: After 20th-century Modernism, which aspired to the international language of abstraction, the aim for the artists of today is to translate into a contemporary language the particularities of their specific cultural identity, their social singularity, and their difference. It is a "translation" in both sense of the word, i.e., the usual meaning of the term and its original Latin sense of something "carried over" or "transferred".' M/M suggested that 'This mutant form of a hybrid culture, this art of resisting the standardization of cultures and of the world economy, might best be called altermodernism.' www.palaisdetokyo.com/fr/presse/communiques/translation/comtranslationen.html.

device almost akin to biography. This historical narrative is one whose elements are locked up within the individual works and reconstructed by the curator through the transcription or placing of each work within a space to tell a particular story. One particularly exemplary illustration of this approach is the 1988 'Stationen der Moderne' exhibition at the Martin Gropius Bau in Berlin. This took the premise that a history of 20th-century art could be presented by the partial restaging of certain exhibitions that might take their place as way stations within a history of modern art, and that this history would be better understood were the works of art that had been shown in, for instance, the travelling Futurist exhibition of 1912 or the 'First Russian Show' of 1922, or the Festival of Fluxus art in Wiesbaden in 1962, to be brought back together again. It was almost as if the experience of seeing these works together for the first time — in 1912, 1922 or 1962, for instance — could also somehow be recaptured now through such a re-staging. Although such a possibility is, of course, ridiculous, it does underpin many exhibitions of historical art. Although this particular exhibition was itself somewhat of a failure and its choice of restaged exhibitions rather wayward as far as one view of post-war art history was concerned (for instance, the choice of exhibitions for the immediately post-war period reflected a need to show how an idea of avant-garde practice — as much as modern art itself — was reborn in Germany and provided the foundations for the 'triumph' of the German neo-expressionists in the early 80s), the exhibition's way of recounting history through an emphasis on a notion of remaking those historical situations within which particular artworks had once been presented is a potent one.

However, whereas 'Stationen der Moderne' remade situations between artworks to construct a form of transcription of a historical narrative in terms of a bogus capture of historical authenticity where a 'true' presentation might deliver an accurate reading or account for those works, [2] my own recognition of the deep splits between the different presentational devices controlled through history or contemporary practice led me to see if, rather than just transcribe a historical narrative, a form of translation between historical and contemporary moments could instead be enacted. Indeed it was felt necessary to ask if the only

2.   Another more recent example is the recent exhibition 'Dada' at the Pompidou Centre in Paris, October 5, 2005 — January 9, 2006. One element of the exhibition was the partial reconstruction of Francis Picabia's 1922 exhibition at the Galerie Dalmau in Barcelona.

way that artworks, now encased within art history, could somehow act within a contemporary perspective was by bringing the forces of translation into play so that history collided with the here and now, almost as a form of second childhood, or as a provocation when understood as a paradox akin to that of a 'pataphysical vision of 'authentic enactment'. If 'Stationen der Moderne' had indeed aimed in part for visitors to recapture the 1912 Futurist Exhibition as if it was being seen for the first time, what was however ignored was the possibility that, by so framing the reception of these works, they might also be understood to be in some way contemporary, have an impact on contemporary practice or, at the very least, reflect it (such a view would tie in with the then contemporary notions of simulacra and repetition underpinning much work made under the banner of neo-geo or appropriation art). To comprehend the action of history in this way would be to confirm it as fluidly contingent on present readings as much as it might have been formed originally from past events. By discussing here projects that I have initiated — as opposed to analysing those initiated by others — I am consciously aware that I am choosing to contravene this book's editorial restriction that asked contributors only to address projects that they had not taken part in. I have taken this view primarily because of my belief that the sorts of authorial slippages that arise within a process of translation, and the effect this has on current practice when viewed from the perspective of history reside at the heart of this book's structure (to account for those activities and practice that have impacted, are impacting or will impact on each of the book's authors), and that this retrospective commentary could perhaps be perceived — more keenly for being personal — as another level of translation.

It was the positive confusion inherent in Alfred Jarry's proposal of a 'science of imaginary solutions' [3] that directly provided one key to the slippages at work in one project carried out in 1996. 'Made New' at City Racing in South London brought together work by Gustav Metzger, Barry Flanagan and Tim Mapston framed by a number of 'pataphysical definitions by Jarry — positioned between his identification of creation

3.   Jarry defined 'pataphysics as 'the science of imaginary solutions, which symbolically attributes the properties of objects, described by their virtuality, to their lineaments' in his *Exploits and Opinions of Dr Faustroll, 'Pataphysician,* unpublished at the time of his death. Looking at that which is beyond metaphysics, 'pataphysics locates truth in absurdity and the contradictory, and holds that every event in the universe be accepted as an extraordinary event. For more on 'pataphysics, see for instance, *'Pataphysics? Definitions and Citations,* London Institute of 'Pataphysics, Merde 130, and Jean Baudrillard (translated by Simon Watson-Taylor), *'Pataphysics,* London Institute of 'Pataphysics, Pédale 133.

as 'clinamen' and the crossing of ideas as 'ethernity' — manifested
in the form of yellow vinyl text skied high on the wall. The works by the
individual artists were all made at early formative points in their careers:
Metzger by his 1959 *Cardboards* installation, his first manifestation of
auto-destructive art; Flanagan by his 1966 sand piece *ringn* which itself
explicitly references Jarry (the inclusion of Jarry in the show had been a
suggestion to me that had been made by Flanagan); and three sculptural
works by Mapston from 1974. In this way the pattern of exhibitions at City
Racing, which explicitly showed work by 'young' or 'emerging' artists
was maintained even in a show of work by much older or established
artists that from this perspective were more usually defined by history.
Furthermore, the work was made in the weeks, or in the case of *ringn*
minutes before the exhibition opened, and as a result had an utterly current
feel (so much so that one collector wanted to buy the Alfred Jarry works
but was rather put out when informed that he had died in 1907, and that
he would put his money to better use by going and asking for his work in a
bookshop): Flanagan's materials had come from a particular sand quarry;
Metzger's cardboard boxes had come from the streets of Whitechapel
and Spitalfields; and Mapston's were largely constructed from MDF.

At the time I described these works not so much as objects but
as events. This was meant in a number of ways. By having the need to
be remade inscribed within each work in a number of different ways,
there was never going to be one particular object that somehow stood
for the work, but instead a continuum of always rather different works. In
being remade, meanings shifted — this was most immediately obvious
in the case of Metzger's cardboards, which shifted from referencing
the Duchampian readymade and Russian functionalism towards those
realisms recording the material waste of pollution and the human tragedies
of homelessness. *Cardboards* was not presented as a set of reliefs on a
wall but now as a brutally realist intervention in a space that was defined
by dimension or aesthetics as much as it was by ideology. [4] The choice
made by Mapston that his work should be remade using MDF, rather
than what had in 1974 been the cheapest but was now among the most
expensive timber, also had the effect of suggesting that newly remade

4.   The nature of this process of translation was further underlined by Metzger's
subsequent remaking of *Cardboards* in 2000 for the exhibition 'City Racing
1988-1998: A Partial Account', ICA, London, 2001. Again the source and
configuration of the cardboards were changed, as was the title to *Been There, Done
That, KS*, making direct reference to Kurt Schwitters.

work could almost mean new work, and through a change in material his three sculptures were allowed to take their place, almost too seamlessly, in the context of the sculptural potentialities of the work of artists such as Liam Gillick in which the material object exists to become a trigger for a possible event or occurrence. By the demands that Mapston's work made to the beholder — beyond just looking — they were continually remade in many ways. Within these sets of contexts the show was asking where 'authentic enactment' could continue to be located.

These historically determined works that made-up 'Made New' had been radically translated by the context in which they had been placed. The particular utterances that they signalled — Jarry, the epistemological break of the first decade of the 20th Century; Metzger, the politicisation of neo-dada in the late 50s; Flanagan, the changing materiality of sculpture from object to process in the 60s; Mapston, the bodying of sculptural objects as potential social structure in the 70s — was levelled out in a rather more complex way. They all existed like illustrations on the same page of a book or magazine so much so that history had not been reduced to a continuum but in such a way as to emphasise that history could be defined by different things from the past happening at the same time now, revealing that they all had the capacity to act as documents of a particular history but could also operate with a peculiarly — because translated — contemporary utterance.

This particular form of slippage whereby historical document doesn't just speak to a contemporary audience but adopts its figures of speech and language was further investigated in two other projects in 2002, 'Poetry will be made by all' for Magnani and the performance event 'A Reading of *Watt*' for Cubitt Gallery. The first used a series of table works by Angela Bulloch as the container and frame for an archival collection of largely countercultural documents which found themselves presented as documents of specific moments of past activity and translated as examples for a current potential practice. 'A Reading of *Watt*' directly embraced issues of reconstruction and translation as six people sat down and read Samuel Beckett's novel *Watt* out loud through the evening without any breaks. This recalled what happened after the editors of *Merlin*, a British expatriate literary magazine published in Paris, approached Samuel Beckett in the winter of 1952 and asked if they could read the manuscript of *Watt* with a view to publishing an extract from it. One rainy afternoon Beckett delivered the manuscript to its editorial offices at the rue du Sabot banana-drying depot. Richard Seaver, an American advisory editor for the magazine (and later director of Grove Press in New York), has recalled how 'a knock came at the door and a tall, gaunt figure in a raincoat handed in a manuscript in a black imitation-leather binding and left almost without a word. That night, half a dozen of us … sat up half the night and read *Watt* aloud, taking turns until our voices gave out.'

It was this particular event, 50 years later that the reading at Cubitt presented. This was the last novel of Beckett's to be written first in English — subsequent novels being translated into English from Beckett's original French. The different national origins of the readers — English, Scottish, American, Canadian and South African — reflected those of the original readers of the manuscript in 1952 who were Jane Lougee (publisher of *Merlin*), Alex Trocchi (editor of *Merlin*), Richard Seaver (Advisory Editor and Director of *Merlin*), Christopher Logue (poet and falconer), Henry Charles Hatcher (poet) and Patrick Bowles (writer). Logue remem-bered how 'Progress was slow because, at first, the text was so comical. Everyone wanted to read. Patrick was the best: deadpan, following the punctuation. As we read on, the writing unsettled us, became frightening and funny by turns — comedy at its most extreme. We found the use of English astonishing. Rhythmically fine-tuned. A first of its kind. Beautiful. For us, it was as it must have been for those who came across the work of Picasso and Duchamp in the 1910s. Or the poetry of Eliot in the twenties. An aesthetically encouraging shock. As is usual when one comes into contact with something good, we felt good.' All of the readers in 2002 were reading *Watt* for the first time and Logue's memory was unsettlingly revisited. Reading out loud without preparation formed one translation; the different inflection and pronunciation of the voices formed another translation — both of which reflected the centrality that translation occupied within Beckett's writing. Staging the reading in front of an audience formed yet another translation in which the private activity of reading became a public performance.

Histories are forever being revisited and most often recuperated in terms of particular present needs and preoccupations. One hope in all this is that Foucault's view might perhaps be doubly reconfigured in such a way that a new understanding of the ever-shifting contemporary condition might appear each time our relationship to history finds itself drastically changed by the present. This underlines the fact that those objects from which histories of art are largely constructed are best read in terms of events and that such readings are themselves part of a larger and continuing process of translation.

CURATORIAL MOMENTS AND DISCURSIVE TURNS

Mick Wilson

"[T]he terrible thing about writing is its resemblance to painting." [1]
Phaedrus

The Discursive Turn

In their introduction to *Curating in the 21st Century* Dave Beech and Gavin Wade cite a question posed by Thomas Crow about the value of conferencing and the proposition that "we should only have a conference when there is a crisis. Otherwise we are just chatting." This ambivalent valuation of "chatting" is played out further as the authors note that during this particular conference a phrase recurred: "Curating, it was mooted, is all in the doing." This phrase was "used, interestingly, both as a defence and then later as a criticism". This prompts the authors to speculate that: "Maybe, even talking is doing something, especially if you are saying something worthwhile. Doing and saying, then are forms of acting on the world." [2]

It seems fair to characterise this as an ambivalent valuation of "chatting" vis-à-vis "doing". Even in the somewhat optimistic speculation — "maybe, even talking is doing something" — the value of the discursive is located in its proxy for actual "doing" — although "doing" may in turn be a source of ambivalence also. This scrupling at the value of the discursive is something that does not appear to have troubled much recent work in the field of contemporary art. Indeed at least since Conceptualism's reception of Austin's *How To Do Things With Words* [3] the productive powers of language have been part of the stock-assumptions of a wide-range of experimental art practices and attendant commentary. This is a tendency that has been given further impetus by the Foucauldian moment in art of the last two decades, and the ubiquitous appeal of the term "discourse" as a word to conjure and perform power. The literalised realisation of conversation has taken on a peculiarly significant role in

1.   *Phaedrus 275d*
2.   Gavin Wade and Dave Beech "Introduction" in Gavin Wade (Ed.) (2000) *Curating in the 21st Century,* Walsall: The New Art Gallery. pp. 9–10
3.   JL Austin [1962] (1975) *How to Do Things with Words,* Oxford: Clarendon Press. In the book Austin asserts that: "To say something is to do something." (p.12) Robert Morris drew on Austin for his 1962 work *Card File.* "*Card File* anticipates the movement of *Conceptual art* which makes an effort, in the Sixties and Seventies, to apply to visual arts a model resulting from the philosophy of language (in particular that of J L Austin) www.centrepompidou.fr/education/ressources/ENS-ArtConcept/ENS-ArtConcept.htm

the current moment in a way that both proceeds from, and exceeds the precedents of Anglophone conceptualism of the late sixties and early seventies.

One of the events scheduled as part of 2005's *Frieze* Art Fair — "Ian Wilson: A Discussion" — although taking place in the immediate past is indicative of an earlier moment in what may be termed the *discursive turn* of contemporary art. It is also indicative of the ambivalence at work in this turn to the discursive. The event announcement in the *Frieze Yearbook* warrants recapitulation in full:

> In 1968 Ian Wilson made his final Sculpture. Since then he has used the unseen abstractions of language as his art form. Today Wilson's ideas are expressed as a series of philosophical discussions with the audience. These 'Discussions' are an extended work in progress about the possibilities of knowledge and allow the audience the opportunity to present their own views, and to question, propose, interject and debate
>
> Over the years Wilson has had 'Discussions' in museums, galleries and the homes of private collectors. The event is never recorded or published, beyond the certificate registering the date, time and location.
>
> Wilson's 'Discussions' exist as a 'fact', yet their presentation utilizes the dynamic of myth, and they in turn become mythologized. Within the current glut of debate on 'social relational practice', Wilson's insistence on clear parameters of articulation is crucial. The works open up ideas about perception and reality but also about what is permissible; the sub-text about freedom of speech and the importance of communication, and – within the context of the art fair – the need for a conceptually critical rather than customer-driven experience.
>
> A Discussion with Ian Wilson will be held on October 23, 2005, at 5 p.m. in the Frieze Art Fair auditorium. [4]

There is ambivalence here as to the value of the discursive — even as a commitment to the discursive is enacted — in as much as Wilson's discrete — within "clear parameters" — discussion is contrasted with an indiscrete "glut of debate." The implication is that the discursive is of value when it is "open" but it must not be excessive or unbounded. On the other hand, the value of the discursive is posited unambiguously in contrast to the values of commerce. Thus a critical communicative experience is opposed to a "customer-driven" experience. There is a rehearsal here of a longstanding Enlightenment value-frame — the theme of the *public sphere* as the condition of possibility of communicative action. This is more than a matter of positing the value of democratic free-speech: this is a question of the independent value of a non-instrumental un-coerced and non-marketised transaction: free speech in the sense of autonomous speech, a speaking together which is free of the constraining action of market relations as much as it is free of censorship through political relations of power or free of obligation through social relations of duty. The public sphere is the promise of multiple sociable *fora* of reasoned discussion which are unconstrained by the imperative of the state and un-tethered from the transactional logic of the market place. This theme of unconstrained communicative reason has taken on increasing significance within one line of development out of conceptualism's engagement with language.

In the wake of Conceptualism's embrace of textual dynamics and the constitutive powers of language, there was in the nineteen eighties and nineties a further inflection of the discursive with the question of social inclusivity realised through dialogue. This is evident in such initiatives as the *Hirsch Farm Project.* Described by Bruce Barber as "probably the purist example of communicative action in action", the project self-describes as "an arts based think tank concerned with public art, the environment and community". The project has brought together different groups of individuals from a "wide range of disciplines to meet in camera for a period of a week to discuss specific topics". Barber continues his description as follows:

Each participant in HFP 'focus groups' develops a proposal or essay that reflects or responds to the conversations generated during the week long discussion sessions, and this results in a publication that is distributed to individuals and organisations in the arts, sciences and humanities. According to Laurie Winter, a co-ordinator the goals of HFP are to 'stimulate dialogue and elevate the standards of conversation between different communities and disciplines whose paths would normally not cross.' [5]

---

5.   www.imageandtext.org.nz/bruce_work_squat_essays.html

The topic of the 1992 gathering at the farm in Northbrook Illinois is indicative of this discursive turn: "the dynamics of how artists and other professionals communicate with a specified audience or community, and how these intentions are received." Of course the advocates and practitioners of the discursive turn in recent art do not necessarily embrace a naïve construal of language and social access. It is worth considering the light shed on these matters by the nuanced and carefully constructed account of the turn to language in conceptual art provided by Harrison in his somewhat hagiographical account of Art & Language:

Once the relevant closures had been relaxed, the critical purport of such things as paintings, sculptures, installations, texts and so on would remain matter for open inquiry. (By open inquiry I mean inquiry that recognizes that there will always be some closure and this will [probably] be nonarbitrary and will [probably] not be cognitive, but that tries to achieve a good match between the conditions of closure and the question asked. An answer to a question about how light switches work is likely simply to exhaust the patience of the inquirer if it has to include material about energy generation, carboniferous deposits, and labour relations within the power industry. Open inquiry stresses that while Verstehen is a condition of any inquiry at all, it is set in a world criss-crossed by different paths... These have to be brought into focus if Verstehen is to be anything more than a condition of absolute relativism.) [6]

Harrison proceeds to indicate that the turn to language in Conceptual Art "was not straightforwardly an injection of language into art, but a militant assertion of art's implication in its own distributive and promotional structures, and of its adjacency to and implication in text". Thus the turn to the discursive is presented as a reflexive attending to the conditions of possibility reproduced in, and as, the art system. There is subsequently a correlation between the turn to the discursive and the explicit thematisation of the infrastructural processes and roles of the art world as evidenced in a very diverse range of practices from Robert Barry's ontological investigations into the limits of the art object to Hans Haacke's social surveys, from Mary Kelly's psychoanalytic meditation and appropriation of the exhibition as system in *Post-Partum Document*

6.   Charles Harrison (2001) *Conceptual Art and Painting: Further Essays on Art & Language*, Cambridge, Mass./London: MIT Press, p.21.

to more recently Tino Sehgal's's theatrical gamesmanship with art market processes. Perhaps out of this admittedly unlikely and somewhat prodigal genealogy, the strange complementarity and synchronicity between the ascendancy of the curatorial gesture and the advocacy of language exchange as a paradigm of practice — the *discursive turn* — might be understood to proceed. Whatever, one may make of this reading of cross-relationships, it is clear that the turn to discursive has entailed as one of its many moments a move to reformulate the various relationships of practitioners, audiences and institutional processes.

Grant Kester, in his (2004) *Conversation Pieces: Community and Communication in Modern Art*, has provided the most comprehensive and robust account of the interrelationship of participatory cultural processes and the turn to discursive practices. Kester proposes that the aesthetic strategies and categories of both modernism and postmodernism converge on "a general consensus that the work of art must question and undermine shared discursive conventions." [7] He itemises the common features of these "avant-garde" frameworks as follows: 1) They promulgate a "relatively reductive model of discursive interaction" based on traditional oppositions between "somatic and cognitive experience" or more simply put as the familiar Cartesian legacy of body/mind dualism. 2) They restrict "the definition of aesthetic experience to moments of immediate, visceral insight." 3) They are based on an "essentially solitary interaction between a viewer and a physical object" which disallows comprehension of collective processes in the moments of production/reception in creative practices. Against this established model of progressive culture or "avant garde" practice, Kester asks "is it possible to conceive of an emancipatory model of dialogical interaction?" Answering his own question in the affirmative, the alternative approach that Kester identifies entails locating "the moment of indeterminateness, of open-ended liberatory possibility, not in the perpetually changing form of the artwork qua object, but in the very process of communication that the artwork catalyses." Kester maps this strategy against a variety of already existing practices including the work of Stephen Willats, WochenKlassur and Jay Koh which he presents as illustrative of this "dialogical aesthetic." This term obviously resonates with Bourriaud's *Relational Aesthetics*, but Kester's construct is arguably more extensively

7.   Grant Kester (2004) *Conversation Pieces: Community and Communication in Modern Art,* Berkeley / Los Angeles / London: University of California Press. p.88

grounded in a considered historical and critical framework that departs significantly from Bourriaud's pop-philosophy citations of Deleuze. [8] Kester also provides a broader genealogy for his "dialogical aesthetic" and is generally less modish in his treatment.

However, Bourriaud's work itself evidences — indeed epitomises — a further inflection of the discursive turn in the last decade with the curious interpenetration of critiques of authorship; the ascendancy of the curatorial gesture — and the curatorial *voice* — as locus and engine of debate; and the multiple orchestrations of conferences, dialogues, interviews, debates and conversations. Liam Gillick in the course of a conversation with Saskia Bos provides a very evocative summary description of this overall pattern of development:

My involvement in the critical space is a legacy of what happened when a semi-autonomous critical voice started to become weak, and one of the reasons that happened was that curating became a dynamic process. So people you might have met before, who in the past were critics were now curators. The brightest, smartest people get involved in this multiple activity of being mediator, producer, interface and neo-critic. It is arguable that the most important essays about art over the last ten years have not been in art magazines but they have been in catalogues and other material produced around galleries, art centres and exhibitions. [9]

Later on in the same exchange Gillick claims that criticism "has become either a thing of record, or a thing of speculation whereas the curatorial voice has become the parallel critical voice to the artist that contributes a parallel discourse." This pattern of development presents itself as the displacement of an exhausted critical discourse — and the partially evacuated role of the critic — by a dialogical process variously facilitated, co-ordinated or enacted by the curator role in conjunction with the role of artists. This broad shift in roles and relationships has yielded multiple outcomes ranging from the de-consecration of the isolated space of the discrete artwork — a revision of established practices

8.   In fairness to Bourriaud, it may simply be that his work has been ill-served by poor translations into English.
9.   Saskia Bos "Towards a Scenario: Debate with Liam Gillick" in Bos et al (Eds.) *Modernity Today: Contributions to a topical artistic discourse, De Appel Reader No. 1.* Amsterdam: De Appel. p. 74

of modernist exhibition design — to the recasting of the exhibition as research instrument or process or performative "event" — a figurative re-positioning of audience expectations and "author" functions. In the first case the individual work is deployed within a tangle of practices according to a metaphor whereby individual works are presented as contingent utterances embedded in the synchronised-cacophony of the ever-mobile conversation. (Molly Nesbit, Hans Ulrich Obrist and Rirkrit Tiravanija's *Utopia Stations.*) In the second case the exhibition becomes a framework of enquiry — in a way that builds upon conceptualism's romance with the exhibition as system — and a metaphor of public education is thus activated. (Catherine David's long-term project series *Contemporary Arab Representations.*) These developments may also be captured under the general heading of a *discursive turn*, in the sense that they point to a literal or metaphorical mobilisation of discursive interchanges as the animating principle informing the orchestration of art practices — they attempt to overcome the hereditary assumptions of the avant-garde as mapped by Kester, but without necessarily invoking his socially-engaged model of participatory culture. However, they do consistently privilege discursive processes as figural or actual paradigms of practice. *Discursivity* is thus a multiply inflected paradigm across a range of contemporary art practices that in various ways articulate themselves with a tradition of progressive practice and simultaneously seek to overcome the impasse of avant-gardism per se.

It may be countered that the metaphor of art as a conversation has a pervasive presence in art commentary throughout modernity, and that modernism's dependence upon an integral strand of critical discourses makes this notion of a discursive turn somewhat overblown. However, it may in turn be argued that precisely the ways in which the metaphor of "the conversation of culture" is being actualised or literalised in recent practices is what marks a significant re-orientation in practice. Consider the following example of the metaphor of conversation in the commentary on modernism, here taken from a recent exhibition — *Dialogues* — examining a pivotal set of interactions across mid-twentieth century American art:

This exhibition traces a dialogue among four great artists of the twentieth century. Stated in this way, that observation might conjure up an image of the four seated at a table engaged in conversation. This, of course, not only never happened, but also would be an inappropriate metaphor for the aesthetic and intellectual exchanges that did transpire when the four of them were working in the same city and knew, or knew of, one another... The relationships were not symmetrical. [10]

This example is worth considering because of its self-conscious reflection on the metaphor employed, and because it illustrates the distance traversed by that metaphor in its literal application in diverse practices of recent years. Thus Mary Jane Jacob's project in Atlanta of the late 1990s *Conversations at the Castle* actualised conversational processes as central to the art process and the image of people seated at a table is perfectly appropriate, just as the desire to enact some kind of symmetry of exchange and interaction is also an apt thematisation of this project also. More recently, and on a much less grand scale, but with a certain critical alacrity and concentrated focus, Sarah Pierce's *The Metropolitan Complex* project has also actualised the conversation between practitioners within a given city in order to tap into the kinds of cross-relationship and micro-networks that undergird and sustain a cultural scene. It is interesting to note also that in constructing a presence for her practice at the Venice Biennale in 2005 as part of the Irish pavilion, Pierce elected not only to produce an iteration of *The Metropolitan Complex* broadsheet — detailing an exchange among artists in respect of a local now superseded music scene — but also to provide a pithy and poetic text by way of contextualisation [11] In this text Pierce describes a set of criss-crossed relationships from recent American art history — Robert Smithson — and the dynamics of micro-sub-cultural initiatives around squatting and urban gardening playing on the potentially absurd correlations of a Grand Canal in Dublin (complete with a Rialto Bridge) and the Grande Canal in Venice. Pierce's text weaves together a set of relationships that is "dialogical" in the classic Bahktinian sense of the term, as well as rooted in the actual processes of conversational exchange and interaction. It is both because of the common turn to dialogical and conversational processes, and because of the breadth of difference across these practices that the broad rubric of *the discursive turn* is employed here. It is not proposed to use the term *discursive* to collapse the differences between these practices, but to characterise

10.   Dorothy Kosinski (2005) *Dialogues: Duchamp, Cornell, Johns, Rauschenberg*, New Haven/London: Yale University Press. (Dallas Museum of Art.) p.13.
11.   www.themetropolitancomplex.com

a broad commonality that marks a significant re-orientation of recent practice.

Within more mainstream institutions this discursive turn has been actualised as an amplification of the explicative function of museums giving rise to such roles as "curator of discussions" and "curator of communications". A review of Martin Creed's work — *The Lights Going On and Off* — as presented in the 2001 Turner Prize Show reveals much of the ambivalent reception of such curatorial roles, and in this regard is worth citing at length:

> It took less than five minutes for the first visitor to crack, although it was unclear whether it was the flashing lights or the explanation from the Tate's wonderfully titled curator of communications, Simon Wilson (recently promoted from curator of interpretation), which was the greater torture. As Wilson gallantly outlined what Creed's installation might signify – the poignance of the dying halogen glow and "the movement towards the dematerialisation of art since the sixties" – there was a barely suppressed roar of rage. A slightly dishevelled man in a leather jacket, shaking with anger, interrupted to ask, "So this is art, is it?" Wilson said that Creed and the Turner jury... certainly thought so. "What, a light going on and off. Really!" he raged, before storming out in the direction of the Victorian Nude, the gallery's new blockbuster show. [12]

In this extract we hear again the ambivalent valuation of discursive performances in relation to the artwork. This review may also be seen as an instance of what Gillick terms a "weak" critical voice, an example of the partial evacuation of criticism. The reviewer's strategy is to render comic both the utterance of the credentialised expert and the unhappy punter. In so doing the reviewer's own mode of utterance becomes privileged. The reviewer is shy of the earnestness shown by both the museum hack and the hapless art-lover. Instead he displays the ironic knowingness that will not be tricked into taking things too seriously. The discursive turn is perhaps to be understood as a turn away from this kind of knowing irony towards a more earnest pursuit of persuasive accounts of what matters, what is worthwhile. In this regard there has been an apparent convergence of institutional processes and avowedly reflexive critical cultural practices: from the *Tate*'s "curator of communications" to

12.   Fiachra Gibbons, The Guardian, Wednesday November 7, 2001.

Manifesta's parallel art college there is a re-situating of the institution as redeemable, as a potential partner and enabler in critical dialogue and not simply the "system" to be negated or to be ironically engaged.

Arguably, the impossibly-multiple curator role — embracing as it does everything from across a spectrum that includes the one-off artist-curator, the hardened local independent, the travel-worn biennale star and the superannuated and institutionally ensconced public servant — has taken over a function of the critic — to produce a persuasive account of value, a rhetoric that produces credible values — and in so doing has served to recast the economy of utterance within these various art-worlds. It has already been indicated that Gillick posits such a shift in the dynamic of roles:

there are moments where artists don't have a fellow critic, as it were, as might have been the case for artists in the late modern period who developed alongside a critical double. My critical double might be the director of the Kunstverein in Munich one week, who next week might be going to do something else. So she is not really my critical double in the sense of classic autonomous critical play. Something more multiple is happening instead which means that we both take on certain roles through pragmatism. [13]

In this context it is interesting to register Michael Diers' intro-ductory essay to Obrist's (2003) *Interviews Volume 1*. Diers points to the emergence of the artist's interview format — noting specifically Warhol's *inter/View* magazine as a key point of emergence for the genre — as a development within late modernism whereby a failure of criticism prompted artist's to "fill the discursive gap with self-presentations in inter-views as well as conceptualisations of contemporary tendencies." Diers contends that artists such as Carl Andre, Donald Judd and Robert Morris took the explanation of their work into their own hands and employed the published conversation as one genre to achieve this goal. This is presented as a response to "the distance and lack of understanding that art criticism exposed in relation to the most recent art". Thus Diers points to another genealogy of the discursive moment in the transfer of a mass-media format — the interview with the celebrity — from pop culture to pop art and beyond to minimalism and conceptualism. It is significant that

13.   Op. cit.

such a trajectory is mapped by way of prefacing a compendious volume of conversational exchanges between a celebrity curator and a broad spectrum of notables including Hans Georg Gadamer, Yoko Ono and Stuart Hall. It is surely significant that in one of these exchanges — Obrist in conversation with Gadamer — there is a rehearsal of the question of the dialogue form in the Western philosophical tradition as founded in Plato.

The conversationalists — Obrist and Gadamer — commence by agreeing that "language only lives in conversation" because "in conversation one is always in motion. By giving an answer the other completes one's own speaking." [14] Gadamer moves to the topic of Plato and the necessity of asking questions to which one does not know the answers in advance. Obrist then questions Gadamer on his first transformative conversation with Heidegger. Gadamer demurs and turns to the counter-topic of silence. Obrist asks "Should we stop now?" seeming to think he is being given a conversational cue for closure. But Gadamer, a consumate professional in the ways of conversation, obliges with a few more turn-taking moves, noting in the process the futility of the search for final meanings in Plato's dialogues. One doesn't have to be philosophically minded to discern that this particular instance of a turn to the discursive is perhaps more than a post-ironical quest for earnestness but rather a full-blown regress to the quest for the authentic and the canonical. Given the tension manifest here between the self-consciousness of a conversation about the nature of conversation, and the seemingly unreflexive move to the canonical — Plato, Heidegger, Gadamer — and the conversational transmission of a tradition, it would seem appropriate to re-activate the theme of ambivalence in the valuation of the discursive at this juncture. By way of doing so it will help to consider a less cheerful exchange of voices as a counterpoint to the niceties of the Obrist-Gadamer exchange. Attention may be turned to a minor cranky squabble over posterity between two authors that have featured already above: Harrison and Crow.

Harrison's account in *Conceptual Art and Painting*, in a manner typical of much of the writing that has attempted to narrate and critically appraise the art of the nineteen sixties and seventies, is threaded with hints at the contentious jostling for canonical position and hegemony in respect of the history of late twentieth century art: "when Conceptual Art is on the conversational or institutional agenda, who is it that gets

14.   Hans Ulbrich Obrist (2003) *Interviews Volume 1*. Milan/Florence: Edizioni Charta/Fondazione Pitti Immagine Discovery. p.144

mentioned?" [15] One aspect of this is his cranky engagement in a footnote with an essay by Thomas Crow — "Unwritten Histories of Conceptual Art: Against Visual Culture" — where Crow questions the constituency, the specific community of discourse, that Conceptual Art engaged. Crow cites both the avowed need for "a changed sense of the public alongside" the proposed "transformation of practice" and Harrison's apparent acknowledgement of a failure by *Art & Language* particularly to deliver in this area: "Realisticaly, *Art & Language* could identify no actual alternative public which was not composed of the participants in its own projects and deliberations." [16] Harrison contends that the quotation is out of context and distorts his original intended statement — which included the sentence "The implication of this circumstance was not that the members of *Art & Language* constituted the only and sufficient audience for *Art & Language* work." [17] It may seem unhelpful to cite these somewhat parochially-minded and often churlish exchanges, contesting the posterity of the recent past, in trying to understand a current moment — the discursive turn in curatorial practice — but these exchanges help to bring into focus the *reputational* stakes of contemporary art. Attending to these *reputational* stakes or *reputational* capital — akin to Bourdieu's sense of cultural capital — may enable a certain insight into the convergence of the curatorial gesture and the discursive turn.

Contemporary art might be helpfully approached as a congeries of systems of work organized and controlled through reputations: specific instances of art (production, display, dissemination, debate, eventing) may then be seen to perform as moves in a game of *reputational* stakes. A description deployed in respect of the sciences might be apposite here:

In... reputational work organizations, the need to acquire positive reputations from a particular group of practitioners is the main means of controlling what tasks are carried out, how they are carried out, and how performance is evaluated. Here, work is conducted with a view to convincing fellow researchers of the importance and significance of the results and hence of enhancing one's own reputations. Jobs and resources

15.   Op. cit. p. 36.
16.   Thomas Crow (1996) "Unwritten Histories of Conceptual Art: Against Visual Culture" in *Modern Art in the Common Culture*, New Haven/London: Yale University Press. p. 215.
17.   Op. cit. p. 214.

are allocated largely according to reputations in the organization so that status ... is dependent on one's reputation in the wider 'community'. [18]

Within contemporary art construed as a *reputational* system, the valency of the discursive turn (especially in connection with the role of curatorship in brokering *reputational* transfer, in the calculation of *reputational capital,* etc.) takes on a specific cast: *discursivity* is a particularly suitable medium for the brokering of reputation. Furthermore, it immediately and tangibly recruits an "actual" public by marking a specific and localisable group as the participant-audience while simultaneously promising an infinitely extensible audience through the ubiquitous promise of the "publication."

Interestingly the promise of publication — the promise of distribution — also surfaces as a point of contention in the course of the conflict of interpretations (and canons) vis-a-vis conceptual art. Harrison again squabbling, this time with Lippard's introduction to an anthology on the subject of conceptual art, asserts:

Insofar as they are in thrall to an increasingly confident global capitalism, the managerial imperatives of curatorship are antielitist only in the absurd sense that universal provision of Coca Cola is antielitist. They are, in effect, powerfully distributive and necessarily imperialistic. [19]

Harrison sounds a note of caution and scepticism in the face of the "distributive" "imperatives" of contemporary curatorship and, by extension, in respect of the participatory "open ended" appearance of discursive processes and practices that characterise the discursive turn in recent art. This is consistent with the Foucauldian proposition that discourse can work to constitute its apparently pre-given objects and be the foundational relay of the various subject positions that seem to animate its production. However, Harrison's inflated critique throws up an all-or-nothing rhetorical move smothering everything beneath the blanket of "global capital", a kind of totalising move that renders all our "chat" crisis-laden, impoverished and inconsequential. It may help to consider, however briefly, a specific instance where the global/local and insider/outsider tensions play out, and a process of *reputational* transfer is in evidence.

18.   Richard Whitley (2000) *The Intellectual and Social Organization of the Sciences,* Oxford: Oxford University Press. P. 25.
19.   Op. cit. pp. 38–9.

    The *Cork Caucus,* devised and managed by *The National Sculpture Factory,* was an initiative that was part of the (seemingly flawed and definitely under-resourced) 2005 *European Capital of Culture* programme. [20] It was a major project developing over 2005 and centred on a discursive network of artists, academics and other cultural workers having its roots in a local initiative by a small artists' group called *art/not art.* Among the *big-name* participants the project was to include Giorgio Agamben, Sarat Maharaj, Catherine David, Gayatri Chakravorty Spivak and Vito Acconci among others — although inevitably, given the hectic schedules and itineraries that many of these figures have to get through in a year, there were one or two no-shows. Charles Esche was also billed as a key curatorial presence collaboratively animating the initiative, his presence on the roster of names flagging the curatorial cachet of the project. The *Caucus* claimed as its purpose an examination of the possibility of "transforming discourse... into social and cultural change." The basic format was a rolling programme of discussions, debates and presentations. A core audience of a hundred or so people appear to have constituted themselves as stakeholders around the rolling schedule of events. The programme thus provided a certain amount of grist for the mill of the familiar biennale-bashing rhetoric in terms of an allegedly uncritical and culturally-conformist capitulation to the prevailing fashions of the globalising-Western art-world circuit, and clearly may be used to concretely illustrate Harrison's critique. However, there is another perspective that needs to be deployed. The *Caucus* event attached value not just to the familiar trope of discursivity as such but also accorded recognition to the already extant informal networks of artists and cultural workers locally and enabled arts organisations to leverage their stake-holders into a more challenging critical environment for practice, to a certain extent puncturing the mythos of the star-system — the dominant *reputational* economy — that so often haunts marginal and provincial sites of contemporary practice. In this instance the attempted transactions of *reputational* transfer, whether successful or not, served to legitimise a field of activity — that of avowedly critical and reflexive contemporary art practices — in a manner that disrupts the safe containment of that field by the predictable "old-grey-cardigan" *grandees* of the local scene. Thus, by providing an impetus to, and a resource for, the contest of reputations locally, and fuelling the possibility and desire for contesting long-established conservative cultural dispensations within the city, the *Caucus* programme "opens" a situation to itself as much as to any external constellation of fashions and tendencies.

The significant issue here is that in describing the system of the *reputational* economy, and the role of discursive exchanges as an especially powerful medium of reputational transfer, it is not intended to negate or puncture such a system by a supposed fiat of ideology-critique. Nor is it proposed that such a reading exhausts the significance of the turn to the discursive. Rather it is proposed to suggest the relationship between a turn to the discursive, the emergence of a diversified and expanded curatorial role and the importance of the ambivalent valuation of the discursive that recurs across this same broad turn to the discursive, the dialogical and the conversational. This ambivalence is a necessary condition for critical thinking amidst the flow of conversations. This ambivalence can be redoubled as we find ourselves in a conundrum of talking-about-talking, discussing the consequences of discussion and even apparently imagining our utterances to already be actions upon the world. This further fold of ambivalence arises as we remember that a value of a certain species of talk might precisely be its possible release from instrumental requirements to effect material change. And this ambivalence may be folded once more if one wishes to attend to Gadamer's demurring response to Obrist on the question of his transformative chats with Heidegger: "Being silent is an extremely strenuous accomplishment, maybe more difficult than talking." [21]

This multiple ambivalence is necessary so that we do not forget that the discursive does not inevitably exhaustively specify experience. Given that the value of discursivity and "critical public debate" appear paramount and the ubiquitously declared values of artists and institutions alike, it is perhaps timely to reconsider that irreducible particularity of matter and sense, their simultaneous residual resistance to linguistic recuperation and abiding problematic *giveness*, that first prompted Baumgarten to frame the notion of aesthetic cognition and set the term "aesthetic" in play for the first time in the philosophical exchanges of modernity. This is not a call for an aesthetic of disinterestedness, nor a nostalgia for objects, nor a quest for authenticity, but for an attending to particularities and opacities that do not easily accommodate themselves to our understanding, our well-worn problematics and our already pleasurable chit-chat.

21.   Op. cit. p. 245.

Biographies

Søren Andreasen

Søren Andreasen lives and works in Copenhagen, as a visual artist and writer. Recent exhibitions include *Manifesta 3*, Ljubljana (2000), *Yokohama Triennale* (2001), *Fundamentalisms of the New Order*, Copenhagen (2002), *Stafet*, Esbjerg (2004) and *Bandit-Mages*, Bourges (2006). He was part of the art-and-text collective *Koncern* (1989–93) and has been collaborating with *Rasmus Knud* (Sebastian Schiørring and Johannes Christoffersen) since 1999. He currently teaches at The Art Academy of Jutland, Aarhus, Denmark.

Julie Ault

Julie Ault is a New York City based artist and writer who independently and collaboratively organizes exhibitions and multiform projects. Ault views exhibition-making as a medium and sometimes assumes a curatorial role as a form of artistic practice. Her recent work includes *Information* in collaboration with Martin Beck at Storefront for Art and Architecture, New York, 2006, and *Points of Entry*, a permanent art project for Powdermaker Hall, Queens College, City University of New York (CUNY) in 2004. Together with Beck she also creates exhibition designs, including for *X-Screen: Film Installations and Actions of the 1960s and 1970s*, Museum Moderner Kunst, Vienna (2003). Ault and Beck are the authors of *Critical Condition: Selected Texts in Dialogue* published by Essen: Kokerei Zollverein, Zeitgenössische Kunst und Kritik (2003). Ault is the editor of, *Alternative Art New York, 1965–1985*, Minneapolis: University of Minnesota Press and The Drawing Center (2002), and of, *Felix Gonzalez-Torres*, Göttingen: steidl/dangin publishers (2006). In 1979 Ault co-founded Group Material, the collaborative that until 1996 produced installations and public projects exploring interrelationships between politics and aesthetics.

Lars Bang Larsen

Lars Bang Larsen is a free-lance critic and curator who lives and works in Frankfurt and Copenhagen. He works with contemporary art and the visual culture of the 1960s, and has published a book on the work of Sture Johannesson, Lukas & Sternberg (2002). Larsen was co-curator of *Pyramids of Mars* in Edinburgh, London and Kolding (1999); *Fundamentalisms of the New Order* in Copenhagen (2002); *Invisible Insurrection of a Million Minds* in Bilbao, (2005) and *Populism* touring Amsterdam, Frankfurt, Oslo, and Vilnius (2005). Currently teaching at the Art Academy of Jutland and the Royal University College of Fine Arts in Stockholm, and writing a book for Afterall Publications about the psychedelic culture of the 1960s in a global perspective. His writing has appeared in *Frieze*, *Artforum* and *Springerin*, among other publications.

Carlos Basualdo

Carlos Basualdo is the Curator of Contemporary Art at the Philadelphia Museum of Art and Adjunct Professor at the IUAV University in Venice, Italy, where he teaches History of Exhibitions. He studied at the Whitney Independent Studies Program between 1994–5. He was Chief Curator of Exhibitions at the Wexner Center for the Arts, The Ohio State University, Columbus, from 2000 until 2002. He is the curator of *Tropicália: Revolution in Brazilian Culture (1967–1972)*, shown at the Barbican, London and the Museum of Contemporary Art, Chicago (2006). He served as curator for *The Structure of Survival*, as part of the 50th Venice Biennial (2003) and was one of the co-curators of *Documenta11* in Kassel, Germany (2002). He also organized the exhibition *Hélio Oiticica: Quasi-cinemas*, seen first at the Wexner Center for the Arts (2001) and which traveled to the Kölnischer Kunstverein, in Cologne, Germany, The Whitechapel Gallery, London, and the New Museum of Contemporary Art, New York, in 2002. Basualdo has written extensively for scholarly journals and art publications, including ArtForum, ArtNews, The Art Journal, The Art Newspaper, Moscow Art Magazine, Flash Art, NKA, Journal of Contemporary African Art, Atlantica, and Art Nexus.

Dave Beech

Dave Beech is an artist, writer and lecturer at Chelsea College of Art. He is a member of the art collective Freee, recently producing public works for the BBC's Power of Art commission in 2006, Hull Time Based Media's Illuminations event, Gavin Wade's off-site project for the Venice Biennale 2005, B+B's Real Estate project at the ICA London 2005, and the Guangzhou Triennale curated by Hou Hanru in China 2005. He is also a regular writer for Art Monthly and other art magazines. He was a prominent member of the young London art scene in the mid-90's, co-authored the book The Philistine Controversy, Verso (2002) and is the co-editor of the new art magazine The Internationaler.

Irene Calderoni

Irene Calderoni is currently assistant curator at the Fondazione Sandretto Re Rebaudengo in Turin. She received her MA from the Faculty of Arts and Design of the IUAV University in Venice in 2005. Since then she has been collaborating with the University on various teaching projects. Her research interests focus on the history of exhibitions and art practices in public space. She is the curator of artLAB, a residency programme for international artists sponsored by the Province of Venice and hosted on the island of San Servolo, Venice's former insane asylum. Since 2003 she has been a consultant for the Percent for Art Programme of the City Council of Venice, where she co-curated the international competition for commissions for the new Law Courts in Venice.

Anshuman Das Gupta

Anshuman Das Gupta was born in 1967, teaches History of Art at Kala Bhavana, Visva Bharati University, Santiniketan. Has taken part in numerous international conferences including: *Curatorial Conference: Berlin Biennale 4*. Has published numerous essays in catalogues and books including: *Open Circle, Yokohama Triennial*, Japan (2006); *Traces Upon the City*, Delhi (2006); *Grey: Options*, Gandhara, Kolkata (2005); *Ramkinker and Some Qualms Over modernity*, Nandan – Visva Bharati University publication

(2005); *Santiniketan Architecture: Nature as Artifice,* Indian Institute of Technology, Kanpur (2002); *Question of Authenticity: Paintings of Our Time* – essay – Lalit Kala Contemporary No. 47 (2003); *Towards a New Art History: Studies in Indian art*, D.K. Print World, Delhi (2003); *Rethinking Avant Garde: A Possible Narrative of Otherness*, Nandan (2002); *Allegories Among the Signs of Our Time*, Nandan (2000); *Contemporary Indian Sculpture; Last Two Decades*, Marg Publication (2000) and *Calcutta: The Rise of Urban Iconography* (2000).

Clémentine Deliss

Dr. Clémentine Deliss is a curator, researcher and publisher who lives in Paris and Edinburgh. She holds a PhD in philosophy (on eroticism and exoticism in French anthropology of the 1920s). Early exhibitions include *Lotte or the Transformation of the Object*, Steirischer Herbst, Graz (1990) and Vienna Academy of Fine Arts, (1991); *Exotic Europeans*, National Touring Exhibitions, Hayward Gallery, London. From 1992 to 1995 she was the artistic director of *africa95*, an artist-led festival of new work in all media from Africa and the diaspora coordinated with the Royal Academy of Arts and over 60 UK institutions. She curated *Seven Stories About Modern Art in Africa*, Whitechapel Gallery, London (1995) and Konsthalle Malmö (1996). Since 1996 she has transformed her curatorial interests into print, and edited and published seven issues of the writers' and artists' organ *Metronome* moving each time to a different location including: Dakar, Berlin, Basel, Frankfurt, Vienna, Oslo, Copenhagen, London, and Paris. Since 2002 she has directed *Future Academy* at Edinburgh College of Art, which investigates the global future of independent art production within the art academy. She is an academic consultant at Edinburgh College of Art and Adjunct Professor at RMIT School of Art, Melbourne, Australia.

Eva Diaz

Eva Diaz is a New York-based art historian and critic. She is a doctoral candidate in art history at Princeton University, where she is completing her dissertation titled "Chance and Design: Experimentation at Black Mountain College", advised by Hal Foster. In 2005 she delivered a talk on the tensions between experimentation and expressionism at the College at the Arnolfini Gallery in Bristol, England, which was published as the exhibition catalogue for their retrospective on Black Mountain. Her writings have appeared in *Art in America* and *Time Out New York*, and numerous exhibition catalogues. She recently co-curated the exhibition *Mind the Gap* at Smack Mellon Gallery in DUMBO, Brooklyn, and her essay for the accompanying catalog examined artists' interventions in and around city spaces and how the privatization of public spaces continues to affect the sites of and for art. Throughout 2006–2007 she is guest curating a series of exhibitions about experiment, art, and performance at Black Mountain College at the Asheville Art Museum in North Carolina. Since 1999 she has served as the Instructor for Curatorial Studies of the Whitney Museum Independent Study Program.

Claire Doherty

Claire Doherty is a curator and writer based in Bristol, UK. As Senior Research Fellow in Fine Art at University of the West of England, Bristol, Doherty leads Situations, a research and commissioning programme devised to investigate the significance of context and place in contemporary art. The programme combines the commissioning of new artworks, with public lectures, conferences, international symposia and publications. Over the past twelve years, Doherty has investigated new models of curatorial practice beyond conventional exhibition models at a range of institutions such as Ikon Gallery, Birmingham, Spike Island, Bristol and FACT (Foundation of Art and Creative Technology), Liverpool. In 2004, she edited the volume of critical essays, case studies and interviews *Contemporary Art: From Studio to Situation*, Black Dog Publishing (2005). She curated *Thinking of the Outside: New Art and the City of Bristol*, a city-wide exhibition of new work by Nathan Coley, Phil Collins, Susan Hiller, Joao Penalva, Kathleen Herbert and Silke Otto-Knapp. In 2006, Doherty will continue to develop the Situations programme and will be the Inaugural International Curator-in-Residence at Massey University, Wellington, New Zealand. www.situations.org.uk

Okwui Enwezor

Okwui Enwezor is Dean of Academic Affairs and Senior Vice President at San Francisco Art Institute. Enwezor was Artistic Director of *Documenta 11*, Kassel, Germany (1998–2002) and the *2nd Johannesburg Biennale* (1996–1997). He has curated numerous exhibitions in some of the most distinguished museums around the world, including *The Short Century: Independence and Liberation Movements in Africa, 1945–1994*, Museum Villa Stuck, Munich, Gropius Bau, Berlin, Museum of Contemporary Art Chicago, and P.S.1 and Museum of Modern Art, New York; *Century City*, Tate Modern, London; *Mirror's Edge*, Bildmuseet, Umea, Vancouver Art Gallery, Vancouver, Tramway, Glasgow, Castello di Rivoli, Torino; *In/Sight: African*

Photographers, 1940–Present, Guggenheim Museum; *Global Conceptualism*, Queens Museum, New York, Walker Art Center, Minneapolis, Henry Art Gallery, Seattle, List Gallery at MIT, Cambridge; co-curator of *Echigo-Tsumari Sculpture Biennale* in Japan; co-curator of *Cinco Continente: Biennale of Painting*, Mexico City; Stan Douglas: Le Detroit, Art Institute of Chicago.

Annie Fletcher

Annie Fletcher is an independent curator based in Amsterdam. Fletcher has curated and co-curated projects including: *Be(com)ing Dutch in the Age of Global Democracy* with Van Abbemuseum (2006–2008); *If I Can't Dance — I Don't Want To Be Part Of Your Revolution,* various locations (2005–2008); *Cork Caucus* with NSF Cork (2005); *The Paraeducation Dept.* at TENT/Witte de With Rotterdam (2004); *Now What? Dreaming a Better World in Six Parts*, BAK, Utrecht (2003), *How Things Turn Out* with the Irish Museum of Modern Art, Dublin (2002) and *The International Language* with Grassy Knoll Productions, Belfast (2001). She teaches on the Curatorial Training Programme at De Appel. Published work includes catalogue essays on Gerard Byrne, Susan Philipsz, Phil Collins, Otto Berchem, and L.A. Raeven and interviews with Liam Gillick, Sarat Maharaj and Nathan Coley.

Liam Gillick

Liam Gillick was born in 1964 in Aylesbury (UK) He has been teaching at Columbia University in New York since 1997. Numerous solo exhibitions since 1989 include: *Literally,* The Museum of Modern Art, New York (2003); *communes, bar and greenrooms*, The Powerplant Contemporary Art Gallery, Toronto (2003);

Exterior Days, Casey Kaplan, New York (2003); *The Wood Way*, Whitechapel Gallery, London (2002); *A short text on the possibility of creating an economy of equivalence,* Palais de Tokyo (2005). Selected group exhibitions include: *Singular Forms*, Guggenheim Museum (2004); *50th Venice Biennale* (2003); *What If*, Moderna Museet, Stockholm (2000) and *Documenta X*, Kassel (1997). Since 1995 Liam Gillick has published a number of books that function in parallel to his artwork including: *Literally No Place*, Book Works, London (2002); *Five or Six*, Lukas & Sternberg, New York (1999); *Discussion Island/Big Conference Centre*, Kunstverein Ludwigsburg, Ludwigsburg, and Orchard Gallery, Derry (1997) and *Erasmus is Late*, Book Works, London (1995). Liam Gillick has contributed to many art magazines and journals including Parkett, Frieze, Art Monthly and a regular column for Metropolis M in Amsterdam.

Jens Hoffmann

Jens Hoffmann is a curator and writer based in San Francisco. He is director of the Wattis Institute for Contemporary Arts and senior lecturer for the Curatorial Practice Program at the California College of the Arts. He is also a faculty member of the Curatorial Studies Program of Goldsmiths College, University of London and a visiting professor at the Nuova Accademia di Belle Arti in Milan. From 2004 to 2007 Hoffmann was Director of Exhibitions at the Institute of Contemporary Arts, London, where he curated group exhibitions such as *Artist's Favourites* (2004); *100 Artists See God* (2004–2005); *London in Six Easy Steps* (2005); *Around the World in Eighty Days* (2006), *Surprise, Surprise* (2006), *Alien Nation* (2006) as well as solo exhibitions of works by artists such as John Bock, Tino Sehgal, Martha Rosler, Jonathan Monk and Cerith Wyn Evans. Since the late 1990s

Hoffmann has curated over 30 exhibitions internationally including: *The Show Must Go On,* New York (1999); *Tropical Modernity* (co-curated with Dominique Gonzalez-Foerster), Barcelona (1999); *Blown Away — 6th Caribbean Biennial* (co-curated with Maurizio Cattelan), St. Kitts (1999); *Indiscipline* (co-curated with Barbara Vanderlinden), Brussels (2000); *exhibition2*, Stockholm (2001); *A Little Bit of History Repeated*, Berlin (2001); *A Show That Will Show That A Show Is Not Only A Show*, Los Angeles (2002); *The Exhibition As A Work Of Art*, Rio de Janeiro (2003); *Institution2*, Helsinki (2003); *An Exhibition in Words*, Caracas (2003–2004); *A Walk To Remember*, Los Angeles (2005); *Me, Myself and I*, Vancouver (2006); *WRONG*, Berlin (2006); *Home of the Free*, Chicago (2006); *The Studio*, Dublin (2006). He was also co-curator of the *1st Prague Biennial* (2003), the *1st Tirana Biennial* (2001) and *Manifesta 4* (2002). His most recent books include *The Next Documenta Should be Curated by an Artist* (Frankfurt: Revolver, 2004), and *Perform*, co-authored with Joan Jonas (London: Thames & Hudson, 2006).

Mark Hutchinson

Mark Hutchinson is an artist. His practice includes writing on art, lecturing, teaching and curating. Recent projects include: co-organising the touring exhibition, publication and symposium *There is Always an Alternative: Possibilities for Art in the Early Nineties*, with Dave Beech; *On Public Art*, a poster produced for Insert Space at the invitation of Hewitt+Jordan; *Escape From Studio Voltaire*, at Studio Voltaire, London: and *Contaminant*, an installation for the Collective gallery, Edinburgh. He is co-editor of the occasional pamphlet and website, *The First Condition* (www.thefirstconditon.com). He is author of the influential essay *Four Stages of*

Public Art, which applies the critical realist dialectic of the philosopher Roy Bhaskar to art. Recent essays include: *Work is the Obscene and Shameful Secret of Art* for the Futurology publication, the Walsall Art Gallery; *Stillness*, on aspects of animation for the touring exhibition The Animators; and *The Terrors of Experts, Curators and Publics*, for The Internationaler.

Bob Nickas

Bob Nickas is an independent critic and curator. He has organized more than fifty exhibitions since 1984, and is Curatorial Adviser at PS1 Contemporary Art Center in New York since 2004. Among his many exhibitions at PS1 are *Lee Lozano: Drawn From Life — 1961-1971*; *William Gedney — Christopher Wool: Into the Night*: *Stephen Shore: American Surfaces*; and *Wolfgang Tillmans: Freedom From The Known*. He collaborated with Cady Noland on her project for Documenta IX (1992). He contributed a section for *Aperto* at the 1993 Venice Biennale and served on the teams which organized the *Biennale de Lyon* (2003) and *Greater New York*, 2005. His book, *Live Free or Die: Collected Writings 1985-1999*, was published in 2000 by les presses du réel. A regular contributor to *Artforum*, his writing has also appeared in *Afterall*, *Purple*, and *Sound Collector Audio Review*. He has contributed to several monographs, books, and catalogues–Felix Gonzalez-Torres, On Kawara, Peter Hujar, Olivier Mosset, Yayoi Kusama, and Jules de Balincourt.

Hans Ulrich Obrist

Hans Ulrich Obrist works and lives in London and Paris. From 2000 to 2006 he was curator of ARC/Musée d'Art Moderne de la Ville de Paris. Between 1998-2000 he was curator at Villa Medici French Academy, Rome. Obrist was recently appointed co-director of exhibitions and director of international projects at the Serpentine Gallery in London. Obrist has edited more than 60 books among which most recently *dontstopdontstopdontstop-dontstopdontstopdontstop: Collected writings 1990 to 2006*, published by Lukas and Sternberg; *Do it*, published by Revolver and *Hans Ulrich Obrist Interviews* published by Charta/Pitti Imagine Milano/Firenze. Obrist has co-curated the Biennales of Berlin (2001) Dakar (2004) Guangzhou (2005) Moscow (2005) and many other exhibitions such as *Cities on the Move*, (1999-), *Laboratorium* (1999), *Utopia Station* (2003-), *do it* (1993-), *Nuit Blanche* (1998), *Life/Live* (1996/7), *Uncertain States of America* (2005-) and *China Power Station* (2006).

Paul O'Neill

Paul O Neill is a curator, artist, lecturer and writer, currently based in London. Since 2003, he has dedicated his time to researching the development of contemporary curatorial discourses from the 1980s as part of a PhD scholarship at Middlesex University. He was Gallery Curator at londonprintstudio Gallery between 2001-2003, where he curated group shows such as *Private Views; Frictions; A Timely Place... Or Getting Back to Somewhere; All That is Solid...* and solo projects: *Being Childish Billy Childish; Phil Collins Reproduction Timewasted* and *Locating: Corban Walker*. He is Co-Director of *MultiplesX;* an organisation that commissions and supports curated exhibitions of artist's editions, which he established in 1997 and has presented exhibitions at spaces such as the ICA, London; Temple Bar Gallery and Project, Dublin; Ormeau Baths, Belfast; Glassbox, Paris and The Lowry, Manchester. He has curated or co-curated over 40 exhibitions and projects that include: *General Idea: Selected Retrospective*, Project Gallery, Dublin (2006); *Mingle-Mangled,* part of Cork Caucus, Cork (2005); *La La Land*, Project, Dublin (2005); *Coalesce: The Remix,* Redux, London (2005); *Tonight*, Studio Voltaire, London (2004); *Coalesce: With All Due Intent* at Model and Niland Art Gallery, Sligo (2004); *Are We There Yet?* Glassbox Gallery, Paris (2000), and *Passports*, Zachęta Gallery of Contemporary Art, Warsaw (1998). He is a visiting lecturer in Visual Culture at Middlesex University and on the MFA Curating course at Goldsmiths College London. He writes regularly for many journals and magazines including Art Monthly, Contemporary, The Internationaler and CIRCA.

Sarah Pierce

Sarah Pierce lives in Dublin where she organises *The Metropolitan Complex*, a practice that incorporates talks, archives, publications and exhibitions. Recent projects include *The Meaning of Greatness*, Project, Dublin; *Monk's Garden*, Scuola di San Pasquale, Venice for the Irish Pavilion at the 51st Venice Biennale (2005); *Archivo Paralelo*, Sala Rekalde, Bilbao (2005); *You can't cheat an honest man,* PS1 MoMA, New York (2004); and *Paraeducation Department* with Annie Fletcher at Witte de With/TENT, Rotterdam (2004). In addition to numerous catalogues for artists, her writing can be found in *Make everything new - a project on Communism*, published by Book Works (2006); *Looking Encountering Staging*, published by the Piet Zwart Institute, Rotterdam (2005); *Put About: A Critical Anthology on Independent Publishing,* published by Book Works (2005); *Meanwhile Some Place Else...,* Sala

Rekalde, Bilbao (2005); *Tracer 1* and *Tracer 2*, published by Witte de With, Rotterdam (2004); and *Printed Project* Issue 01, for which she served as the Guest Curatorial Editor. Pierce is a Research Associate in Curating and Documentation at Interface, University of Ulster (through May 2008).

Simon Sheikh

Simon Sheikh is a curator and critic who lives in Berlin and Copenhagen. He is Assistant Professor of Art Theory and a Coordinator of the Critical Studies Program, Malmö Art Academy in Sweden. He was director of Overgaden – Institute for Contemporary Art in Copenhagen, 1999-2002 and Curator at NIFCA, Helsinki, 2003-2004. He was editor of the magazine Øjeblikket (1996-2000), and a member of the project group GLOBE from 1993-2000. Curatorial work includes exhibitions such as *Exclusion*, Consul, Århus (1993); *I Confess*, Nikolaj – Copenhagen Contemporary Art Center (1995); *Escape Attempts* in Christiania, Copenhagen (1996) (with GLOBE); *Do-It-Yourself — Mappings and Instructions*, Bricks+Kicks, Vienna (1997); *Models of Resistance*, Overgaden, Copenhagen (2000) (with GLOBE); *Naust* Øygarden, Bergen, Norway (2000); *In My Room*, Nordic Video, Musee d'Art Moderne de la Ville de Paris. *Circa Berlin*, Nikolaj – Copenhagen Contemporary Art Center (2005); *Capital (It Fails Us Now)*, UKS, Oslo (2005) and Kunstihoone, Tallinn (2006). Recent publications include the anthologies *We Are All Normal* (with Katya Sander), Black Dog Publishing, London (2001); *Knut Åsdam* (monograph), Fine Arts Unternehmen, Zug (2004); *In the Place of the Public Sphere?* b_books, Berlin (2005) and *Capital (It Fails Us Now)*, b_books, Berlin (2006). His writings can also be found in such periodicals as Afterall, AnArchitectur, Springerin & Texte zur Kunst.

Mary Anne Staniszewski

Mary Anne Staniszewski, PhD is an Associate Professor and Graduate Director in the Department of the Arts, Rensselaer. She has written about art and culture for a diverse range of academic, art world, and general interest publications for twenty-five years. Staniszewski investigates art and culture in relation to social issues and as a means of promoting progressive aesthetic, cultural, and political perspectives. Her major research projects form a "trilogy" of books that are interdisciplinary investigations of modern culture as articulations of the modern self: *Believing Is Seeing: Creating the Culture of Art*, Penguin USA (1995) is a critical history of modern art and culture; *The Power of Display: A History of Exhibition Installations at the Museum of Modern Art,* MIT Press (1998) frames installation design as an artistic medium in its own right that creates displays not only for artworks, but for those who view them. The third book, which she is writing, examines the myths and contemporary definitions of race, sex, and life and death in the United States.

Grant Watson

Grant Watson is a writer and curator based in Antwerp. He works at the Museum van Hedendaagse Kunst Antwerpen (MuHKA). He was the Curator of Visual Art at Project from 2001 to 2006 where he worked with a range of artists including: General Idea, Heather Allen, Klaus Weber, Goshka Macuga, Martha Rosler and Gerard Byrne. He has worked extensively in the field of contemporary Indian art collaborating with the curator Suman Gopinath on exhibitions such as *Drawing Space; Contemporary Indian Drawing*, inIVA (2000), *Room for Improvement*, The Crafts Museum New Delhi (2001); *City Park*, Project (2002);

Retrospective as Artwork, by Valsan Koorma Kolleri, Project (2003) and BQ gallery (2005) and *Mural*, Project (2005). and has undertaken research in this area for Documenta 12. He has edited several publications including *Make Everything New*, Book Works (2006), *To What Extent Should an Artist Understand the Implication of His or Her Findings*, with Bojan Sarcevic, Project/The Model Arts and Niland Gallery (2006); *The Meaning of Greatness*, with Sarah Pierce, Project (2006); *Fatfinger (HAITCH.KAY.EKS)* with Martin Westwood, Project (2003); *Drawing on Space*, The Drawing Room, (2001); *Drawing Space; Contemporary Indian Drawing*, inIVA (2000); *Woof Woof*, Austrian Cultural Institute (2001); *WOA*, Thames & Hudson (2000) and *Victorya* (1997–1999). His writing has been published widely including with Phaidon, Flash Art, Neue Review, Zing Magazine, Printed Projects and The Douglas Hyde Gallery.

Andrew Wilson

Andrew Wilson is an art historian, critic and curator based in London where he is curator of modern and contemporary British art at Tate. From 1997–2006 he was deputy editor of the British contemporary art magazine *Art Monthly*. Over the last ten years he has curated or co-curated, amongst others, *Wyndham Lewis*, Austin/Desmond Fine Art: London (1990); *From Here, Painting in the 90s* (with Karsten Schubert and Hester van Roijen), Karsten Schubert Gallery and Waddington Gallery, London (1995); *Made New*, City Racing, London (1996); *I Groaned with Pain...Sex, Seditionaries and the Sex Pistols* (with Paul Stolper), Eagle Gallery, London (1996); *Sluice Gates of the Mind, The Collaborative Work of Dr Grace W. Pailthorpe and Reuben Mednikoff, 1935–1940*, Leeds City Art Gallery (1998); *The Situationist International*, a collection of material curated and presented for *Unconvention* by Jeremy Deller, Centre for Visual Art, Cardiff (1999); A Reading of *Watt* (performance event), Cubitt Gallery, London (2002); *Poetry will be made by all,* Magnani, London (2002); *Punk: a true and dirty tale,* (with Paul Stolper), The Hospital, London and Urbis, Manchester (2004–2005).

Mick Wilson

Mick Wilson is currently Head of Research at the National College of Art & Design, Dublin, Ireland. He is active as an educator, artist, and writer with a range of current research interests that include contemporary art; cultural practice and technology change; and critical research practices. Trained in art practice, art and design history, information technology and education, he has taught on a wide variety of undergraduate and postgraduate programmes. He recently completed doctoral research project on the rhetoric of discipline-based knowledge conflict in the university. Recent published work and essays includes "Tricks of Trade and Terms of Art" in *Third Text*, Volume 19, No. 5 (2005); "Invasion of the Kiddyfiddlers" in Robert Atkins and Svetlana Mintcheva (Eds.) *Censoring Culture: Contemporary Threats to Free Expression*, (New York: The New Press, 2006); *Jeanette Doyle: Gifting*, (Dublin: Broadstone Gallery, 2005); and *Incompletions: Brendan Earley*, (jointly with Declan Long), (Dublin: Temple Bar Gallery & Studios, 2006).

Editor's Acknowledgments

A big thank you to all the authors for their inspiration, knowledge and commitment throughout the editorial process. To Okwui Enwezor for permission to publish our conversation; to Ann Demeester and the De Appel Foundation; Jon Bird, Adrian Rifkin and Middlesex University for assisting my research throughout the last three years; to AA Bronson, Vaari Claffey, Carlos Basualdo, David Blamey, Dave Beech, Hans Ulrich Obrist, Mark Hutchinson, Annie Fletcher, Matt Keegan and Mary Anne Staniszewski for their advice and editorial suggestions at the right time; to Suzanne Mooney for her patience and understanding and to all who generously gave of their time for discussions, interviews and conversations over the last three years including; Heather Anderson, Ami Barak, Iwona Blazwick, Saskia Bos, Nicolas Bourriaud, Thomas Boutoux, Dan Cameron, Lynne Cooke, Papa Colo, Neil Cummings, Catherine David, Barnaby Drabble, Patricia Falguières, Tom Finkelpearl, Andrea Fraser, Rainer Ganahl, Lia Gangatano, Teresa Gleadowe, Jérôme Grand, Hou Hanru, Anna Harding, Matthew Higgs, Jeannette Ingelman, John Kelsey, Pierre Léguillon, Pi Li, Maria Lind, Julia Maier, Ute Meta Bauer, John Miller, Stephanie Moisdon, Lynda Morris, Molly Nesbit, Brian O'Doherty, Michael Petry, Steven Rand, Andrew Renton, Jérôme Sans, Nicolaus Schafhausen, Seth Siegelaub, Polly Staple, Robert Storr, Emily Sundblad, Gilane Tawadros, Eric Troncy, Alexis Vaillant, Alice Vergara-Bastiand, Gavin Wade, Brian Wallis, Lawrence Weiner, Catherine de Zegher

Editor's Note:
I encouraged each contributor to write in the style that they are most used to working with. The resulting variations, from text to text, offer the reader a reflection of the range of approaches to writing within the field as a whole.

Authors' Acknowledgements

A further version of "For a... Functional Utopia?" will be published in Liam Gillick, *Proxemics: Selected Writings 1988 – 2004*, ed. Lionel Bovier, (Zürich: JRP Ringier, 2007)

Bob Nickas's "To Be Read (Once Every Two Years)" also appears in *25th International Biennial of Graphic Arts Ljubljana,* ed. Christophe Cherix and Madeleine Goodrich Noble, (Ljubljana: International Centre of Graphic Arts, Ljubljana, 2003) 41 – 43.

Carlos Basualdo's "The Unstable Institution" was translated from Spanish by Vincent Martin. This essay was commissioned by the Philadelphia Exhibitions Initiative, a program of The Pew Charitable Trusts, administered by The University of the Arts, for its publication *Questions of Practice: What Makes A Great Exhibition?* ed. Paula Marincola, (Philadelphia: Philadelphia Exhibitions Initiative, 2006) and is reprinted here by permission of PEI. All rights reserved.

Parts of Julie Ault's "Three Snapshops from the Eighties" were excerpted from Julie Ault, "Exhibition: Entertainment, Practice, Platform," in *Agenda*, ed. Christian Kravagna, (Vienna: Folio, 2000).

Series Editor
David Blamey

Series Art Director
Stephen Kirk

Editor
Paul O'Neill

Design
Jonathan Hares

Font
Stephan Müller
Unica Neue Regular & Light

Print
G&B Printers
+44 (0) 20 8755 1822